MAKING SENSE OF A CHANGING ECONOMY

'Economists know a lot about economics but not much about the economy.'

Conventional economic theory and policies are increasingly perceived as irrelevant and out of touch. While the economic system continues to change rapidly, the dominant theories which guide economic policy have largely remained unchanged for the last fifty years.

In *Making Sense of a Changing Economy*, Edward Nell presents an unorthodox and original view of the current state of economic theory and policies. Deriding the general trend for 'econobabble', he explains the reason why economic theory and policy now seem anachronistic. In so doing, he provides a clear and sharp explanation of how the economic system actually works. The book is divided into four parts covering all the major economic principles. The understanding of economic theory is simplified by placing it within real-life contexts, while technical and more difficult topics are explained in separate appendices. Coverage includes:

- a guide to the function and rationale of the market, including an analysis of the Keynesian versus monetarist debate;
- management of the system and possible alternatives;
- markets and morals – the Machiavellian versus the traditional code;
- outlook for the future – current controversies, the environment, and the transformation of consumption and production.

Professor Nell employs a lightness of touch and wit that makes the book entertaining throughout. The result is an enjoyable and accessible read which requires minimal prior knowledge of economics. The book will be a valuable guide to those who find conventional economics texts formidable or irrelevant.

Edward J. Nell is Malcolm B. Smith Professor of Economics at the New School for Social Research.

MAKING SENSE OF A CHANGING ECONOMY

Technology, markets and morals

Edward J. Nell

London and New York

First published 1996
by Routledge
11 New Fetter Lane, London EC4P 4EE

Simultaneously published in the USA and Canada
by Routledge
29 West 35th Street, New York, NY 10001

© 1996 Edward J. Nell

Typeset in Garamond by
Florencetype Limited, Stoodleigh, Nr. Tiverton, Devon.
Printed and bound in Great Britain by
Clays Ltd, St. Ives PLC

British Library Cataloguing in Publication Data
A catalogue record for this book is available from the British Library

Library of Congress Cataloguing in Publication Data
Nell, Edward J.
Making sense of a changing economy : technology, markets, and
morals / Edward Nell.
    p.   cm
Includes bibliographical references and index
1. Capitalism – Moral and ethical aspects.   2. Consumption
(Economics) 3. Individualism.   I. Title.
HB501.N368   1995   95–40964
330.12'2–dc20   CIP

ISBN 0–415–13639–3 (hbk)
ISBN 0–415–13640–7 (pbk)

CONTENTS

PREFACE

This book is intended for anyone and everyone with a genuine interest in the important and alarming economic issues of our times. I say 'genuine' interest, because it takes hard work just to understand what these issues are, let alone to assess the different proposals for dealing with them. So this book is not for the casual consumer of sound bites. But it's not only for students and scholars – it is addressed to everyone who cares about what is happening to the economy. Anyone who has ever taken an economics course ought to be able to follow the argument – even if, perhaps especially if, they found that economics course less than inspiring. One of the goals here is to explain why the conventional wisdom in economics is out of touch. To do that it will be necessary to range far afield at times, touching on issues in Philosophy and Politics, as well as Economics. The borders between disciplines are as porous as those between nations – but crossing one of these borders without proper documentation may be just as dangerous! The reader will have to judge.

Economics aspires to be a scientific subject, and some familiarity with the technical language is necessary. I have tried to define all such terms, and show how they are used, whenever they come up, but it may be useful to consult a good basic textbook, from time to time. The crucial sections to note are those that explain the basics of supply and demand and prices, on the one hand, and the adjustment of the whole economy through savings, investment and the multiplier, on the other. But be careful! *Understand*, but don't be too quick to *believe*, what the textbook says. It should be there, readily at hand, not only for consultation, but also as an example of what can go wrong in thinking about the economy, since it is an important part of the argument here that the textbook approach can be misleading on many important issues!

ACKNOWLEDGEMENTS

Robert L. Heilbroner repeatedly and graciously read drafts of most chapters and offered invaluable editorial advice. George Argyrous read both drafts of the manuscript and helped to clarify and simplify a number of difficult passages. Bertell Ollman also read an early draft and offered helpful comments and sound advice. Garrett Bekker went over the manuscript at a late stage and helped to enhance its readability. He also drafted the glossary. Stephanie Clark and Tom Phillips helped with proof-reading and final editing. Teaching with Willi Semmler improved my knowledge of mathematical dynamics, and discussions with Martin Hollis clarified my ideas on philosophy and economics. Marsha Nell provided support and comfort, a bit of sharp criticism, and a good deal more than encouragement, without which it might never have been finished. Finally, my mother, Marcella Nell, had long urged me to write this book, and I am sorry she did not live to see it in print. I dedicate it to her memory.

KEY TERMS

Aggregate demand

This refers to the level of demand present in the economy as a whole, at a particular time. Demand refers to 'effective' demand, that is, desire backed by money. Normally, aggregate demand is taken to equal the sum of the spending on Consumption plus Investment plus Exports minus Imports plus Government.

Balance of trade; balance of payments; exports and imports

'Balance of trade' refers to the difference between what is bought from other countries (imports), and what is sold to them (exports), during a specific period of time. When imports exceed exports, a trade deficit results. The balance of trade refers only to the exchange of goods, whereas the balance of payments takes into account all transactions between countries – goods, services and financial transactions.

Banks and banking

In the US, the Glass–Steagall Act has separated banks into two broad types: commercial banks and investment banks. Banks serve as 'intermediaries', by channeling the surplus funds of savers to borrowers. Commercial banks do this by accepting deposits and granting loans, earning a profit on the difference between the rate they pay out on deposits and that which is charged for loans. Such loans are primarily for current business purposes. Investment banks raise money for corporations and government agencies by issuing bonds and stocks; such funds are capital funds. In recent years, however, the distinction between commercial and investment banks has become increasingly blurred; both types of banks now engage in practices that were once the exclusive domain of the other.

Business cycle

Refers to the ups and downs of the economy over time, i.e. contractions and expansions of GDP. The term 'cycle' implies that there is some regularity to such occurrences, as opposed to the (neo)classical view that recessions are simply random events. The character of the business cycle appears to have changed over time; in the nineteenth century price fluctuations were the chief concern; in the twentieth century changes in output and employment have moved to the foreground.

Capacity; capacity utilization

Refers to the maximum amount of output that the economy could produce if all of its resources (land, labour, capital, etc.) were being fully utilized. Capacity utilization is a specific measure of the former, usually expressed as a percentage of maximum capacity, a concept which has proved difficult to define precisely.

Capital

Refers to a particular configuration of legal rights and relationships establishing control over the means of production and claims to the output of those means, thereby giving rise to valuations of both outputs and inputs. 'Capital' may refer to the heterogeneous collection of inputs, or to the *value* of that collection, or it may refer to a fund of purchasing power, or to the value of a claim to a stream of payments generated by some production process. These are not three separate definitions – goods, funds, stream of payments – they are three phases or stages in the regular turnover of capital, as funds are converted into productive goods, which are used to generate a stream of earnings from the sale of output.

Credit and finance; financial markets

Credit is a device whereby individuals and businesses can consume more than their present income would allow, by borrowing against future income. The price of credit is measured by the interest rate. Mainstream theory views the interest rate on credit as representing an individual's preference for present versus future consumption. In other words, the greater the desire to consume now versus the future, the higher the interest rate consumers will pay for that privilege. Credit can take many forms, the most common of which is bank loans. Finance refers to the ability of firms to raise funds to pay for investment and production; credit is only one form of finance. Financial markets refer to the array of markets where financial assets are traded, including credit instruments.

Consumption; consumption function

Outlays by households and businesses for goods and services. The consumption function analyses the relationship between income and consumption. It is typically assumed that as income rises, consumption rises; in other words, income and consumption are positively related. However, this relationship is not proportional; as income rises, consumption will tend to rise by a smaller and smaller amount.

Deficits; government budgets

Deficits simply refer to an excess of expenditure over income during a specific period of time. A government budget deficit, for example, occurs when the government spends more than it receives in the form of taxes in a given year. This can result from an excess of spending, a shortfall in taxes, or some combination of the two. The Government does not separate capital and current expenditures; hence a 'budget deficit' may reflect capital spending. The Government does not calculate capital gains on its assets, either, nor does it revalue its assets to reflect inflation. The deficit should tell us whether the Government is increasing or decreasing its asset position; moreover, we should be able to learn whether the Government is stimulating the economy or holding it back. As conventionally measured, it answers neither question.

Dynamics and statics

Statics, or comparative statics, refers to a type of economic analysis in which various positions of equilibrium are compared to one another after a disequilibrating change in one of the variables under study. For example, two equilibrium positions can be compared after a change in the money supply. However, static analysis says little or nothing about how, or if, the economy moves from one equilibrium position to another, which is the central concern of dynamic analysis.

Economic growth

Refers to the increase in GDP from year to year, expressed in percentage terms, as a rate.

Employment; unemployment

In simple terms, the percentage of the work force who have jobs. Unemployment therefore represents the percentage of the work force without jobs. It is important to note that official unemployment figures only count as unemployed those who are willing and able to work, and are actively seeking employment. Workers who have given up looking for work, or who are employed part-time when they would like to have a full-time job, are not considered 'unemployed'.

Equilibrium

A fundamental theoretical tool in mainstream economic analysis, used to describe a situation where the system is at rest, i.e. there are no forces pushing the system toward further change. This conception of equilibrium derives from nineteenth-century physics. Equilibrium canalso be used to describe a situation where prices adjust so that supply and demand are equal, and therefore all markets "clear". In such a situation, sellers are able to sell all that they want at the market-clearing price, and consumers can purchase all that they wish to consume. Macroeconomics draws on a different conception of equilibrium, a kind of hydraulic concept, in which 'injections' of purchasing power just balance 'withdrawals'.

Free trade (see protection)

An economic doctrine dating back to the mercantilist period, based on the idea of comparative advantage. The essential point is that if there are no barriers to exchange between nations (tariffs, quotas etc.), then all nations will be made better off by specializing in the goods that they are best at producing and exchanging them with other countries, rather than trying to produce at home all the goods that they need. Free trade is the driving force behind recent trade agreements such as NAFTA, the US–Canada Free Trade Agreement, and GATT (the General Agreement on Tariffs and Trade). Free trade means that a country gives up control over its balance of payments; hence it may be forced to adopt austerity to protect the value of its currency.

GNP; national income

Gross National Product is the supply corresponding to aggregate demand. It is a statistical measure designed to reflect the dollar value of the goods and services produced and sold by a given country in a particular period, usually a year. National income is the mirror image of GNP – since all sales constitute income to someone, we can measure GNP by either adding up the value of all goods sold or by adding up the value of all incomes earned in the process of producing those goods and services. Thus, National Income will consist of wages, salaries, bonuses, profits (distributed as dividends or held as retained earnings), capital gains, rents, commisions etc., interest, and any other payments that are made for productive services. Transfer payments are not included.

Households and firms

Households are simply the individual economic units in the economy. A firm describes any business enterprise, whether organized as a corporation, partnership or proprietorship.

Inflation

A rise in the average level of prices, as measured by indexes such as the Consumer Price Index (CPI) or GDP deflator. Both the CPI and the GDP deflator measure inflation by comparing the current level of prices to the price level in some base year, chosen periodically. The CPI measures the change in prices for consumer products only. The GDP deflator is broader, encompassing the prices of raw materials and inputs for manufacturers and businesses, as well as consumer prices.

Infrastructure

Basically, all the items that help make our economy more productive – highways, schools, hospitals etc. Since private investors may have difficulty reaping the benefits of investment in such projects, the state of our infrastructure is usually dependent on government spending rather than private investment. It follows that cuts in government spending tend to weaken our infrastructure and indirectly curtail our overall economic prosperity.

Investment

The addition to the nation's capital stock: goods, machinery, technology etc. Note that the economist's definition of investment differs from the standard definition. Economists are only concerned with the increase in the nation's ability to produce goods and services; therefore, the purchase and sale of existing assets is not considered 'investment'. For example, putting your savings into stocks and bonds only serves to transfer wealth from one party to another, without increasing the nation's productive capacity.

Just price

A theory of price formation descended from the Middle Ages, based on ethical values and 'justice'. As the market system of production extended its reach over society, moral philosophers and theologians grappled with the ethical implications of trade and commerce upon everyday life and spirituality. The basic idea of a 'just' price was that it would allow both parties to a transaction to benefit equally, so that neither was taken advantage of. 'Just' prices were ethical, or fair. In practice, however, just price came to mean simply the conventional price established by the market, generally believed to be equal to the direct and indirect labour embodied in the good or service.

Macroeconomics

The branch of economics dealing with aggregates such as the rate of unemployment, inflation, GDP growth etc. It studies the economy as a whole, rather than its individual parts – firms, households etc.

Margin

A 'marginal unit' is the last unit added to a particular stock, such as the labour force, the money supply, etc. Economists typically study changes at the margin, such as a one-unit increase to the existing capital stock, rather than analysing the entire capital stock.

Marginal productivity; marginalism

Marginal productivity theory holds that as more resources are applied as inputs, output will increase, but at a diminishing rate. That is, marginal products decline. This is held to provide a basis for the theory of wages and prices. No one would pay a worker more than the worker could produce, i.e. more than the marginal product, what one more worker will add to output. Competition will push the wage down to that level. Similarly, price will be governed by marginal cost; no one would sell for less, and competition will push price to that level. The theory that develops these ideas fully is known as 'marginalism'.

Markets

Institutions that bring together buyers and sellers of a particular good or service. Not necessarily a physical location; the money 'market', for example, isn't an actual place where people buy and sell money, as is the case with the stock market.

Market-clearing

A result that occurs when supply and demand are equal, such that all supplies are demanded and all demands are fulfilled. When markets clear, there is no tendency for further change and the system is said to be in equilibrium.

Microeconomics

The study of the individual units that make up the economy and their behaviour – households, firms etc.

Multiplier

A multiplier relationship occurs when a change in one variable leads to a succession of further changes in other variables, producing a 'ripple' effect. For example, an initial amount of investment spending provides income to someone, who in turn spends that sum, providing income to someone else etc., leading to a cumulative expansion of income in the economy as a whole. The end result is a multiplied increase in economic activity beyond that of the initial investment.

Money

Not simply what we put in our wallets. Economists have a more precise definition for the green stuff – they call it 'currency'. In economic jargon, 'money' usually refers to currency and purchasing power held in checking accounts, or 'M'. Furthermore, 'money' is not what we make at work; this is called 'income' by economists. Money should also not be confused with 'wealth'; when non-economists say that an individual has a lot of money, what they really mean is that they are 'wealthy'.

Monetarism

The doctrine of economics developed by Milton Friedman, and which was the driving theoretical force behind the period of high interest rates and attempted control of the money supply during Paul Volcker's reign as Chairman of the Federal Reserve System in the early 1980s. The basic conclusion is that inflation is the result of an oversupply of money, and therefore limiting growth of the money supply is the ultimate cure for inflation.

Neo-classical

A broad, catch-all term used to describe economists and economic theories that are based on the notion of supply and demand, Say's Law, and marginal productivity theory. In general, neo-classical economists are in favour of free markets, arguing that the economy will correct itself in the long-run if government and other obstacles are removed.

Optimal; optimizing

Optimal outcomes are the best that can be attained under given circumstances. Optimizing is a method of studying the choices consumers and firms make in economics. Since agents are assumed to be 'rational', we can make the further assumption that they will always choose the course of action that provides them with the optimal outcome. For example, in consumer choice theory, optimizing allows us to predict that consumers will choose the good that provides them with the most 'utility', or satisfaction. This allows for the development of theories of how consumers actually behave.

Principal-agent

Refers to a fiduciary relationship where one person or group acts on behalf of another, as 'agent'. It is typically used to refer to the 'principal-agent problem', whereby agent(s) tend to act in ways that are contrary to the interests of the principal(s). For example, in a corporation, the managers of the firm are supposed to act in the best interests of shareholders, as their 'representative agent'. However, many studies have indicated that agents frequently take actions that are detrimental to the needs of the principals.

Production function

Describes the relationship between the number of workers employed and aggregate output in the economy. It is typically assumed that as the volume of employment rises, the level of output rises also, but at a diminishing rate. In other words, while higher employment increases output, each additional worker adds less to output than the previous worker. In economic jargon, increasing employment is subject to diminishing returns. Mathematically, the first derivative is positive while the second is negative.

Productivity; productivity growth

Productivity is the relation between output and input in some time period; the phrase usually refers to labour productivity. Productivity growth is the annual rate of increase of labour productivity, reflecting technological improvements or improvements in labour organization.

Protection

Establishing trade barriers to protect domestic industries and jobs from foreign competition. Widely believed to permit or encourage inefficiency, although there is little evidence to support this. However, protection clearly does permit a country to adopt an expansionary stance without fear of creating a balance of payments crisis.

Rate of interest; rate of profit

Basically, the price that is paid for the use of money. If you are a lender, the rate of interest is your compensation for providing someone with the temporary use of your surplus funds. Since all rates of interest in the economy tend to move in the same direction, economists frequently speak of 'the' rate of interest, even though in reality there are numerous different rates of interest. The rate of profit refers to the profit made (or expected) on a particular project, relative to the initial investment, expressed as a percentage. Economists frequently use rate of profit and rate of interest interchangeably since, in equilibrium, the two will be equal. This is because borrowers will only borrow if they believe that the rate of profit, which is what they make on the project, is at least equal to the cost of borrowing the money, represented by the rate of interest.

Real wages/money wages

Real wages are the amount that workers receive in terms of its ability to purchase goods and services. Money wages are simply the face value of the income received by workers, not adjusted for the price level of goods and services.

Rent; rent-seeking

Feudal rents were originally per capita payments owed in virtue of status, like tithes. They only later became attached to particular plots of land. Differential rents – sometimes called 'Ricardian rents' – arise because of differences in the fertility of different lands or in the productivity of equipment. (Both plots of land or pieces of equipment produce the same good for the same price, both pay interest at the same rate; the more productive land or equipment can charge rent.) Monopoly rents are based on monopoly control of a desired resource or needed asset. 'Rent seeking' behaviour refers to activity designed to establish monopoly control.

Savings

Savings represent individual income that is not consumed, i.e. spent on goods and services. Savings are typically deposited in accounts at financial institutions, which can then be lent out to firms and others who need to borrow. According to orthodox theory, a higher rate of savings is therefore necessary for investment to increase.

Stability

This can be used in two ways in economics. One usage refers to the stability of equilibrium. In this sense, a stable equilibrium would exist when the forces of competition or supply and demand tend to push the variables of the model back toward equilibrium after a disequilibrating disturbance. An unstable equilibrium would tend to push variables farther and farther away from equilibrium, so that the equilibrium would never be regained. Stability can also be used to refer to functional relationships, such as the demand for money. The basic idea is that the demand for money is based on a number of factors, most of which aren't subject to frequent and drastic fluctuations. As long as money demand is stable, predictable relationships will develop, which can be used as a basis for policy recommendations.

Supply and demand

The basic idea that prices and quantities are determined by the free interaction between producers' desire to supply a particular product and consumers' desire to purchase that product. In general, producers will increase quantity supplied as price rises, while consumers will demand less. If the quantity supplied by producers at a given price exceeds the quantity demanded by consumers, the price will fall, as producers attempt to eliminate inventories of unsold goods. The converse holds for an excess of quantity demanded over and above the quantity supplied. Eventually, a price will be arrived at for which supplies and demands are equal, and thus prices will have no tendency to change further.

Transformational growth

Theory developed by the author which recognizes that the way the economy functions changes over time. By implication, any economic theory must incorporate these changes if it is to offer a realistic assessment of economic life. Hence, the principles of economics – the basic theory of how markets work – are likely to be different in different eras. In particular, S&D is a plausible account of nineteenth-century market adjustment, while simple Keynesian theory describes the advanced world in the post-War era. This theory is in direct contrast with most orthodox approaches to studying the economy, which are basically ahistorical – they treat the economy as essentially unchanging over time, and economics as a science devoted to discovering timeless truths.

INTRODUCTION
Economics at the Alumni Club

It was late; the cocktail hour was over and people had begun to settle in at the dinner tables, while the speakers gathered at the podium. I had been delayed by some small departmental crisis, typical of academic life. Standing in the wide doorway, I checked out the large round tables one after another, hoping to find former room-mates. Ignoring the mural, its struggle to be quaint a lost cause, showing life at P.......n thirty years ago – as glowingly remembered by loyal alumni. Should I sit down? Would the dinner be worth it? Would the wine be drinkable? (. . . European conferences; the older Universities have excellent wine cellars.) Activity at the speakers table had increased; mikes were tested, and then the group was called to order. We were to hear how the Crash had happened, what to expect next from the economy, why we were declining, straight from the horses' mouths, the men who knew how the system worked . . . I decided to stay.

These evenings fade into one another. The speakers are always different, the speeches always the same: America's decline, hopes for rebirth, which will come when virtue is restored in the family, righteousness to public life – provided we curb our extravagance, cut deficits and government spending, so we can save enough to get accumulation going again. It can be embarrassing to listen to these speeches. (Always by men, none of my classmates were women; they came to the University later, after much opposition.) Yet it can also be illuminating. 'Econobabble', one might call it. A set of clichés, phrases, and postures designed to sound important and appear profound, but which can be easily mastered by anyone with a minimal education. The need to tighten our belts, the dangers of deficits, the importance of sound finance, and of saving, the need to provide adequate incentives, the rigours of competition and the efficiency of markets – the litany goes on.

Yet econobabble can be too easily dismissed. These are the ideas according to which the country is run – tidied up and made presentable and well-seasoned with self-congratulations. Of course, not every after-dinner speech is the same, even if delivered in econobabble. Businessmen are chiefly interested in profits; academics and economists tend to put the well-being of the public first. There can be major conflicts, although sometimes they go

1

together. But taking this into account, the major problem is that these speeches – and the ways we talk about the economy generally – simply don't connect with how the system works. It's not just wrong facts, or misunderstandings of technical details. That would be no surprise, and nothing to worry about. It's a question of the whole picture, the *vision* of the economy and how it works. Free markets, efficiency . . . everyone will be better off. It all works automatically: supply creates its own demand. The picture that underlies econobabble is what is disturbing, because it shows that the vision guiding our political discourse is dramatically out of focus.

FINDING A TABLE

By now, the room had largely filled up, and as I looked around there didn't seem to be any seats left at the dinner tables. Nor had I spotted any of my former room-mates. I stood off to one side, near the door to the kitchen; it was noisy but I had an unobstructed view of the podium. The introductions were being made. The main talks would be after dinner; now each speaker whetted our appetites. A first speaker, for example, having dined on taken-over firms for lunch, told us how he had cut unprofitable routes from his airline. If the customers weren't there, you didn't do it. Sales, not prestige, not tradition, was what mattered. You had to be hard-headed, and you couldn't count on building up sales by cutting prices. Sometimes that worked, sometimes it didn't. You had to know whether the customers were going to be there.

Common sense, I thought; business should design its operations to appeal to the markets where the sales are expected to be. What else would you do, after all? But that is not what most of the textbooks say; they'll tell you to design operations to be the cheapest, and they won't even notice a possible problem. There is something to be said for plain common sense.

I wasn't the only one without a seat. An organizer and his wife were also high and dry – an old friend with a new job, retired early from telephones and now working for anti-pollution. And not alone; a number of other class-mates were involved in environmentalist projects. He arranged a table for us; at dinner he drank sparingly. Once fat, now trim. Wife the opposite – and smoked, too. I looked around the room; only wives – well, women – seemed to smoke. Or to be fat. No one drank hard liquor. Fish first, good. But then rubber chickens. Why bother to jog if you ate rubber and drank sulphites? Mass production, for all its real benefits, certainly came with costs.

THE MAIN COURSE OF EVENTS

The platform stirred again, as plates were removed and mouths opened for business. New introductions and the conqueror of airlines, successor to Howard Hughes, took the floor again. No Jane Russell, no outlaws. Not even a spruce goose. But then, with eloquence, we heard that the cause of our problems was too much wasteful consumption, too little saving. American companies are soft; they squander money on Lear jets and executive suites. The country is the same; everyone has a VCR and nobody works hard or saves. If there is no saving how can there be growth? The other speakers nodded sagely and agreed. American executives didn't save and they didn't take hard decisions, either. American management was run by committee; everyone got along with everyone else, and no one rocked the boat. The result: no innovation, no dynamism. The whole country was going soft. Business had given up on competition.

And why not? I thought, as I had so often on similar occasions. Wouldn't you? Competition was war; dangerous, unpredictable, and a source of unending stress. Business leaders celebrate its virtues, but in practice keep it at a distance. Now an interruption from another panelist, a venture capitalist. The problem is the shortage of venture capital. Correct this and competition will be restored through the dynamics of American ingenuity, operating through the free market. Incantation, rather than analysis? After all, why has the free market failed to provide enough venture capital? Perhaps because moneyed wealth does not enjoy the risks of competition? Could that be? Just as business itself unfailingly moves to restrict competition?

Is this so hard to understand? Consider what we see in the health clubs every day: There's too much stress in life. Which is the reason for all the jogging and carrot juice. Why not make a deal? Competition is right up there with apple pie and the Fourth of July, but in practice no one wants it. Yet the panel nodded solemnly, and Venture Capital subsided, pleased. An economist once said the only people who really like competition are economists who write textbooks. A metaphor for the modern economy: the textbook writer who lavishes praise on competition, hoping to edge out the competing books and establish a monopoly.

Too much welfare, too much government regulation, the speaker continued, too much government spending – a familiar litany, but in recent years a new element had emerged – especially in regard to the military. Weapons waste. This is where our savings go – and it's mostly garbage. First, the Cold War is over and we'll never use it; if we negotiate a deal with the Russkies, we'll never need any of it. And God help us if we ever did have to use it, because the stuff won't work. It's not the right stuff; it's the wrong stuff. Contracts awarded non-competitively, compliance improperly audited, and whistleblowers booted; the whole military mess is a waste, and it is dragging down the rest of the economy. We've squandered our savings.

I could agree with a lot of that, I thought, but is military spending the only 'waste'? What about packaging? Advertising? The waste of our best talents in protracted lawsuits, or in blowing speculative bubbles in the financial markets? What about the neglected and under educated kids in the cities, or for that matter, in the suburbs? And why do speakers on these occasions invariably go on about 'savings' all the time? Savings is just not-spending-on-consumption; there's no magic in that. *Investment* is what counts. It is a mystery why so many people believe that more not-spending-on-consumption will encourage more spending on investment. If people are buying *fewer* consumer goods, why build a new factory to make *more* consumer goods? After-dinner speakers often started from common sense: markets are indeed the key to progress and prosperity. But almost invariably there would follow a disastrous move: the country is just like a household or a business. You and I should not run ourselves into debt – so neither should the country. You and I should not over-spend, so neither should the country. Spending on what you don't need is waste, for us, so it must be for the country, too.

This is the hardest point, probably in all of economics. The system as a whole is not just the projection of its parts onto a larger screen; it is not the household or the firm writ large. It is a different *kind* of system; it works according to different rules. And there is no obvious reason why this should be so. Even worse, at one time – and not so long ago – it wasn't so, and the system as a whole *did* (more or less) replicate the workings of the house-hold. The word 'Economics', in fact, is derived from the ancient Greek for household management. How to explain all this? Write a book?

ADDITIVES IN THE FOOD FOR THOUGHT

More wine; more, but not better. And dessert, cake made with white sugar, whipped cream from the can. Now, wait a minute, just where do all these derogatory judgements come from? Let's be superior and show that we have taste? Are we being a little defensive? Well, perhaps. But consider this: the richest school in the richest country in the world has a dinner and the chickens are rubber, the wine has additives and the whipped cream is from a can. The point is plain enough – mass production is why we became the richest – but the taste of the additives and the rubber shows why we are slipping now. The dinner may say more, more eloquently and more to the point, than the speakers. Pushing dessert away, I turned towards the podium.

Now, black hair slicked down, peering through rimless glasses, impeccably dressed financier, of New York and Paris, was presenting elegantly phrased thoughts about international flows of funds and the causes and consequences of the twin deficits, those of government and foreign trade. The government deficit absorbed private savings and so drove up interest rates, attracting foreign funds, which drove up the dollar, which created the trade deficit. Very simple. So we need to save more, and spend less, especially on the part of the govern-ment. We can't afford welfare, we can't afford extravagance, certainly not on the part of the military, which should set an example of efficiency. We can't afford to shell out money for the poor and the homeless, much as they need it, shameful as their plight is, unless we can curb some other forms of spending – such as the military or Star Wars. Or Social Security.

It sounded good, especially delivered with a slight foreign accent, which lent authority and an air of European sophistication. It's what we've been hearing recently from the Chairman of the Federal Reserve, and from the Clinton Administration. It is also completely and obviously wrong. A quick look at the figures will show that there is simply no correlation between larger deficits and higher real (that is, inflation-adjusted) interest rates. To take the most obvious case: the largest deficits in relation to GNP in the twentieth century occurred during World War II, when real interest rates were near zero or even negative. In the 1950s and early 1960s, GNP grew faster than debt, so deficits fell in relation to GNP. But during a good part of this period, real interest rates rose. In the 1980s and 1990s deficits/GNP and real interest rates have sometimes moved together, sometimes in opposite ways. There's no reliable or systematic pattern. Yet the Clinton Administration built its economic policy on reducing the deficit in order to bring down interest rates! It did bring the deficit down – but as of late 1994 and early 1995 interest rates are going back up!

It should be added that the rest of the argument is no better. It went: high interest rates lead to a high dollar, which cuts into exports and creates a trade deficit. High interest rates relative to those in other countries will tend to attract an inflow of short term capital, and this will tend to drive up the dollar – sometimes. Other factors are also involved. A high dollar will cut into exports. But high interest rates will tend to cut domestic investment and create a slump at home, which will tend to reduce imports. So the total effect on the trade balance may not be at all clear-cut. But these are technicalities. The issue is the *vision* of the economy. According to the after-dinner speakers, deficits are dangerous. They are one of the major causes of our problems. By contrast, a better focused vision of our system will tell us that the deficits are a symptom, an effect not a cause, and that they are not only not particularly dangerous, but kept within limits they actually serve a useful function.

The next speaker continued the litany. Governor of our neighbouring state, the one where it's dangerous to breathe and the rivers are firetraps, he told us of the need to cut government spending, to bring budgets under control. Tough decisions had to be made; priorities had to be clear. Unless the budget deficits were controlled, the country would spend itself into ruin. At present we were heading, as a country, for bankruptcy; governments were out of control, consumers were piling up debt, firms were doing so even faster, and as for banks, the whole system was on the brink. The problem was a moral one; as a people we had lost sight of the old virtues, the eternal verities, 'neither a borrower nor a lender be/ for a loan oft loses both itself and friends / and borrowing dulls the edge of husbandry'. Miss Shipley, too, had stressed that, in 9th grade, not realizing that Polonius was a pompous old fool, and his advice to his son was meant as a parody.

Instead of making things better, the Governor's prescription – and his successor's even more – could only make them worse. Cut back on government when rivers are catching fire? To say nothing of centre cities. Reduce taxes instead of solving problems? This was being part of the problem, not part of the solution. How could that be? The Governor was smart, had been a fine student, and after a flirtation with the teaching of history, had spent the whole of his adult life in public service. Like the banker and the take-over artist, he knew his trade; he knew how the world worked well enough to rise to the top. Like them, and like his successor, he started out his remarks from eminently common-sense premises. Good, clear, sharp observations about politics and money. How could he, or they, be wrong? How could people who run the system not know how it works?

BORN IN THE USA MEANS BORN TO RUN

Well, for one thing, you get to the top by knowing how to climb a pyramid, not by knowing how it was made or what mysterious forces it contains. I remembered my trip to Egypt, my second year at Oxford. It was not long after Roger Bannister had broken four minutes on the track in Cowley; everyone was doing a 'four-minute' something or other. Art Buchwald defined the track for a 'four-minute Louvre': main entrance – *Mona Lisa* – *Winged Victory* – *Venus de Milo* – and out. Now we were going to try a four-minute Great Pyramid – a race, we agreed, that would prepare us for corporate America. Real training. We were perhaps more right than we knew – it's not just corporate America, it's the same in the academic world, too. Everything seems to depend on how skilfully you can climb the Great Pyramid. (Don't try a four-minute pyramid; the rock crumbles unexpectedly as you get near the top, and it's a long, steep fall to the bottom. More training for corporate America!)

But preparing for the climb, and all the mountaineering skill in the world, doesn't tell you anything about what to do when you finally get to the top. Witness Ronald Reagan. Or, for that matter, some CEOs of major companies. To reach the top personal political skills are needed; to govern, knowledge and wisdom. Knowledge of how the system works, and how it can be made to work better. Wisdom to know when and how and for whom to make it work better. None of this is learned or needed in the scramble up the ladder. Indeed, one of the worst things you can do is show that you know more about how things work than the boss does.

Yet this is only part of the story. After all, once at the top someone smart enough to have made it there should surely be able to figure out how things work. Why not? In previous eras the reflections of active leaders – at least the smart ones – told us how the system worked.

A few summers back my son, getting ready to go up to Oxford, joined me on a summer seminar programme – August in a cliffside hotel on the Adriatic. He brought along Machiavelli, both *The Prince* and *The Discourses*. Talking to him about his reading, I was once again impressed by the sweep and above all, the modernity of Machiavelli's thought. He was a political activist, at one time defence secretary of Florence, who, when forced out of political life, reflected on his times. He was the quintessential outsider, trusted neither by the republicans nor by the Medicis, but needed for his talents and his connections. He never quite rose to the top, but he was never far from it either. Kept outside the innermost councils, but privy to their secrets, he was the ultimate observer – shrewd, detached, unsentimental, with a keen eye for detail. Very like my classmate speakers at Reunion evenings – also outsiders: a corporate raider, a venture-capitalist, a foreigner, a Southerner, and a liberal in a party gone conservative. Yet when Machiavelli reflected on his experience and examined the way the system worked, on the whole, he got it right. He saw through the system, to how it really worked. My class-mates got it wrong. Why? Of course, they cannot be expected to write a new theory for our times and must be pardoned for not being the stature of a Machiavelli – who today among our public figures is? But Machiavelli's advice on the issues of the day was sound and theirs – and Stockman's and Reagan's, to say nothing of Bush and Sununu, or the Democrats from Dukakis to Clinton – is not. Why?

It is not a question of the subject matter, for Machiavelli did address economic questions, taxes and the revenues of the state, for example, as did later writers, such as William Petty, Francois Quesnay and Adam Smith. Their advice was not only sound; it became the prevailing view of the day. Moreover, dissent and alternative proposals could usually be understood in terms of conflicting views as to who should benefit, and who pay, in matters of policy. There did not exist a clash of diametrically opposed visions of how the system works, giving rise to diametrically opposite policies to achieve more or less the same ends. Yet that is what we have today: austerity vs. expansion as alternative routes to growth and prosperity.

Machiavelli was acutely aware of the influence of worldly incentives and of the resulting differences between appearances and reality in people's actions. This led him to the conclusion that mercenaries would fight as little as possible, so as to prolong the war, and therefore their period of pay. Florence finally agreed when its mercenary captain was seen beating back his own troops with the flat of his sword from the breach in the walls of Pisa, lest they succeed in taking the city they were hired to besiege. In replacing mercenary forces with a citizen militia the Florentines may have become more worldly-wise, abandoning illusions about the moral force of solemn oaths, and recognizing that market incentives worked perversely in the case of 'public goods'. But they did not in any way adopt a policy at odds with their own personal life experience. For a contrast, consider the policy of increasing state expenditure and indebtedness in a depression: every one of us, from our own experience, knows that in hard times you have to cut back on spending and keep out of debt – or you'll end up in the bread line. But if the state cuts back in time of depression it makes things worse, not better; the correct (Keynesian) policy is for the state to expand and run a deficit.

Machiavellian insights into motivation generalize to many professions, and are no less relevant today. Nor are the crude and obvious cases, like Captain Vitelli at Pisa, the most important. More serious by far were the rules of conduct and precepts of strategy that led to hard-fought battles like that at Anghiari, where after a day-long struggle the two armies left but one casualty on the field, and that an accident. Of course the battle decided nothing, but the participants had to be paid for combat. The parallel today might be the performing of unnecessary surgery, or dragging out a case at law. The orientation of medicine today, and its strategy of research, is to make war on disease, to concentrate on curing, which earns handsomely, and wins plaudits in the press. Yet the greatest successes by far have been due to public health and sanitation measures, simple prevention, carried out by public agencies, by which we have wholly eliminated formerly endemic plagues. However, the process has generated very few opportunities for private gain. And cutbacks on public health spending have allowed diseases that had been defeated, like TB, to rise again.

People don't like to believe this sort of thing, now any more than in Machiavelli's time. It runs against the grain to suggest that a whole profession, whether soldiers or doctors, has changed its standards and procedures, even unconsciously, in order to maximize pecuniary gains. It's even harder to accept that this has been supported by the political process. How could pillars of the community be involved in such a thing? How could the free market permit it? Private enterprise and monetary rewards are supposed to bring about the optimal allocation of scarce resources. Making money is as American as apple pie. (Gnawing doubt: do commercially grown apples cause cancer? But doubts, too, are unAmerican.) Like Wall Street and just as fervently, Main Street believes in the virtues of the market.

Yet we have all been short-changed in the market one way or another. We've bought a used car that didn't run, we've had an operation we didn't need, or bought a coffin too expensive by far for someone whose experience with their used car or unnecessary operation was more fateful than ours. Or less carefully regulated by government. We've all met this in practice, yet we have trouble facing up to Machiavelli – we call his kind of clarity about motives and intentions, and the resulting implications for state policy, 'Machiavellian', with sinister connotations.

If we have trouble accepting a way of thinking that fits our everyday life, how much more difficult, then, to accept an approach to state policy that runs directly *counter* to our everyday experience? That is what macro-economics calls on us to do – when we are at our most down-and-out, when the state is taking in least in revenues, that is when it should borrow and spend the most!

AN UNEXPECTED CALL

One problem with being an intellectual is that sometimes you find yourself thinking when you should be paying attention. The Chair had just called on me by name: 'Now let's hear a completely different point of view, one that puts people ahead of profits.' Objections on the speakers' platform; no one there put profits ahead of people, nor was there any possible conflict between them. The Chair was genially unconvinced, and gesturing, called on me to stand and deliver. What did I think of these proceedings? On the spot. What was I to say?

So I said what I had been thinking: that in earlier times the best and the brightest had generally been able to get it right on the burning issues of the day, and the consensus tended to form around a broadly sensible, if sometimes watered-down, vision of the working of the world. Conflicts over economic issues were clearly understandable in terms of the different classes and interests. But in our time, in the twentieth century, on questions of the economy, the best and the brightest apparently not only could not get it right, but generally got it all wrong, upside down, and the consensus more often than not tended to form around an almost absurdly wrong vision of the working of the world. Keynes was the exception that proved the rule. But now, at a time when the economy has been weak or stagnating for nearly two decades, *austerity* is advocated! The problem that this evening posed for me, was how could we have arrived at such a state of affairs, where a group of proven leaders, men of stature, echoing the opinions current in the corridors of power, could have set forth views so totally wrong and so disastrous for the well-being of ordinary people?

There are many tricks in public speaking, techniques that help you get out of tight spots, overcome awkward moments, and smooth over difficulties. College lecturing provides plenty of practice. But nothing could have helped me out of that one. After a long pause I sat down. Silence. Then a scattering of applause; a few isolated souls approved. The meeting pulled itself together, and moved on as if nothing untoward had happened.

But it had, and when we broke up for conversation, I was besieged. What did I mean, 'totally wrong'? Keynesian economics is *passé*. How could I be so sure? How can we be sure of anything? Could I come to study with you, and learn why my husband is always wrong? (I know he is, but I can't explain it properly.) What did I know of real markets? Had I ever met a payroll? Made make-or-break decisions? Why Machiavelli? Is economics immoral? I know business is. And finally, suppose I was right, how do we explain it that the best and the brightest tend to get it wrong when it comes to the economy?

OLD WINE IN NEW BOTTLES – OR VICE VERSA?

To tell the truth I couldn't answer any of the questions that night. I had spoken out of turn; caught almost dreaming, I had come out with what was running through my mind, but nothing had been worked out or thought through properly. Yet the questions are answerable, and the main question is the last one, the one I had started with.

To answer it we have to see that in modern times we face a new kind of problem in coping with the world, one that only emerged with the development of the industrial economy. For this was a change that transformed not just industry, but the whole society, and it did so in a way that continued, and carries on to the present. What changed at the most fundamental level was the complex of forces keeping the society together: from being essentially static, and holding the system in an equilibrium, as a result of the unleashing of market forces – competition – this complex array had become dynamic and now drove the society along a path of unending development!

In a static world, in which technology is simple and small-scale, the parts will tend to replicate the essential relationships of the system as a whole; the principles of household management as expounded by Isocrates, for example, will hold for Athens as well. Not so in a dynamic world; when the technology is large-scale, and production aims at the gobal market, the principles which explain the workings of the part will no longer hold for the whole. Indeed, perversely, at times the whole will appear to work in a manner almost exactly opposite! This creates difficulty in understanding the economy; common sense will be indispensable, but followed to its logical conclusion, common sense will now lead to paradox! This will take some explaining, but it will make it clear why modern economics – and therefore modern politics – is so difficult, and why so many well-placed executives and political leaders harbour so many mistaken views.

Yet we had better proceed slowly, especially since these views are not fully consonant with the received wisdom of the profession. Is it not presumptuous – and dangerous – to depart from the canons of the general consensus? Dangerous perhaps, if you want promotions and tenure. Or to publish in the leading journals. And yet . . . The average economics journal article has 2.4 readers. Even the profession is not interested. Moreover, there is no longer much of a consensus. Perhaps it is time to break free – hardly any one takes the textbook stories seriously any more. Textbooks tell parables, usually about a single market, studied in isolation. But of course markets are not isolated; they interact, and we know that a set of interacting markets can behave in unpredictable and bizarre ways. Unfortunately there is no agreement about how this should be expressed theoretically. A recent Nobel Prize winner was awarded the prize for his theoretical and empirical studies of the aggregate growth of the economy. *The New Palgrave*, a four volume, four million word compendium of received wisdom in economics – the definitive word according to more than 900 contributors – lists ten articles dealing with this prize-winning work. Nine of them declare it to be based on fundamental errors, while the tenth supports it in principle, but holds that it was carried out incorrectly. Where is the consensus?

Academic economics can be 'academic' in the worst sense – and it usually is in textbooks, which are too often the product of compromises between competing schools of thought. Doctrine is watered down to boost sales. Professional economics is a kind of game; there are rules – certain kinds of arguments are acceptable, others are not. Playing by the rules you had to reach one or another acceptable set of conclusions. There are 'Whites' vs. 'Reds', like the two teams at my daughter's former school. 'Whites' came out for the unrestricted free market; 'Reds' for mild and occasional government intervention. The more effectively you argued within the rules, the better you played the game, the faster you would be promoted. Very few economists I knew had ever been in business on their own, or worked in a blue collar job. A few worked in bureaucracies, for banks or for government agencies, but not for manufacturing companies, or for distributors. In my experience professional economists knew a lot about economics, but not as much as one would expect about the economy. They were just as narrow and blinkered in their own way as businesspeople. Why didn't we require our students to get to know each of the main sectors of the system? To spend some time working in each? A recent poll of graduate students showed that only 3 per cent thought it important to know about the real world. 'Important' in what sense? Passing exams in economics, I expect. I think they're right; you don't have to know anything about how the real world works to get good grades in economics. In fact it may cause you trouble. I always had secret sympathies for the Maoist project of sending the top bureaucrats out to dig ditches, to do some real work, manual labour, for a change. What if our economics professors had to do some real work for a change?

But if the conventional wisdom of professional economics is a poor guide to how the system works, where will we find a better one? How will we know it? And who should the reader trust as a travel guide and interpreter in these uncharted seas? A professional economist? We've all had much the same training – mathematics, conventional theory, econometrics, and all that. A clue: most of my professional colleagues, who regard our subject as a science, tend to scorn the older writers as out-of-date. Who reads Adam Smith and Ricardo? or Marx? Or even John Maynard Keynes? Yet these are the great books, the foundations on which everything rests, including the conventional wisdom. And they emphasized dynamics – growth and structural change, problems of cycles and instability – rather than allocation and static efficiency. In short, they saw the development of the economy as part of history.

This will guide our approach. Our understanding of markets will be based on the history of the automobile, and television, and electronics, the rise of industry and the decline of the family farm. From these kinds of studies, the path will follow insights gleaned from sociology and industrial relations, subjects very much out of favour with the leading schools of economic thought today. Rightly enough, in a way; for what we learn from sociology and industrial history must give rise to doubts about the conventional wisdom. It will take a hardened academic ideologue to seriously argue that 'markets allocate efficiently' after studying the history of American labour and unemployment, or the waste, fraud, strip mining, and dust bowls generated by American business, along with its goods, goodies, and bads. But we will find, nevertheless, that markets are the key to understanding the development of modern technology and the prosperity and power it brings.

And if we economists are so smart why aren't we rich? Well, Ricardo and Keynes *were* rich, and they made their money themselves, by putting their principles to work. As for me, at least I've met a payroll, which is a lot more than most corporate lawyers, or for that matter executives, can say. In fact two different payrolls, and both gave me headaches. Maybe even heartaches; the business system face-to-face is pretty rough. For four years I ran my co-op, in SoHo, downtown Manhattan. Then I started a business with some friends, producing a board game, called Class Struggle. We did well at first, but got in trouble when we tried to expand too fast. In the end, no losses, but no profit either. (I did better in real estate.) So I have met a payroll, although I never got rich.

Still, why should anyone listen? Why, indeed? Surely because we need to know. Maybe it might be right ... The record shows that no one official, private or public, understands the economy very well. And this bothers us; it is not a lone voice here or there raising questions, but a chorus from all walks of life. People want to know how the system works, the system *as it actually is*, not 'as if' it were competitive or rational or whatever. The economy – how it works, why it breaks down from time to time, what we can do to make it work better. More fairly and justly. And where is it going? Will it get there? Will the Japanese and the Germans already be there? And what will happen to us, to our children? Practical questions can't be answered by theories based on mythology.

In the end, it doesn't matter how much you have studied a problem; the question is whether you can deal with it convincingly, in ways that will help in practical matters. Economics is not an experimental science. To some extent we can test our theories by seeing if the policies they imply work the way we expect. But if we can't get our policies put into effect the only test may be to see if we can persuade others, that, yes indeed, we have got it right, that's how things work and the other answers lead us up blind alleys. And we want to know how the world works so we can make it work better. It may take time to build coalitions and create institutions necessary to put our insights into practice; but first we must have the insights.

So what follows is my attempt to persuade my fellow classmates from that famous University in the state where you must not breathe too deeply, that this is how the world works, that while they started out those Reunion evenings from common sense, they slipped on a tricky bit of it, early on – and that one slip set them sliding off on the wrong course altogether, ending up not with common sense, but with common nonsense – mere econobabble. Common sense tells us that the economy responds to demand, to sales – and that is right. Common nonsense tells us that the economy as a whole works just like an individual household or business – that what is true of the part is true of the whole, that the household is a microcosm of the world. Would that it were so! And perhaps once it was. But in the world of modern technology it is no longer, and the result is a nest of paradoxes which has trapped popular thinking. Let's see if we can work ourselves free from these entanglements, and look at the world with a fresh vision.

Part I

UNDERSTANDING AND MISUNDERSTANDING MARKETS

There's no getting around the fact that economics is tough. It's about making money, and if that were easy we'd all be rich. This will be the most difficult Part, and within it, Chapter 1 will be the hardest chapter. Nevertheless, the main drift of the argument should not be at all hard to follow. It will be signposted throughout, a path marked out through the thickets and brambles of economic argument. And the predatory economic theories inhabiting this jungle will be kept caged – on display, but not allowed to run wild in the text.

From the author's point of view there is another problem. No matter how much ingenuity is deployed, the subject remains difficult and some readers will be tempted to throw up their hands, feeling it has all become too technical. Other readers, however, adept in technical reasoning, may be inclined to skip over the carefully pruned analytical passages, feeling they are fit for kindergarten, but beneath the notice of the initiated.

If this chapter is successful – and much hard work has gone into it – both these reactions will be wrong. The analytical passages have to be technical in order to be correct, but there's no reason they have to be hard to understand. The reader will have to do some work – no pre-digested sound bites can do it for you – but the effort will be rewarded. Nor should the technically adept reader skip over these passages too lightly, for, simplified though they are, they tie the argument to the basic assumptions about the economy. Part of the message here is that scientific economics has unwittingly helped to foster econobabble by failing to adapt its analyses and models to changing historical conditions.

The textbook account of markets stresses their role in efficiently allocating scarce resources, whose supply is given, among a set of pre-determined competing ends. Such efficient allocation is supposed to describe the way markets actually work. The textbooks make an important point – agents making rational choices certainly do 'allocate'. But models of optimal choice are important in *improving* economic activities; they are relevant to innovation, rather than normal operations. They are prescriptive, rather than descriptive. For that very reason *markets* engender dynamic pressures which lead to changes in the 'givens' of the economy.

Markets adjust. Supply and demand describes a process of market adjustment in response to changes in prices. This looks a lot like the models of optimal choice, but the two should not be confused. Furthermore, markets can adjust in other ways; in particular, they can adjust via the multiplier, in response to changes in aggregate demand. The great 'Neo-Classical Synthesis' – the 'billabong' of the title – was an attempt to fit together these two mutually exclusive patterns of market adjustment, each correctly describing the way markets worked in a particular historical era. Conventional Keynesians, Monetarists, and their successors all come to grief over this point.

'Transformational growth' is the process of change which results from market pressures. Changes in the 'givens' lead eventually to different patterns of market adjustment – so that the market works differently in different historical periods. In particular the Craft Economy adjusts through price changes, so that the economy as a whole tends to behave like its constituent parts. But the pressures of competition lead to innovations in technology, resulting in the system of Mass Production. As we will see in Chapter 2, this system has an independent dynamic, so that the behaviour of the whole is quite unlike that of the parts – the macrosystem does not behave like a firm or a household.

The price mechanism in a Craft Economy tends to act as a stabilizer. Market adjustment in such a system works more or less as the textbooks say. But prices are not flexible in a Mass Production economy; there is no 'price mechanism'. Adjustments take place through the 'multiplier-accelerator', and tend to be de-stabilizing. The market needs guidance and correction. But it remains the driving force of the economy, generating technological innovation.

The dynamic force of the market, and its revolutionary nature, are glossed over by the conventional wisdom. Indeed, that wisdom does not even adequately describe the more ordinary impact of the market, namely to provide incentives to people to carry out the functions of normal life. To see this we need an account of 'institutions', the subject of Chapter 3. Production institutions are arrangements of reciprocal obligations designed to achieve some objective or objectives. From a study of the duties assigned to different roles it is possible to define their 'natural intent', and once this is known, to develop an account of the 'general good' for the institution.

The market generates incentives that propel people to act as they should in their social roles, to carry out their duties energetically, promoting the General Good. But also, and more importantly, it generates incentives to *improve* the system of production. This latter, conceived in a very general way, consists of two kinds of institutions, socializing roles and production roles, that fit together as an interdependent whole. Socializing institutions – families, schools, churches – train and prepare people for roles in production

– agriculture, manufacturing, services – where they produce the goods and services that support families in both kinds of institutions, and also, of course, replace the goods and services used up in production. Normally production will generate a surplus, a net product, over and above the goods used up in production and in supporting the households of workers and managers. In a feudal system this net product is appropriated in the form of rents, taxes and tithes, and spent on public works, ostentatious display and the arts, and supporting military projects. Under capitalism it appears chiefly as profits and taxes, although some portion will often go to wages and salaries as well. Taxes support public works, defence, policing, social infrastructure and the like, net wages and salaries support luxury consumption – but also investment in 'human capital', and profits largely underwrite new investment.

Markets set up material incentives to harness agents to do their duty; the *economy* may be seen as the combination of markets and systems of natural intent. But we will see that markets can only effectively create incentives to achieve *private* aims; public goods and services, meaning things that have to be used or consumed collectively, will not be provided by market pressures, at least not without distortion. But over time, as the economy becomes richer, the ratio of public goods to private tends to rise – an issue we will examine more fully in later chapters. But the problem can be seen even at this stage: as public goods and services become more important, the market will become progressively less able to promote the General Good.

1

MAINSTREAM OR BILLABONG?

WHAT THE TEXTBOOKS TELL US AND WHAT THEY DON'T

Once lecturing in Australia I referred to 'mainstream economics'. A famous teacher there corrected me: not mainstream, he said, but 'billabong economics'; a 'billabong', it seems, is a raging torrent that in spring rushes down the hills, sweeping all before it, only to run out in the desert and dry up in stagnant pools. It struck me that that is just what has happened to mainstream economics. The mainstream today refers to the ideas of the 'Keynesian Revolution' blended with the traditional principles of supply and demand, or 'marginalism'. When first propounded in the late 1940s this new synthesis swept all before it, rushing on into the desert wastes of high theory. Everyone thought, now will the desert bloom, and fruitful policies be harvested! But it has been a billabong.

Nowhere is this more evident than in the arid reaches of neo-Classical high theory. Take a major topic: the 'existence' of general economic equilibrium. This doesn't mean finding out and identifying actual, real-world cases of overall economic balance. It's the search for a mathematical solution to a set of highly abstract equations that supposedly represent consumer and producer preferences for goods and techniques. But to manipulate the equations it has been necessary to make such drastic 'simplifying' assumptions that the actors are no longer recognizable. Nothing is left of society. No one any longer pretends that the topics being studied are 'realistic', or even plausible. No one cares. Both questions and answers are abstract and mathematical; they have nothing to do with anything so common and ordinary as everyday business.

Perhaps this doesn't matter all that much. High theory is written by and for high theorists. It's the textbooks that count, as was often brought home to me at Reunions, in after-dinner conversation. Practically everyone who finishes college takes a basic economics course – and what do they learn? 'You teach economics – how can you say that deficits don't matter, that protection could be helpful, that regulation is necessary. Don't you read the

19

textbooks you teach?' The textbooks – they really are the stagnant pools in the desert, the torpid residue of that great flood of scholarship immediately after the war.

STALEMATE

Why this stagnation? And what does it mean to say the theory has dried up? To understand this we have to start with the post-War synthesis of Keynesian (macro) and traditional (micro) thinking, which unleashed the flood of new work. 'Macro' economics, in its modern form invented by Keynes just before World War II, deals with the big economy-wide questions – unemployment, inflation, growth. By contrast, 'micro' economics deals with consumers and households making their best choices, and how these various choices can be reconciled through the market. Putting the issue in its simplest form, if the market does reconcile everyone's *optimal* choices, so that each person gets what they want subject to what everybody else gets, there can't be any 'involuntary' unemployment, nor could there be any inflation. For if there were either, somebody would be out of equilibrium. Being involuntarily unemployed is not anyone's optimum, nor is losing one's savings in an inflation. But Keynesian macroeconomics is designed to explain 'equilibrium' (persistent) levels of unemployment and inflation. Does macro-economic analysis therefore rest on the failure of markets to work at the micro level? The post-War synthesis provided a straightforward answer, designed to please everyone: Yes and No. Yes, markets fail, compared to *perfect* markets. But No, it isn't actually a failure, because that's how markets work in reality. Like most such answers, however, this satisfied no one, and the great debate began.

One side, later labelled 'Keynesian' developed the view that the market system was not necessarily defective; institutional factors required markets, especially labour markets, to work in certain ways that could be considered 'imperfect' from the point of view of pure theory, but which reflected actual and important, perhaps even desirable, social and political pressures. As a result there existed wage and price rigidities that not only made Keynesian unemployment, etc., possible, but made it necessary for these things to be analysed by means of macroeconomic theory. Microeconomics was not enough. The mainstream full equilibrium picture, while acceptable as pure theory, was unrealistic.

Not so, said the other side, first appearing dressed as 'Monetarists', later as 'New Classicals'. Paraphrasing the poet,

> 'Macro is micro, micro macro' – that is all
> We know on earth, and all we need to know.

There cannot be two theories, or two kinds of theory; there is only one and it is the traditional one. If markets are imperfect, and so give suboptimal results, the solution is not to invent new forms of intervention; it is rather to find ways to remove the imperfections. Then the system will work properly.

This second position draws on a central concern of Neo-Classical theory, namely, demonstrating the virtues of free markets, usually at a very abstract level. Unfortunately this has often meant ignoring how actual economies work, perhaps since that would require, among other things, explaining how they periodically break down and recover. (Which, in turn, suggests that free markets have important and possibly inherent, shortcomings, a point perhaps under-appreciated by after-dinner speakers everywhere.) Free markets are supposed to provide the venue for optimal choices; everyone will situate themselves in their most preferred position, subject to the choices of everyone else. Roughly, free markets will bring the best of all possible worlds. We should expect that all productive resources (most significantly, labour) will be fully employed and that the important economic problem is scarcity in relation to what people want. And since this is what the textbooks teach us, it is quite natural to believe that this is what real-world markets are all about.

In practice, as the Keynesians tirelessly point out, nothing could be further from the truth. Markets do perform important social functions, and it is a pity that so many economists analyse the workings of fictitious and abstract institutions, thus failing to notice what real-life markets actually do, since their working is both interesting and important. Markets do involve choice, and do bring about the resolution of potential social conflicts, just as the theory suggests. But what happens and how it works is completely different from the story told by the abstract picture – as we shall see.

This does not mean we side with the conventional Keynesians, even though they win our sympathies. For early on, they accepted a fatal compromise, which dramatically weakened their position. They accepted the view that supply and demand – the picture of markets adjusting through flexible prices – should be based on the theory of rational choice. 'Rational choice' means that agents know what they want (precisely and in detail), know what stands in the way (the constraints) and maximize, which means, get what they want to the highest extent possible. 'Rationality' is arguably the same at all times and places; it can plausibly be claimed a universal in human experience. (Some philosophers will not agree, however!) Hence, many economists contend, the behaviour of markets will be the same anywhere, anytime, subject to different imperfections and interferences. The *core* patterns of market behaviour – resource allocation by the price mechanism – will be a universal constant in human experience, disturbed, inhibited or 'shocked' by historically different external influences.

This is not the only way to interpret supply and demand (henceforth S&D). Marshall, for example, understood the price mechanism quite differently, as reflecting practical (rather than optimal) responses guided by working rules designed to govern normal operations in conditions of open competition (Andrews, 1964). He developed what has become the first take on the traditional picture – demand curves sloping down from left to right, with supply curves rising from left to right. This is often called 'partial equilibrium analysis' – looking at particular markets – and Marshall based it on *specific* assumptions about institutions and technology, as is made clear by his examples. Supply was provided by family firms, operating processes subject to diminishing marginal returns; demand came from households whose consumption patterns exhibited diminishing marginal utility. The resulting curves showed how the market adjusted through the variations of prices.[1]

Statistical data from the late nineteenth and early twentieth century confirms that up to World War I money prices were indeed flexible in both directions, and in fact, tended to drift downwards over time. Money wages also moved in both directions, but their movement was smaller and slower. Real wages – money wages adjusted for purchasing power – behaved as S&D would predict – high real wages were associated with lower levels of employment and output, and vice versa. By contrast, after World War II, prices moved only upwards, as did money wages – but money wages rose faster, causing real wages to rise. High real wages went along with high employment and output, rather than low.[2] The S&D picture appears to describe the period in which it was developed, the period of family firms and family farms, but not to describe the later era of giant corporations and mass production. On this view, then, S&D is a theory of *market adjustment*, based on specific assumptions about institutions and technology, which applies only to certain periods and circumstances.

Neither Monetarists nor conventional Keynesians will accept this. Both rest S&D on rational choice theory. Both are trying to build a general picture of the economy, and each has chosen a set of building blocks containing incompatible parts. The conventional Keynesians wish to accept the S&D theory of markets and resource allocation, while at the same time explaining unemployment, inflation and the business cycle in Keynesian macroeconomic terms. But if the market brings about an optimal allocation, how can there be unemployment? Monetarists and 'New Classicals' more consistently base their approach to all economic issues on the basic theory of 'rational choice' supply and demand, but this compels them to try to explain unemployment, inflation and the business cycle as the results of optimal allocation when disrupted either by chance events or by political intervention. But this means that the causes of unemployment and inflation are not to be found in the world of business and markets! Everything is for the best there, and it is someone else's fault when things go wrong in the economy. This sounds like PollyAnna.

Equally seriously, because it affects us all, innovation and imagination have departed the realm of policy-making. Few, if any, new policy instruments have been developed since World War II, and significant ones, such as planning and various kinds of controls, have fallen into disuse and are no longer discussed, even by liberals. Policy questions have been largely confined to the relative merits of fiscal and monetary measures. Fiscal policies work by manipulating taxes and spending; monetary policies are concerned with interest rates and the money supply. Which is better, when?

- Keynesians argue that both are effective under the right conditions, and that the mix should be chosen according to immediate problems – 'fine tuning'.
- Monetarists argue that the economy cannot be 'fine tuned', because fiscal policies work only temporarily, while monetary policies have effects that are both powerful and unpredictable. The best policy, therefore, is a balanced budget and a steady moderate expansion of the money supply, following a rule that will keep it in line with anticipated (or desired) output growth.

Little has changed in this argument, on either side, in more than thirty years.

THE VIRTUES OF THE FREE MARKET

So much for general positions. Let's consider what the conventional wisdom has to say about the important problems that bother us all. There are lots of them: unemployment, inflation, high interest rates, the government deficit, foreign competition and the trade deficit, poverty in the midst of plenty, pollution and the environment. Other worrying problems could be mentioned, but this is more than enough. The textbook position is that the free market can, in theory, handle them all. If the markets worked perfectly, then the adjustment of supply and demand would provide a solution – although it might not be the one that voters would most prefer. On the other hand, if markets are imperfect, there may be no solutions – or horrible ones.

Each of the above cases must be treated somewhat differently, but the central idea is the same – employment, the price level, the level of interest rates, the distribution of income, even the amount of pollution will be determined by supply and demand, and if market conditions are competitive, the results will be 'optimal', in a limited and rather technical sense.

This should be explained – which requires some economic reasoning. Left to itself, a free market system would solve these problems through the interaction of supply and demand, if only the market could operate unimpeded by institutional rigidities (unions, minimum wage laws), government interference, the working of special interest groups, and quite a lot of other factors. However, there is a serious catch: institutional 'rigidities' and government 'interference' exist because influential groups, perhaps the majority, *want* them, often for very good reasons. Government regulations, for example, protect the public and force businesses to recall unsafe products. Automobiles, for example. Labour unions, in spite of the bad press they typically receive, defend the interests of their members. Employers cannot summarily fire unionized workers, there are grievance procedures, lay-offs are organized in a fair manner, and so on.

In other words, market solutions, although the 'best' attainable under the circumstances, might not be acceptable to many, perhaps even a majority, of those in the economy – for the market records *dollar* votes. Those with the most dollars have the most impact. 'The circumstances' under which the free market solution is optimal include the initial distribution of resources. Those who own the most at the outset have the most to say about the outcome, but the result in a 'one-person, one-vote' election might be very different. Furthermore, this tells us: change the distribution of resources (e.g. change the inheritance laws) and you will almost certainly change the market result.

So the free market solutions are conditional. They may nevertheless be important. Let the political process correct the distribution of property, and the free market will then provide the optimal result. Perhaps surprisingly, the textbooks do largely agree on how this works, though this may reflect a move to the centre for the sake of sales as much as genuine scientific consensus. But here's the basic story:

• *Start with the case of unemployment.* Unemployed workers will be willing to work for less and so will bid down the price of labour, and with the price of labour lower, more workers will be hired – as long as the extra revenue generated by adding workers exceeds the wage they have to be paid. For labour will be hired up to the point where the additional output from employing more workers just equals their wage. With a fixed amount of plant and equipment a point will be reached where the increase in output achieved by adding more workers will be less than proportional to the number of new workers. In other words, diminishing returns will set in. Since firms will pay workers a wage equal to the additional output they produce, if more workers are employed, the real wage must be declining. So the labour demand curve must slope downwards from left to right. Further, the labour supply curve rises from left to right. Workers face a choice between working more or taking more leisure time. Since work is unpleasant (by assumption) wages must rise to induce them to work more. With lower wages some workers may withdraw altogether from the labour pool. (What unemployed workers live on is not explained in this story. Moreover, who does the working and who the hiring depends on the initial distribution of resources). With a downward-sloping demand curve and a rising supply curve, the level of employment will be determined along with the level of real wages. A labour shortage means that wages are too low, and unemployment simply means that wages are too high.

• *Next, consider inflation.* Too much spending drives up the price level. But the market will correct this automatically, unless there are imperfections or interference. For people's holdings of money lose value with higher prices, since the pre-existing stock of money can purchase fewer goods.

Faced with diminished wealth, households and firms – anyone with cash holdings – will cut back spending, reducing the pressure that was driving up prices. Who has the wealth? That depends on the initial situation. (Notice the assumption that inflation is caused by demand pressure – 'too much money chasing too few goods'.)

- *Now take a different kind of problem next, the effects of government over-spending.* High interest rates are said to be caused by government deficits; the government is competing in financial markets with private investment for the pool of available savings, which will go to the highest bidder. The high interest rates in turn will attract foreign investors, who bid up the dollar, which will hurt US exports, and stimulate imports – since a higher dollar makes US goods more expensive to the rest of the world, while imports become cheaper to Americans. So a government deficit will supposedly drive up interest rates and bring about a trade deficit.

According to this view, then, the market tends to bring about a clear-cut determinate result, optimal when markets are free of regulations and inter-vention, problematical otherwise, although the case can always be made that the initial endowments were unjust, or unacceptable (or even inefficient – if the best resources went to the least talented.) But, *prima facie* what the market brings about must be considered at least as *potentially* optimal; it has to be established in every case that the market result is tainted by imperfection, before it is legitimate to tamper with it. Keynesians tend to assume that such imperfections exist. Further, they tend to add that, since market outcomes reflect the distribution of property, which is highly unequal, voters – one person, one vote – may legitimately wish to amend those results.

KEYNESIANS VS. MONETARISTS

We saw earlier that conventional Keynesians and Monetarists both accept the view that markets are social devices for allocating scarce resources. This compelled Monetarists to look outside the economy for the causes of unemployment, inflation and the business cycle, and forced Keynesians to postulate imperfections that inhibited the market from adjusting properly. The argument between them provides a good introduction to the issues we must consider, and will help us to see the importance of looking at the economy historically.

Keynesians see government intervention and institutional influences in markets as unavoidable, and sometimes, as with trade unions, even desirable. The free market solution is a theoretical curiosity, nothing more. Its only practical significance is as a guideline. Market forces are important, but in general they have to be helped along by policy. Even in the absence of rigidities, etc. markets often don't reach equilibrium, and where non-market factors are important, as in the case of labour, social policy will have to be paramount. Market forces do reflect free choices, choices backed by money, but not all such free choices are socially desirable, nor do markets always produce the best results from society's point of view. Why shouldn't the political process of one person/one vote correct or modify the economic process of one dollar/one vote?

Monetarists agree that institutional factors, technical and social rigidities *et hoc omnia genus* all tend to prevent the market system from working optimally. But the solution is not to throw more obstacles of the same kind in the way. Instead the aim of policy should be to remove obstacles, reduce government and institutional interference and generally smooth the way for the price system to work its magic.

So Keynesians have defined a set of policies that will tend to stimulate the economy, expanding it towards full employment, or deflating it if it is over-heated. These are the fiscal and monetary policies mentioned above. Suppose there is unemployment: Keynesians would urge deficit spending to stimulate the economy, so that with higher overall demand, more workers will be hired. Alternatively, the same goal could be achieved by loosening up the money supply, bringing lower interest rates, which would encourage businesses to borrow more for investment purposes, and the higher investment spending would then lead to higher overall demand.

Keynesians, however, note that there are possible difficulties in using each form of policy to manipulate demand. In the case of monetary policy, even when interest rates have fallen, businesses may not borrow and spend more if the economy is in a really bad slump. True, the funds are available cheap, but why spend any money, even cheap money, on constructing new productive facilities, when the economy is in a slump and already existing facilities are lying idle? So, in a deep slump, Keynesians would have to fall back on deficit spending. On the other hand, manipulating the government budget is not that easy. Budgets have to be approved by Congress, which takes time. Moreover, political considerations will be paramount, so policy-makers may find it hard to get their way. In an inflation, for example, spending should be cut – but Congress will not easily let its sacred cows be slaughtered. Even if the 'right' budget were finally approved, the timing might well be off, yet timing is often the crucial element in successful policy.[3] For these reasons monetary policy is often preferred: it can be administered by experts, the timing can be precise, and it need not be subject to the politicians – to put it another way, it is independent of the will of the people. This is a touchy subject!

If S&D determine the amounts exchanged in all markets, including the labour market, then government spending can only have temporary effects on the system. Manipulating the money supply can have quite powerful effects, Monetarists think, but not in the way Keynesians expect. Basically the money supply affects prices; inflation is the long run result of Keynesian monkeying around with the economy. Monetarists reject the basic premises of Keynesian policy analysis. The government should fix the growth rate of the money supply and leave the market system to its own devices. New Classicals by and large agree, but some would go further, and eliminate government control over the banking system.

So – a plague on both houses, will be our motto. For the debate has gone on endlessly, with no resolution, and no real development. Enormous ingenuity has been displayed, but the basic positions have hardly changed. There doesn't seem to be that much more to say, but it's hard to declare a winner. Certainly Monetarist policies have been a disaster, both here and in the UK, but Keynesian policies have also fared badly. Monetarist predictions have been so wide of the mark at times as to verge on the ridiculous, but while the Keynesians may have seemed more sober, they were probably wrong just as often. Like the Bourbons, the two sides in this quarrel have learned nothing and forgotten nothing. Unlike the Bourbons, there is a good reason for this: each side has got hold of an important part of the truth. Keynesians understand how market adjustments can lead to unstable processes resulting in unemployment, inflation and fluctuations, while Monetarists and New Classicals portray stabilizing market adjustments. Both kinds of market adjustments exist – the question, as we shall see, is to understand when and why the economy will adjust one way or the other.

So nobody's got it right. Meanwhile the economy has been throwing up new problems. Not only that, there is evidence that the way it adjusts has changed in the past and is changing once again now. This suggests that perhaps *both* schools are both wrong – and right! But for different times and circumstances. Maybe we need a new approach altogether, a new current of thought that is not going to end up in stagnant pools.

SUPPLY AND DEMAND (S&D)

Every one of these arguments is based on the rational choice/resource allocation interpretation, treated as if it were virtually self-evident. When prices are high, e.g. the price of labour, demand will be low, but supply will be high; and vice versa when prices are low. Somewhere in the middle there will be a price at which demand and supply just balance. This is the price that the market will tend to seek out and establish. This price, and the quantity (of whatever it is) bought and sold at this price, will be the best for everyone, in the reasonable sense that this is the freely chosen position, given the initial circumstances (which include the distribution of property.) Of course, this conclusion depends on people knowing everything they need to know about the various commodities, and about all the other possibilities – technologies, natural resources, how peoples' tastes might develop in different circumstances, and so on. It also requires the absence of institutional frictions, such as government intervention, or coalitions of special interest groups, or political pressures forcing changes in the distribution of property. Any of these can disrupt an equilibrium reached by the working of the free market.

Swimmers in the mainstream, whatever their other differences, all do agree on one thing: namely, the *nature* of markets and the price system. Allowing for blemishes and for the fact that no human institution works the way it is supposed to, markets are understood to be devices for allocating scarce resources optimally among competing ends – which also means competing groups – and prices measure the values attached to foregone opportunities. 'Foregone opportunities' – sometimes called 'opportunity cost' – is basic to the mainstream vision. The idea is simple: you choose this and not that, and pay its price. Since you chose to pay the price, it must therefore be worth more than (or at least equal to the value of) the next best thing, the one you didn't choose. What you *didn't* choose is the 'opportunity cost' of what you did. That cost in turn is just less than what the good is worth to you, since you paid the price of what you did choose. So the price you paid is an indicator of cost relative to preferences. Costs, of course, reflect payments in proportion to marginal productivity as factors are shifted among alternative uses. Prices will lead to allocating factors to the production of the goods most highly desired.

The Classical economists, Smith, Ricardo and Marx, and their modern followers, did not view markets that way, and, arguably, neither should we. Rather than mechanisms for achieving optimal allocation, in the Classical view, markets are arenas of conflict. They are settings in which struggles over wealth take place, but where the combat follows reasonable rules, which set limits to the social damage. But markets themselves are not a system for resolving the conflicts – who wins and who loses will be determined by many factors. Yet the gap between these views is not unbridgeable – it could be agreed that the market is the arena for power struggles, but that the rules contribute to finding the best outcomes. The real difference comes when we look at prices and the role the price mechanism plays.

The very meaning of the word 'price' is at issue. (In the old days the controversies were over 'value', a word even more heavily laden with impli-cations.) On the one hand prices are held to measure availability relative to preferences. That is the conventional view. On the other hand, there is the tradition extending from the Ancient Greeks through the Classical economists to the present day, which explains prices as the exchanges required to enable the *system of production* to continue functioning. Goods are used up in making other goods. (Steel is used up in making machines, machines are used up in making steel.) At the end of the process various producing institutions (firms, households) have on hand their *outputs*, but to carry on, they need their *inputs*. There will therefore have to be exchanges. These are necessary to maintain the material basis of the social system.

So we are faced with two complicated sets of ideas with far-reaching ramifications. Indeed, this is the deepest, and most treacherous, water in all of economics. We are asking for the basis of value in exchange.

First, the textbook view, in summary form. A market is supposed to consist of a large number of firms, each supplying an identical product, and a large number of households that wish to purchase the good. Since both households and firms can easily switch trading partners, no arbitrage opportunites can persist, so the equilibrium price will be the same for all transactions. Many textbooks tend in practice to follow Marshall, although they pay lip service to rational choice. Firms produce subject to 'diminishing marginal returns'; households consume subject to 'diminishing marginal utility', (terms to be explained in a moment). This means that prices and quantities will be determined by the intersection of two kinds of curves.

- First there are supply curves that rise from left to right, reflecting diminishing returns. (Returns diminish when you put twice as many men to work on the farm, and you get less than twice as much corn from it; which means that when you set three times as many to work, you get less extra corn than you did from the first increase. This means that costs per unit produced rise.)
- The other curves are demand curves that fall from left to right, exhibiting the influence of diminishing marginal utility (you enjoy the second ice cream cone less than the first, and the third less than the second. So the more you eat, the less you'll be willing to pay for each additional cone.)

Supply requires choosing the best combination of factors (should you put all these extra men to work on the farm, or should you buy a tractor for the original workers?) Nature is niggardly; serious effort and rational choice are needed to overcome the difficulties of extracting desirable goods. Demand is a matter of choosing the most preferred combination of available goods (instead of a third ice cream cone, whose marginal utility will be very low, a piece of cake). The balance between S&D will be a balance between costs and utilities, and will thus reflect availability in the light of preferences. This is what prices are all about, according to the mainstream view. The pressures of the market establish prices that measure relative scarcities.

There is a certain common-sense plausibility to this – how else could it have become so widely accepted. Diminishing returns are often met in everyday life; it's too much work, given what you expect to get from it, to extend the garden any further. Utility diminishes, too – a third scoop of ice cream is a little too much. On the other hand, constant and increasing returns are frequently encountered also – think of mass production – and many ordinary consumer items can only be purchased in conjunction with other goods or services. (Think of all the complementarities among ordinary household goods.) In other words, it's plausible, but it may not fit a lot of circumstances. This will prove to be the key, as we shall see, shortly.

It's worth remarking on what the rational choice – RC – approach adds to the story. (Having a textbook at hand might be a help here.) S&D is based on households and firms, acting in particular circumstances. It asks how the system adjusts when there are small changes. Is there an equilibrium and does the system tend to move towards it. By contrast, RC aims to be fully general. All possibilities, and all agents are considered together. Moreover, it dismisses institutional and technological details as irrelevant. The agents are abstract 'rational individuals', who possess *complete* preference orderings – they know which they prefer of *any* two bundles of goods, made up of whatever you like. Faced with comparing a bundle of 12 sofas, 14 Chevrolets, and 3446 ice cream cones to 16 sofas, 9 Chevrolets, and 1341 ice cream cones, they will not hesitate for a moment. They know which they like better, and they prefer that bundle absolutely, i.e. whatever job they hold, whatever their other circumstances. Nor will their preferences change as the result of their consumption – not even if it includes travel and education. In any case they already know and have access to all technological possibilities. Any agent can draw on any technology at any time. But they begin with given 'endowments' of factors, which they then choose to trade or to combine to produce goods and services which they will trade. The object is for each agent to attain the highest point possible on his preference set, subject to other agents' doing likewise.

This means that diminishing marginal returns and utility, respectively, are replaced by the mathematical assumption that the relevant sets of possibilities are *convex* (Koopmans, 1953; Walsh, 1970). Such assumptions are described as 'more general'; but they are also *different*. The RC approach considers a vast variety of *hypothetical alternative* production facilities, and consumption possibilities, which are arranged according to their unit costs, or preferred status, respectively, assuming that orderly relationships will exist. The Marshallian approach considers the intensity with which *given* specific production facilities are operated. It notes the variation in unit costs when currently existing plant and equipment is operated at different levels. Marshallian firms know how to operate a specific technology, the one they are using, and they know the conditions of their own industry, but not of other industries. Marshallian households consider consuming extra amounts of some good or goods, in the context of an already existing pattern of household activity. They are unaware of other consumption patterns. Marshallian costs are 'real' costs, that is, actually used up energy and resources; RC costs are 'opportunity costs', that is, the hypothetical value of what might otherwise have been done with the resources. Marshallian 'utility' is the satisfaction gained or lost by a small consumption change in a specific setting.[4] The Marshallian approach is tied to a particular time and place; the RC is designed to hold for all times and places.[5] In short, the Marshallian system is concrete and specific, while RC is abstract and general – but also unrealistic.

AGGREGATE S&D

As a result of the 'Keynesian compromise', mentioned earlier, the S&D apparatus can supposedly be adapted to macroeconomics. (Again, a textbook will be useful). The same curves can be drawn, a demand curve sloping down from left to right, and a supply curve sloping up. But the curves are re-labelled: the *general price level* (an index of the effect of inflation, e.g. the consumer price index) is put in place of the supply-and-demand diagram's 'price' variable, and *aggregate expenditure* appears in the place of 'quantity demanded', while *aggregate output* replaces 'quantity supplied'.

- *For demand*, the curve shows that at lower price levels more will be demanded in the aggregate, and at higher, less. In a nutshell, the reasoning runs as follows: Businesses and households both hold money for transactions purposes. When the general level of prices is low, holdings of money will be more valuable. (Note that holdings of debt have been ignored!) So holders of money will spend more, and conversely, they will spend less when the price level is high.
- *For supply*, the curve shows that at lower price levels less will be supplied, at higher, more. The argument: the real wage is what employment depends on. At high real wages workers are expensive, so few will be employed; at low real wages, labour is cheap so more will be employed. But the real wage is the money wage divided by the price level. At lower price levels, the real wage is high, so fewer workers will be employed and less will be produced; conversely when the price level is high, the real wage is low, so more workers will be employed and more will be produced.

So we have two curves. One slopes down from left to right, the other rises from left to right – just like the basic micro diagram! Hence, given certain natural assumptions, we can expect the two curves to intersect, so that *aggregate* demand and supply will determine equilibrium aggregate output – GNP – and the price level, in the same way that S&D determine equilibrium prices and outputs in individual markets.

It should be clear, however, even from this abbreviated summary, that the rationale for the aggregate version of S&D is much weaker than that of ordinary S&D. It lacks the intuitive plausibility and it is riddled with difficulties (See Appendix I). Moreover, the ordinary story, based on diminishing returns and diminishing utility, can be extended to large aggregates, for example, consumption goods as a whole, or capital goods. But when it is so extended, this gives us a different kind of aggregate demand and supply; there is no longer any room for the textbook Keynesian story. The 'Keynesian Compromise' faces serious problems.

PRICES AND PRODUCTION

We said there was another perspective on prices. It could hardly be more different. Scarcity doesn't figure at all; technology and production are central. Let's try to work it out in the simplest terms, (although it still won't be easy). Consider Crusoe's island, with two shipwrecked people who find they can do different things.

31

- Robinson can use tools and consume food to grow food.
- Friday can use tools and consume food in order to make tools.

In each case, we shall assume, the exact amount of tools and time required for production is given by the technology. When things are done correctly, we shall assume, then the amounts of inputs per unit output are strictly fixed. (If more labour is applied to the tools, there will be diminishing returns. We assume that the fixed amounts just indicated are those corresponding to the minimum points of the Marshallian U-shaped average cost curves.) Let us suppose that Robinson can grow just enough food to support both of them for the time it will take to grow food, and in that time Friday can just manage to make enough tools to replace the ones used up by both himself and Robinson.

Now consider the situation at the end of such a period of time. Robinson is out of tools, but has more than enough food for himself, enough for both of them, in fact. Friday is out of food, but has more than the tools he needs – he has the ones Robinson needs as well. There is therefore an *exact exchange* – Robinson's surplus food for Friday's surplus tools – which will enable both to repeat their operations. This exchange is unique and determinate – for a numerical example, see Appendix II. It defines the price of food in terms of tools. Such a price has nothing to do with preferences or with alternative uses of resources; it simply reflects the interdependence of technology, given the requirement that the system continue to operate.[6]

Now consider what happens if Robinson or Friday – or both – were able to speed up their operations, so that they completed production before the food supply supporting them is used up. Then there would be a *surplus*, more being produced per period than is needed to repeat the process exactly. Under these conditions there will be a number of different possible prices which will permit repeating the operation, but which will each assign the surplus differently. This is when it gets interesting. For we have to consider what determines who gets the surplus. In general the answer is likely to have something to do with the distribution of power in the social order, e.g. Robinson, it should be remembered, rescued guns from his shipwreck! Moreover, there are further questions: should the surplus be consumed as is, or should it be used to support the work needed to produce luxuries? And the technology might be improved; this would very likely change the kinds of skills needed, and it will also change the prices.

Our example is awfully oversimplified. To examine capitalism we have to show how the surplus can be distributed as a rate of profit on capital – which is the value of the means of production – at the same time that the exchanges required by the technology for reproduction take place. This is more complicated, but it's not different in principle. The reasoning, however, is very close knit. (Sraffa, 1960) It's not something we can go into here. In Appendix II, however, the numerical example is worked out for full-scale capitalism where profits are earned in a growing economy.

This argument is a piece of pure economic theory in the Sraffian mode. In practice, of course, industries do not swap goods and services back and forth. Outputs are sold for money, and money revenues are ploughed back in investment. The view that prices are determined by replacement and invest- ment needs is often embodied in more practical models. In these, prices are set by firms in terms of the *mark-up* over labour costs. The mark-up covers the expenses of replacement and maintenance, and provides the profit that firms will need to cover their planned investments. These models have been developed in many directions, and are frequently used in econometric work.[7]

How are we to choose between these two different views of what prices mean? On the one hand, prices are supposed to reflect relative scarcities; on the other, they reflect technology and the power to influence distribution. And what difference does it make? Why can't both be right, at least in part? We will come back to these questions over and over again.[8] For now the important point is to understand that there are deep-seated differences in the basic approach to understanding markets. The S&D picture concentrates on the optimality of markets in given circumstances – it takes a *static* perspect- ive. Insofar as it considers market adjustment, it pictures a simple, stable process. When there is a shortage, prices will rise and call forth more supplies; when there is a glut, prices will fall, until supplies are cut back. The market tends to equilibrium, in which S&D balance. Given the basic conditions, markets are supposed to guide us to the best possible arrangement of activities. Surely this is often what happens.

On the other hand, markets can also get out of hand. The other view – that exchange depends on the technology and who gets the surplus – leads to a focus on how the surplus is produced, since that will have a bearing on who gets how much of it, and what is done with it. It therefore leads to a *dynamic* perspective: competition leads to pressures to increase the surplus, hence productivity, investment and growth move to centre stage. Markets will tend to generate innovations and to provide the means to invest in them. There is no reason to expect these processes to be stable. Investment, in particular, can displace labour, and lead to unemployment – as Ricardo pointed out long ago. A rise in investment can lead to expansion, creating demand pressures that lead to an even greater increase in investment, and so on.

ALLOCATION AND THE SYSTEM OF PRODUCTION

To assess these different views let's first examine the conventional thinking about the market. Both Keynesians and Monetarists agree that competitive markets 'allocate scarce resources optimally', i.e. answer the questions what? how? and for whom?, and that enough present-day markets are sufficiently competitive – and non-competitive markets are sufficiently similar – that the theory is at least a useful approximation. The main difference, according to

the textbooks, is that non-competitive markets can't be trusted to answer
what? how? and for whom? *optimally*, for the best in the best of all possible
worlds, as Candide was told.

If we forget about the textbooks for a moment, and trust to common
sense, we will find that the institutions that organize production may be
more important than markets in answering these questions, partly because
they may determine how markets actually work. Prices, according to the
second view considered earlier, follow from the requirements of continuous
production, given the social power system that decides who gets what. Real-
life market processes, especially in the years following World War II, often
seem to work quite differently than textbook models; at other, earlier times,
or in developing countries, actual markets do seem to exhibit a 'price mechanism'. In particular, it may well be that early capitalism – a system of family
firms and family farms – functioned in much the way suggested by the theory
of competitive markets. But the economy of giant corporations and modern,
hi-tech industry does not, and hasn't since the advent of mass production.
Whether the firm is a small family affair, or a bureaucratic hierarchy, may
be crucial. (And we may be on the verge of another change in the nature
of business organization.)

Let's take the questions in order, and consider how they were answered in the
post-War era. What? in this period was not answered in any simple sense by
the market; it tended to be settled by bureaucratic infighting in the great
corporations. To be sure, new products – Fords and rubber chickens – would
be 'market-tested', and in the case of hot new items, e.g. computers and
software, there would be a competitive scramble, sometimes between divisions
of the same company, sometimes between different companies. But if products
are adjusted to consumers' preferences, it is equally true that, when markets
settled down, consumers would be adjusted to what corporations decide to
produce. It is a race, and the spoils go to the winner. Big fish eat little fish;
the victor will end up with the dominant market position. This is not what the
textbooks mean by a 'movement to equilibrium'.

As for How? that, too, is answered by committees as much as by the market.
A prospective technology will emerge from the company's labs, and then must
be carefully examined from all angles. Assembly lines, robots, antibiotics,
pesticides – all have to be tested, developed, and re-tested. Pilot projects will be
set up and evaluated, cost studies under various conditions are made. Finally,
the studies will be sent to the board and a decision reached, a decision that will
very likely exercise a determining influence on many careers. So, besides the
(more or less) objective economic factors, other considerations, including institutional politics, will definitely intrude. And the role of the market? There's no
simple answer. Costs are crucial, but product quality is equally so. And safety,
pollution, the technology's demand for operator skills, and other factors all
figure in. To say 'the market will be the final judge' is saying no more than we
will see how it works out in practice. There is no decisive market test.

For whom? the system produces for those with the money to pay. Health care goes to those who can pay, not necessarily to those who are sickest. The higher a family's income, the more visits its members make to the doctor and the dentist during the year. Homes do not go to the homeless, nor food to the hungry. Oversimplifying, the system exchanges goods for money, and provides money incomes to those who have property and/or were able to find a job on the basis of their education and training. Parents can no longer educate their children at home; everyone must manage to attend an appropriate school, or otherwise obtain suitable training. Even unskilled labour requires social skills, many of which were unknown a century ago. Since the ownership of property is treated by the textbooks, but not by the Robber Barons or for that matter, by Robinson Crusoe, as a *given*, an assumption from which we start, the market cannot be said to 'determine' anything significant about for whom the system works.

AND COMPETITION?

As for competition, why is it supposed that a competitive market system is a stable, self-sustaining or self-perpetuating structure? In some respects, this is quite a strange idea. Competition is a form of war; businesses are out to wipe the floor with each other. Losers go bankrupt or get taken over; winners fatten up, expand, and go on to scale new heights. So the number of firms progressively gets smaller, while the firms themselves get larger. Taking the long view, it is clear that competition is not at all stable. In fact it might be argued that the 'competition' in question is a kind of race – the race to get the monopoly. In practice, the race usually stops about three-quarters of the way along, with a few big firms dominating the market and making peace among themselves, while permitting a number, sometimes a large number, of small, often specialized firms, to continue to operate, as long as they follow the lead of the giants.

Indeed, a simple formal argument can be advanced to show this. Suppose, as seems reasonable, that a firm's *future* sales and market share will be proportional to its *current* success or failure. Start the analysis from a hypothetical situation where a large number of firms, operating plants of about equal size, are competing vigorously for customers, who have little reason to prefer one firm to another. Under these conditions we may suppose that the result will be a normal distribution of success. There will be a few firms, who through effort or good luck, attract and serve a large number of customers. And there will be an approximately equal number, who, through bad luck or poor management, attract very few or virtually none. The great majority will fall in the middle, and the distribution itself will appear on a graph to be 'bell-shaped'.

Now the successful firms will have to expand their plants, while the unsuccessful will have to scale them back. So at the end of this first stage, an initial group of firms of equal size has turned into a group with a normal (bell-shaped) distribution of size. But the next step is decisive; in the next round of effort, success will tend to be proportional to previous success. The largest firms will tend to make the largest gains, the previous losers, the biggest losses. But the effect will not always hold; each firm will have a statistically normal chance of growing (shrinking) in proportion to its previous achievement. The result of this is to produce a distribution of sizes that is greatly skewed – the famous 'lognormal distribution' – there will be a very large number of small and very small firms, and a small number of very large ones.

And why should businesses allow this process, and others even worse, like bankruptcy, to continue unabated? Why permit the war of all against all to be waged on all fronts? Thomas Hobbes certainly thought that in the political sphere people would be driven to accept 'articles of peace'. Surely a similar point must hold for wars in the marketplace; the natural response must be to strike a deal, to sue for peace and settle on terms that will permit business to prosper without the dangers and uncertainty of perpetual competition in all spheres. Moreover, as some businesses reach a dominant size and position they will be able to exercise leadership and lay down terms that others will be hard put to resist, especially if the terms are crafted to reflect the common interests of all in establishing and maintaining a peaceful and orderly market, one without 'cutthroat competition'.

THE SOCIAL FUNCTION OF MARKETS

So our argument suggests that how markets work depends on their history, and on the development of technology, and its impact on the organization of production. We can start from the common-sense observation that the economy runs on sales. Times are prosperous when markets are good, depressed when they are bad. So the question is, what makes for active, swinging, expansive markets, and what for weak, slow-moving ones? We start with the question of booming vs. slumping sales, for the system as a whole, and then we look more carefully at how the parts work, individually, and how they fit together. How does the market, as an institution, work – and how and why does it sometimes misfire? How do business strategies fit into this, and do they make things better or worse? What is the role of technology and innovation?

By contrast, the textbooks start with the making of rational choices in conditions of scarcity. Ironically, this is often presented in terms of Robinson Crusoe – conveniently forgetting that Robinson, a shipwrecked slave-trader who had managed to rescue his firearms, was able to cajole and coerce Friday into doing most of the work for him.[9] Such 'institutional detail' is swept aside as irrelevant to the grand project, which is, in deliberate imitation of what is believed to be the method of natural science, to establish general principles good for all times and places. These are supposedly derived from a study of the process of rational choice, as made by abstractly conceived 'individuals' in abstract settings. But we already saw that when Robinson and Friday are mutually dependent, operating simple technologies, they must engage in exchanges, which will in fact be determinate. If there is a surplus, the exchanges depend on how it is distributed. But if Robinson has the firearms, that will not be hard to answer. Robinson's calculations, as carefully depicted by Defoe, were not concerned with optimal allocation, within a given context, but with finding better ways of doing things. He was *innovating*, changing the givens, in order to increase productivity.

Abstract rational choice is not very helpful as a descriptive approach. The economy is here and now, not everywhere and forever – and actual choices are made by real people in real circumstances, with real and limited powers, information and obligations. The general principles are not very interesting because to derive them, it has proved necessary to abstract from virtually everything of actual importance. What's left is largely tautology, and where it's not the theory is inconclusive. Nor is this an accident; the 'imperfections' which have been put aside – physical constraints, differential access to information, materials, and talent, problems of finance, and so on – form the basis for most business decisions. To 'abstract' from them is like abstracting from the terrain in developing a theory of strategy on the battlefield. If you leave out what counts your theory is bound to be empty.

The reply will be that the general theory can be related to particular cases by 'relaxing' the assumptions – instead of assuming that the agents know everything they need to know, we can allow for uncertainty and ignorance. Instead of abstract individuals we can start from the current situation of a specific business. This can certainly be done; various engineering subjects, like 'operations research' do just that. But 'relaxing' the assumptions even a little turns out to make an enormous difference in the results. As soon as the assumptions become specific in even one area, let alone in all, the generality of the argument evaporates. Things become indeterminate; the outcome depends on the exact nature and specific content of the new assumptions. The optimizing approach may be quite useful – linear programming, queueing theory, critical path analysis and other management/operations methods have proved their exceptional worth in many contexts. But their usefulness depends precisely on their *flexibility*. Given circumstances can be analysed in different ways by different models; indeed, the same model may be used to determine different courses of action.

A powerful theorem, central to optimizing, in fact, implies just this. The 'Theorem of the Alternative' shows the relationships between the profitability of outputs or activities and the valuations assigned to the limited resources or constraints used in those activities.[10] If an output figures in the most profitable mix, its costs will be just covered; conversely, if its costs are not covered it will not be produced. If a resource is fully used, it will have a positive 'shadow price' or value, if not, it will have a zero value. The first of

37

these – most profitable mix – implies the second – resource valuation. But the first is a version of the usual optimizing problem for the firm. The second, valuation of input constraints, tells the firm how much it will increase its profit by shifting each constraint. If a firm behaves according to the first, it accepts the givens and chooses the best market strategy. But it can just as easily follow the implications of the second, and increase its profit by *changing* the givens. Which should it do? That will depend on the cost and technology involved in shifting a constraint, on the likelihood of such a strategy working, on the possibilities of an even better innovation becoming available at a later date, and so on.

So it is not obvious that the economic problem should be formulated as one of making optimal choices in given conditions. For one thing, this makes the market's working appear static – the market reconciles everyone's best choice with what everyone else chooses. And that's that. But this leaves out growth, innovation, and development – aren't these market phenomena, too? Furthermore, aren't they also, at least in part, chosen by rational methods? We have just seen that we cannot separate the optimizing analysis that chooses the best course of action in *given* circumstances, from that which determines the best way to *change* those circumstances. In many cases the economic problem is *not* a matter of choosing the best set of goods or factors from a pre-established list, but rather of choosing the best way to develop a new list. In general, the optimizing agent has no reason to take the circumstances as given. It is highly likely that it will be possible to change at least some among the given circumstances.

Economic agents do not passively accept the world as they find it. The history of the West has been one of vigorous, innovative change, suggested by science or by experimentation and carried out by rational methods. An active mind provides a better perspective on rational choice – rather than *descriptive*, it should be seen as *prescriptive*. Models of rational choice, including management science and industrial engineering, as well as economic models of optimizing, are designed to be applied in concrete circumstances in order to decide how best to *improve* the situation, both how to manage within the givens and to determine which of the givens should be changed.

But the textbook set of 'assumptions' effectively *precludes* the hypothetical agents from taking a serious look at their situation. This, indeed, is the point of such assumptions. By postulating many small firms who are price-takers, with full information, easy mobility of 'factors', facing diminishing marginal returns, suppliers are put in the position in which the only variable over which they have any control is output. Hence the optimizing problems are reduced to determining the best choice of output, and the best combination of inputs. The same is done on the demand side; the only effective choices left open to households are selecting what to buy, and how much labour and savings to offer. Hence the optimizing model can be interpreted descriptively; it predicts what the agents will do. But once the assumptions are relaxed, and a more realistic situation considered, the optimizing approach offers a variety of possibilities. It is a *tool* for the agents, a way of assessing their circumstances and deciding how to improve them. Optimizing comes into play when agents set out to *make a change*; when acting in a routine manner, agents will follow the conventional norms.[11] Neither Marshallian nor Keynesian accounts of market adjustment have to be based on 'optimizing behaviour'. These are descriptive accounts, so if optimizing models are brought into the argument, they have to be 'limited'. Behaviour in response to market signals can be determined by economically sensible 'rules of thumb'. (Indeed, the 'New Keynesians' have developed a category of models of 'limited rationality'.)[12]

The conventional wisdom treats the market as arranging the *coordination* of the optimal choices of the individual units, each solving its problems in the given conditions. This overlooks some prior questions. How did the given conditions come to exist and how do they continue to be supported? Where did the individual units, the choosers, come from, and how did they come to be endowed with the skills they have been assumed to possess? How are they replaced when they die out or cease to exist? This is the problem of the exchange between Robinson and Friday. It is not an optimal choice problem at all. It is the question of how the economic system as a whole manages to support itself, and how it produces and distributes a new product. Exchanges enable the system to keep running. Outputs are recycled as inputs to keep the system going – but in the process output may be expanded, new processes or products introduced, new jobs created and old ones scrapped; the system is constantly in motion, constantly recycling, using itself up and regenerating itself.

TWO INTERPRETATIONS OF 'S&D'

To explain this further we have now to face a difficult and subtle point in economic theory. In the textbooks, 'S&D' *determine* the equilibrium – prices and outputs. This makes sense when S&D are derived from optimal choice. But we have just seen that the theory of optimal choice could and arguably should be understood as a prescriptive theory – along the lines of linear programming, say – and that it does not make sense as a descriptive theory. This would seem to remove the foundations of S&D. We have further argued that prices can and should be thought of as determined by technological interdependence together with the distribution of the surplus. On the other hand, we have also argued that at least for early capitalism, S&D seemed to provide a plausible account of market processes, at least in some circumstances. If it does not rest on optimal choice theory, and if prices are determined by technology and distribution, what is the role of S&D, and how is it to be interpreted?

Consider Robinson and Friday again, only this time let there be lots of Robinsons and many Fridays. The Robinsons are farmers, the Fridays, tool-makers. Each can work more or less vigorously, with diminishing marginal returns. There will be a point at which unit output will be 'least-cost' in terms of effort. (This is *implied* by the usual assumption of diminishing marginal returns.) This will be the normal supply position. Each will also have a preferred pattern of consumption, likewise a normal position, characterized by diminishing marginal utility. Farmers and tool-makers can be aggregated into 'industries'. S&D curves can then be constructed, showing the reactions to deviations from normal activity. When an unexpected 'shock' drives demand above normal, for example, supply will be increased, but at a higher cost. Prices will rise, real wages will fall, employment will rise – but not much. With a fall in real wages, and only a small and delayed rise in employment, *consumption spending* (household spending of the wage bill) will tend to fall. Thus the system will have generated an *offsetting reaction* to the initial, externally caused and unexpected, rise in demand. This is stabilizing.

The S&D curves intersect at the normal position. But this 'normal position' is the one described earlier, on the assumption that the amounts of input per unit output were rigidly fixed. We showed at that time that Robinson and Friday would produce, and then exchange their outputs, in order to continue their normal activities. Prices arose naturally from the mutual dependence of industries which use each other's products. (In the Technical Appendix, we show how this conception works for a growing capitalist economy.)

Now in this new conception we have allowed the activities to be variable, ranging around a normal position that is the point of least-cost production. As we just saw, by making production and consumption variable, we allow for *market adjustment*. What the S&D curves do now is tell us how the market responds to changes, how prices tend to bring the system back to the least-cost position. The equilibrium prices – that is, the pattern of exchange when production is at the normal least-cost point – are determined by the technology (of the normal or least-cost positions) and the distribution, just as in our original account of Robinson and Friday; but the adjustment process is governed by S&D.

So S&D can be interpreted as providing the dynamics of markets under conditions of diminishing returns. Prices will rise when supplies are short, fall when they are excessive. Moreover, when prices rise, the real wage falls, so employment will tend to rise, and vice versa, when prices fall. These changes will tend to adjust output to the right level – the market system will tend to be stabilizing. This suggests that when the RC influences are removed, there is a core of truth in S&D, when considered in relation to the appropriate historical periods. For the story depends on diminishing returns, and small-scale craft technology, operated by family firms.[13] Under conditions of mass production, markets will adjust very differently.

To summarize our discussion of different kinds of economic analysis: we need to explain how production, exchange and distribution *maintain and support* the system, including the agents who make choices. The trade between Robinson and Friday is an example of such an analysis. We also need to say whether and how market incentives will enable this system to adjust, when various 'shocks' take place, e.g. changes in external trade, new products, etc. Both Keynesian and Marshallian models take up this question, basing their arguments on institutional and technological specifics. And we need to know how agents can use optimizing models to analyse the system in order to improve it or introduce innovations. But optimizing models are prescriptive – they are tools for making improvements. The one kind of economic model that we will not find useful is a purportedly descriptive abstract, general market analysis based on rational choice.

THE WHOLE AND THE PARTS

So what we have to do now is examine how 'the system' can be maintained through production and show, in outline, at least, how it works. As we shall see, there are at least two patterns of market adjustment – one described by S&D, and another by the Keynesian multiplier-accelerator. The first tends to be stabilizing, the second, explosive. The first is consistent with a 'Night Watchman' state, the second requires Keynesian intervention.

But 'the system' cannot be purely economic – for economics, after all, only deals with one aspect of the whole society. So it will be necessary to separate economic from political questions, for example. Traditionally, of course, political theory distinguished between the state and civil society, with the former the province of political rivalry and the latter resting partly on the social life of households, and partly on the working of the free market, where this adjusted in a stable way. In such a case the state's role with respect to the economy is that of the famous 'night watchman'. But markets drive technology and as innovations develop, costs change. When the structure of costs changes enough, as we shall see, markets come to work differently. They change the way they adjust. In particular we will see that with Mass Production, they tend to become unstable. When the market cannot effectively or adequately adjust itself the state must become more active – or face periodic economic breakdowns. But an interventionist state then comes to play a role in the development, even the definition of civil society, and the traditional distinction between the spheres of politics and economics becomes harder to sustain.

And why exactly does the market no longer automatically adjust? (If, in fact, that is the best way to describe what it did . . . let's not beg the important questions. We must be careful what we mean by 'adjust' – one person's adjustment could be another's depression.) This is what we shall have to look into next – why are there fluctuations in the economy's output and employment? Have there always been, or has this changed significantly? Can the market be trusted to ensure that things will operate smoothly? In a Mass Production economy, and even more in the coming Information Economy, we shall see, fluctuations call for state controls. The 'Invisible Hand' can be made out if you look carefully – but when last seen clearly, it was waving goodbye!

TECHNICAL APPENDICES

These Appendices treat two technical topics on which the textbooks can't altogether be trusted. The first is generally not treated adequately, while the second is seldom even mentioned at all.

Aggregate Demand and Supply are often explained quite well but the *weaknesses* of the approach are usually not covered. To take an empirical example: like an ordinary demand curve, the Aggregate Demand curve slopes down from left to right, implying that at lower price levels Aggregate Demand will be higher. The suggestion is that increases in Aggregate Demand occur when the price level falls. In the 45 years from 1950 to 1995, in the US and in other major industrial countries, Aggregate Demand frequently rose, sometimes quite strongly, but at *no* time, in any country, during this whole period, did the price level *ever* fall significantly. In the great majority of the years, in all of the advanced countries, it *rose*. Even if the alleged relationship between Aggregate Demand and the price level had no analytical weaknesses, it would be practically irrelevant. And as we shall see, it does have many such weaknesses – but no one is likely to learn any of this from a major textbook.

The problem with the other topic is even more severe. As far as most textbooks are concerned, prices are determined by supply and demand, and that's that. S&D means scarcity. A good has value because it is scarce, relative to human wants. No other possible explanation is considered. Yet the account we sketched earlier shows that there is another way to look at the question. Exchange values might reflect the trades that are needed to enable a system of mutually dependent production to keep going. We illustrated this with the trading of tools and food between Robinson, the farmer and Friday the tool-maker. This approach has a long pedigree, going back to the Classical economists, especially David Ricardo, and before them to the Physiocrats. It is the core of truth in the often misinterpreted labour theory of value. Of course, a version of it was espoused by Marx, and textbooks shy away from four-letter words. But in modern times it has been developed into a fully articulated theory, of great mathematical sophistication.

There's a reason for taking the trouble to understand this theory, not so much the details as the central idea. For a 'scarcity' theory implies that factors of production will be fully employed in equilibrium. When economists claim that 'prices depend on scarcity', they mean that in equilibrium (that is, when everything has settled down, and random factors have been excluded) prices will mirror the ratios between what people want, and the basic 'endowments', or supplies, of factors of production, like land, labour and capital. People want goods, of course, so demands for factors are derived from the demands for goods. People only want factors to use to make the goods they intend to consume. How much they demand of a factor depends on which goods they prefer and the productivity of that factor in producing those goods. So prices will reflect wants, constrained by the scarcity of factors, given their productivity as determined by technology.

Now consider a factor that is *not* fully employed in equilibrium; some of it is not needed. If there is more of it than is needed, it is not scarce. If it is not scarce, then it has no value – its price must be zero. This is what the theory says: now let's draw the important conclusion – if wages are not zero, then labour must be scarce. So in equilibrium labour must be fully employed.

Keynes, however, argued that *in equilibrium there could be unemployed labour*. Keynesian theory, then, cannot be combined with a scarcity theory of value. Assuming both theories to be free of logical difficulties, we are faced with two different and incompatible accounts of equilibrium. Keynesian theory determines output and employment, together with the rate of interest. It says nothing about relative prices. There is room, therefore, for a theory of relative prices, but it must be a theory which is compatible with the possibility of unemployment. Deriving prices from the requirements of production provides the core of just such a theory.

Textbook aggregate demand and aggregate supply

This has to be regarded as one of the flimsiest constructions in the whole panorama of textbook jerry-building. Aggregate Demand will supposedly be higher when the price level is lower, because a lower price level means a higher real value of cash balances, i.e. greater household and business wealth. Such higher wealth is supposed to lead to more spending. So the Aggregate Demand curve slopes down from left to right – a lower price level means higher demand. That's the story. Now let's ask two basic questions, one about the money holdings, the other about the possibility of counter-balancing effects.

The first question: do households and businesses actually hold sufficiently large money balances that a change in their value would significantly change household or business spending patterns? Such money balances have to be *wealth*, held in money form instead of being placed as stocks or bonds. Money accounts that are turning over as agents receive revenue and pay expenses reflect *income*, not wealth, so do not count. For a change in the general price level – a change in the value of money – will affect *both income and outlay equally* (if it does not, then there will be distributional effects, a separate and complicated matter), resulting in a *net* effect of zero. But these are the largest money balances, in technical terms, most of M_1.

However, there are monetary holdings of *wealth*. These include savings accounts, money market funds, etc. – in technical terms, $M_2 - M_1$. But some of this can't be counted either. Money balances held by financial institutions, non-profits, etc. should not be included because such organizations typically don't spend on goods and services – they don't consume or build new factories. So only those money balances of wealth held by households and manufacturing or service-providing firms are at issue. This is quite a small part of total wealth. Such holdings would be affected in the manner suggested, but in so far as they are marketable, their value will also depend on the rate of interest.

In any event, against such holdings we must set *nominal debts*, which will be affected in just the opposite way. When the general price level falls, a savings balance is worth more, i.e. will buy more – but a mortgage is a heavier burden. A given number of dollars has to be repaid, but because prices have fallen, more goods or more labour will have to be sold to earn those dollars. So households and businesses will feel *poorer*, not richer, and this effect will lead them to curtail, rather than increase, their spending. Nominal debts are a very large item in the balance sheets of households and businesses. But only if the effect on money balances outweighs the effect on debts could we suppose that a change in the price level would change aggregate demand. This is not likely, and empirical studies tend to confirm that the burden of debt effect is significant, while the real-balance effect cannot be detected.

As for the supply story, it is even more ragged. If the price level changes, with *money wages fixed*, then the story is easy to tell – but a change in the real wage implies a change in distribution, e.g. in profits. This will affect both investment and consumption, so is likely to *shift* the Aggregate Demand curve. But if both money wages and prices move together, so the real wage is constant, then Aggregate Supply will be unchanged. To get around this, stories have been made up about different patterns of expectations. These tend to be *ad hoc*, and implausible. But even if they weren't, there would still be a problem: if firms, for example, believed that because prices were changing, the real wage was changing, they would not only alter employment, but also their investment plans. The expected change in the real wage implies a change in profitability, which will normally affect investment plans. But a change in investment will shift the Aggregate Demand function. So a movement *along* the Aggregate Supply curve – from one point to another – will imply a *shift* in the position of the Aggregate Demand curve. The two curves are not sufficient to determine the two variables.

The conventional Aggregate Demand and Supply story is fundamentally unsound. Textbook writers appear to have been seduced by the prospect of using the same supply-and-demand diagram for both micro and macro – quality sacrificed on the altar of efficiency.

Classical prices, profits and growth

Next let's examine the idea that prices are determined by the needs of production. To understand this consider a numerical example:

Suppose initially that we have two mutually dependent industries:

	Tools	Food		
Tools	3/8 T	1/2 F	---->	1 T
Food	5/8 T	1/2 F	---->	1 F
	1 T	1 F		

Each industry *produces* one unit, each period of production, and the economy as a whole *consumes* one unit of each during that period. At the end of the period tool-producers will keep 3/8 of their output and be ready to exchange 5/8 for the 1/2 F which they need. Food-producers will keep 1/2 their output, and be ready to exchange the other for the 5/8 T they need. Hence 5T exchange for 4F; the price of tools in food is 4/5.

Now suppose that through cajoling or coercing the workers in each industry are persuaded to move twice as fast. The labour input will therefore be only half as much:

	Tools	Food		
Tools	3/8 T	1/4 F	---->	1 T
Food	5/8 T	1/4 F	---->	1 F
	1 T	1/2 F		

A *surplus* has emerged, consisting of 1/2F. If the workers were paid in proportion to their increased productivity, the wage would be doubled and would absorb the whole surplus. The price would then be unchanged.

But suppose that the surplus were appropriated by the *owners* of the industries, to be invested in expanding. Each industry will have to 'plough back' a combination of the two goods in the proportion in which it uses them. So the surplus will have to consist of *both* goods, in the proportions in which they are used overall. So the relative sizes of the two industries must change; we will assume *constant returns to scale* here. That means that changing the relative sizes of the industries will not change the coefficients. (This is an extreme assumption, but it simplifies the story a lot, and, anyway, is not so wrong for mass production.) Given the coefficients, we have to determine at what rate the system can grow. Let the growth rate be G, and the relative size be q:

	Tools		Food		
Tools	G[3/8 T]q	+	G[5/8 T]	=	q
Food	G[1/4 F]q	+	G[1/4 F]	=	1

The best way to understand this is to imagine that all the profit will be *invested*, ploughed back into each sector. But if there's no technical change, each sector will need for its investment a bundle of the *same goods* it already uses as means of production. So, in the aggregate, the surplus has to consist of the *same* goods in the *same* proportions as the aggregate means of production. That way each sector can have the goods it needs for investment. Hence, the ratio of the surplus to means of production is a *pure quantity ratio* – since the bundles making up numerator and denominator consist of the same goods in the same proportions they can be compared without recourse to prices. So this ratio – the surplus being invested to the present bundle of means of production – will be the rate of growth, i.e. the ratio of net investment to physical capital.

Solve each equation for q and set them equal. Then re-arranging, we will get

$$2/32 \ G^2 + 5/8 \ G - 1 = 0,$$

which is a quadratic. Applying the formula, we find that the positive root is

G = 1.403, and solving for q, q = 13/7

That is, the *net* rate of growth is 2/5, and the tool industry should be 13/7 the size of the food industry. To see how this works out, multiply the tool industry by 13/7. This will change the relative sizes. (We are *not* asking how this comes about, how goods and labour are transferred from one sector to the other, so the economy shifts from being a stationary system to growing. That is a separate and important line of inquiry; instead we are comparing the systems.)

	Tools	Food		
Tools	39/56 T	26/56 F	--->	104/56 T
Food	35/56 T	14/56 F	--->	56/56 F
	74/56 T	40/56 F		

The ratio of the output of tools to the total used up is 104/74, the ratio of food produced to food consumed is 56/40. Both are equal to 1.4, allowing

46

for rounding. So in the aggregate the output is now in the right proportions to be invested!

What about exchange? Consider profits in *value* terms. In each sector, the output – food and tools, respectively – multiplied by price is the revenue. Revenue minus replacement costs – the food and tools to replace what was used up in production – equals profits. The rate of profits is the ratio of profits to replacement costs. So *prices* have to be such that the ratio of the net output of each sector to its means of production is the rate of profit. But if all profits are invested, then the rate of profit *has* to equal the pure quantity ratio defined above. It is easily seen that if this is true, then the net output of each sector will exactly exchange at these prices for the bundle of means of production each sector needs for investment.[14]

Taking the equations above, multiply both sides of both by 56, to clear the fractions, and write R for the rate of profit, and p. for the price of tools in terms of food. Then,

$$R[39p + 26] = 104p$$

$$R[35p + 14] = 56$$

We know that R = 1.4. Substituting and doing the arithmetic, p =.74. In intuitive terms, this means that tool producers hold back 1.4 x 39 = 54.6 units, and exchange 49.4 units for 1.4 x 26 = 36.4 units of food. Food producers hold back 19.6 units and exchange 36.4 units for 49 tools. Allowing for rounding off, this gives us the price ratio, determined by investment and the requirements of production. Neither preferences nor endowments figure in the story. Scarcity plays no role. By implication labour is paid what is necessary to enable it to work, and to be productive. Nothing is implied about full employment, one way or the other.

2

INVISIBLE HANDS
The price mechanism or the multiplier?

How many economists does it take to change a light bulb?
None. Economists just sit in the dark, and wait for the Invisible Hand to do it.

'My husband says Reagan set the markets free – at least, he made them freer
than they had been since before Roosevelt. So if markets make everyone better
off, why are there so many homeless now? Why are there so many more poor
now that the rich are better off than ever before?' Wife of a classmate.

I don't remember exactly what I said that night. I tried, but it's a bad sign
when people's eyes glaze over. There's too much technical language in
economics. It's true that the terms are scientifically designed; the precision
is useful and important. But it does inhibit communication.

The eye-glazing answer to my classmate's wife was that markets may not
adjust in an orderly fashion – meaning, for example, that labour markets
won't necessarily provide everyone who wants to work with a job, even when
business needs workers, and the two sides could, in principle, agree on a
wage. How could this be? Remember, the labour market depends on other
markets – business has to sell, and households have to buy; so adjustment
in the labour market depends on what's happening in those other markets.
This market has to adjust to what that market is doing, which in turn requires
adjusting to what is happening in this other market – and once the system
is out of sync the processes may never catch up. Sudden shocks can set
markets off on a path of adjustment that increases unemployment even if
the equilibrium were at full employment. Economics really is complicated.

Later, teaching, I appreciated her reaction to this technical precision. The
classroom was hot, and I was having trouble keeping awake. It was my
co-teacher's turn to lecture, and the subject was market adjustment, the way
markets moved to establish equilibrium. Jacobian matrices, negative diagonal
dominance ... Sitting in front, I couldn't let students see my drooping
eyelids. Face blackboard, back to class. Gross substitution, weak axiom of
revealed preference. No, sit up straight, no slumping. Force eyes open – face-
to-face with a D-stable matrix; its principal minors alternating in sign. Partial
derivatives swimming. If I shook my head, it would look bad. I shifted a

little to sneak a glance – my assistant was watching. If I tied my shoe . . .
Multiply by a diagonal matrix of reaction coefficients . . . And the conclusion
to which we were glacially moving, '. . . which it has taken the profession
thirty years of high mathematics to reach . . .' The lecture, I had to admit,
was very good, very well organized . . . 'And which has not yet trickled down
through the textbooks to the public, an unwelcome conclusion, reluctantly
reached . . . That free markets, adjusting under ideal conditions, need not
and most likely will not reach equilibrium, but can oscillate or diverge
in all sorts of erratic patterns.' Advanced mathematical analysis has now
shown us what mainstream theory actually implies: that anarchy rules in the
marketplace![1]

I sat up straight, wide awake. We, in the graduate schools, now take this
for granted. But what do the textbooks say? The news doesn't seem to have
reached them.[2] For the most part they still tell the story of a 'price mechanism'
which allocates 'scarce resources' optimally, in the process, not altogether
incidentally, solving a lot of serious social conflicts, since one of those
resources is labour. Markets made up of large numbers of small firms, running
small-scale operations, adjust efficiently in response to prices. The price mechanism moves resources around until equilibrium is reached; it is stabilizing.
This is the Marshallian story and there is evidence to support it – for the
nineteenth century. Of course, it looks like a fairy tale today, when we face
large bureaucratic corporations operating Mass Production technologies,
under conditions in which unexpected events can set off cumulative movements resulting in mass unemployment or dangerous inflation. But, as we
have just seen, advanced economic theory, based on RC, doesn't support
any story of movement towards equilibrium. So the conventional wisdom
is caught between a rock and a hard place. If it adopts the Marshallian
picture, equilibrium exists and is stable. But the models are tied to specific
assumptions which are simply not true today. On the other hand, if it takes
the general RC approach, it is free of specifics. The models can be applied
generally – but they need not be stable!

RELYING ON MARKETS

The conclusion that a general model of markets (based on RC) may be
unstable has led many economists to a critique of the actual economy,
of the kind I gave that night. Since markets may be generally unstable,
clear and forceful policies are required to keep them in line.[3] But the more
I thought about it the less satisfactory that answer seemed. Sometimes
markets run wild, out of control, but most of the time market processes
work fairly well. As we pointed out earlier, markets with large numbers of
small firms operating craft-based technologies tend to adjust through flexible
prices, whereas – we shall see – giant corporations engaging in Mass
Production typically generate cumulative movements, swinging explosively in

one direction or another. But there were unstable breakdowns in the nineteenth century, and long periods of stability in the post-War period, even apart from government intervention.[4] Market processes have many dimensions, and we need to explore these, not only in economic theory, but also in the light of common sense.

What happened when Reagan set the markets free was not random or disorderly; markets adjusted quite well to deregulation. Unemployment and the growing impoverishment also proceeded in an orderly way. It may have been a movement away from equilibrium, but it was not disorderly. There are different kinds of instability, and the Keynesian kind, for example, is not disorderly at all. In fact, disorderly markets are relatively rare. Most of our daily business is conducted in markets whose smooth performance we rely on. We go to the supermarket, buy commuter tickets, make travel plans, mortgage our house, take a loan for the car, and wait for our pay cheque, all in the firm belief that we will face no great surprises in regard to prices and payments. Quite the reverse; businessmen, government officials, even university administrators, in fact, just about everyone who has to deal with the practical world, turn to 'the market' for help in dealing with day-to-day issues. This would not be possible if markets were erratic.

What should you pay a new assistant professor? to take a question I've had to face as a Department Chair. Well, you consider equity, what the other ranks are making, what are the current costs of living in the city and ... then you begin to ask around, what are others paying? You consult 'the market', in other words. What should you charge for your book (if your publishers allow you to influence the price!)? How much should you ask for a lecture fee? How much should you bid for the lot adjacent to your house? These are all questions involving many different kinds of factors, but an important, indeed indispensable, element in settling them is going to be the verdict of 'the market', understood in a very practical sort of way. In day-to-day business, we can't afford erratic markets, and whenever we have to face them – more often on Wall St than on Main St – the result is a far-reaching crisis. High theory, starting from the 'scarcity' idea, and ending up with the conclusion that markets are as likely to be erratically unstable as not, may just have gone off the track altogether.

Businesspeople concerned with launching new products do not need to be reminded of the importance of the market's judgement; they may be surprised to hear that academics are no less concerned with exactly that same judgement when they launch new programmes. Or again, suppose you are managing an important resource in limited supply – electrical power in a rural area or underdeveloped region, or building materials, say. To whom do you provide this resource? One important answer will be, to those who can outbid the others. Their willingness and ability to pay means that it is more important to them, or contributes more to productivity when used by them, than when in the hands of others. Of course, there may well be other considerations, ethics, for instance, or questions of public welfare, or the fact that some bidders are simply much richer than others, so that money means less to them; but the verdict of the market will surely figure in the outcome.

The market sums up and expresses opinion, in a very simple, crude and powerful way – in dollars and cents. It is a gauge, a barometer, that sets a value on things. It isn't, and shouldn't be, the final word in many matters, but it is always important. Very simply, the market is where opinions, backed by money, compete. And the idea is that the best, not the absolute best, but the best value for money, tends to win out. So the market does more than just sum up and express opinion; it tends to sift it and judge it as well. The market brings out the best values; the goods that make it big, in some sense deserve to; the assignment of resources is in some way, the right one, or the best. Always subject to qualifications of course. But the Invisible Hand holds a few aces.

As we have seen, the idea that market outcomes are somehow optimal, is basic to the textbooks, and also corresponds to the prevailing wisdom among economists and business leaders, even though it is no longer sanctified by high theory. But this last is ignored, since, as I've just argued, reliance on market results is rooted in our everyday experience. Not that market outcomes are *optimal*, but rather that they have a certain objectivity and reflect robust good sense. If you pay attention to the market signals, you ought to do all right; if you don't you will run a serious risk of going under.

THE INVISIBLE HAND

The textbook doctrine of the 'Invisible Hand' carries this a good deal further, making a twofold claim: that the pursuit by each agent of purely selfish aims, will be resolved into the common good, and further that the market would see to it that this common good was realized in practice. The argument is on the basis of RC, and claims that, in general, markets will adjust; they are assumed to be stable, contrary to the findings of high theory. Each individual pursuing his self-interest would be led, as if by an invisible hand, to act for the common good.

Now we all know that, taken at face value, this is simply not true; individuals pursuing their self-interest are quite likely to cheat the rest of us. Not to mention destroying themselves, as the story of *The Treasure of Sierra Madre* will remind us.[5] Nor will it do to say that, in the long run cheating doesn't pay, cheaters will get found out in the end, etc. John D. Rockefeller died a very rich man, and so did most of the other great Robber Barons. Ivan Boesky was caught, but how many others were not? Plainly, crime does pay, and, in fact, pays quite well, as is proper since it is very risky. Nevertheless, there is some common-sense truth in the doctrine of the Invisible Hand, and we must try to establish just what it is.

What common good is brought about by the pursuit of private gain? 'It is not from the benevolence of the butcher, the brewer, the baker, that we expect our dinner, but from their regard to their own interest.' (Smith, 19xx, p. 14) The common good in question is the efficient division of labour, giving rise to high and expanding output and wealth. Prosperity, in short. Here is the famous passage:

> As every individual, therefore, endeavours as much as he can both to employ his capital in the support of domestic industry, and so to direct that industry that its produce may be of the greatest value; every individual necessarily labours to render the annual revenue of the society as great as he can. He generally, indeed, neither intends to promote the public interest, nor knows how much he is promoting it. By preferring the support of domestic to that of foreign industry, he intends only his own security; and by directing that industry in such a manner as its produce may be of the greatest value, he intends only his own gain, and he is in this, as in many other cases, led by an invisible hand to promote an end which was no part of his intention. Nor is it always the worse for the society that it was no part of it. By pursuing his own interest he frequently promotes that of the society more effectually than when he really intends to promote it.
>
> (p. 423)

This passage occurs in the context of a discussion of whether capital should be employed in the home trade or in foreign. Self-interest, declares Smith, will lead to its being employed in the home trade (for security), and in the most profitable lines (for gain). Hence the aggregate capital will give rise to as much employment, and produce as much output as possible, when owners of capital choose how to use it freely, rather than being coerced by restrictions and laws promulgated by statesmen and lawgivers.

The prevailing wisdom claims – as we saw, unjustifiably – that the market answers the questions 'What? How? and For Whom?', i.e. what products (from among all possible) will be produced, by what methods of production, and to whom the proceeds will go. It further claims that if markets are competitive, these results will be optimal. This is a considerable step beyond Adam Smith, and beyond common sense, too. Nor is it supported by economic theory, as we have seen. It is one thing to argue that market arrangements set up powerful incentives to expand output and to innovate; another to hold that such arrangements can reach socially optimal judgements about such complex and fundamental questions as the distribution of income and wealth, or the list of 'the furniture of the world'. Of course in reality these questions are partly answered, and certainly strongly influenced, by the market – but such outcomes can hardly be considered *optimal*.

FROM THE CRAFT ECONOMY TO MASS PRODUCTION

At the time of Adam Smith, market incentives probably did lead, as Smith argued, to maximum output and employment, and at a later date, as the market became more fully developed, it is likely that the price system did encourage the efficient use of resources, including the best choice of consumer goods, in terms of value for money. This is the grain of truth in the Monetarist and New Classical argument. But it is not a *general* truth: certain conditions have to be met, the economy must be organized in a certain way. Firms must be small and family-run; the technology must be small-scale, and dependent on craft skills. Mechanical energy, e.g. steam and water power, can replace human or animal power, as in the early factories. But the work is still performed by craftsmen, and the process is organized in accord with traditional principles. The craftsmen no longer have to provide the power, but they still guide the tools. Hence production processes are dependent on their workers, who work together as a team. The team organizes the process, and often decides on various aspects of the division of labour. The whole team must be present for production to take place at all – an absent worker means an essential task will be left undone.

In these circumstances firms will tend to have only two options when the demand they are facing fluctuates: either produce with a full complement of workers, or shut down. If the plant is running at all, it requires the whole work force. When demand is strong they will work hard, when demand is weak, they will take it easy, and perform clean-up and maintenance. So, in such an economy, employment will not vary all that much when demand fluctuates, as long as the fluctuations are not too large. Since employment doesn't vary much, money wages won't either. Prices, on the other hand, will tend to rise in periods of strong demand, since output can only be increased marginally by working harder, and will fall in the face of weak markets, since if it is worth while staying open at all, the normal output should be produced and sold for whatever it will bring.

In other words, market incentives are effective, and market adjustment will tend to be stabilizing, in a Craft Economy, where skilled workers, operating in complex teams, produce at a pace which they largely control. When demand is strong they will work intensively, when demand is slow they will take it easy. Productivity will vary when demand varies, but employment will not. Money wages will be set along with employment, much as the price of any commodity is established by market processes along with the normal amount exchanged. Since in these conditions, employment does not vary much with changes in demand, neither will money wages. And since output only varies marginally with demand, the prices of produced goods will tend to fluctuate in the same direction as demand. So when, for example, there is a general fall in demand, we can expect prices to decline as firms try to keep up their sales. Employment and labour costs, however, will remain fixed, unless the decline goes too far, in which case businesses would have to close down.

Now consider what this means when, for example, there is a decline in demand. The fall in demand will bring in its wake a *rise* in the real purchasing power available to working families – for money wages will tend to remain constant, while prices are falling. Thus consumption in real terms can be expected to rise. So in a Craft Economy the market mechanism *automatically* counters a falling off in demand with an increase in consumption. (This will tend to have a stabilizing effect, as statistics confirm.[6] Furthermore, if good years are averaged with bad – and if the variations are not too wide – a pattern of 'normal' resource use can be defined, and it can be argued that this normal level of usage is what the price system is supposed to make efficient.)

In early capitalism, the nature of technology led to the development of small firms, typically craft-based family firms, that were relatively inflexible in terms of adapting output and employment to changes in demand. Firms grew to an optimal size – the size that a production team could most efficiently work. Fluctuations in demand were accommodated, on the one hand, by varying the intensity of the production team's effort and, on the other, through price changes dictated by the marketplace.[7] In the first case, output was varied by varying productivity, a solution that could not be satisfactory to either employers or employees. Employers would not wish the slower pace of hard times to become a norm; employees would not wish to be held to the faster pace of booming times. In the second case, output would be maintained, but with fixed supply and weaker demand, prices would be driven down. Again this could not be satisfactory; firms would take losses on their inventory, and the market might become 'spoiled'.

But the technology did not make varying output in line with the market easy. In some cases, the nature of the production process, for example, water or steam power, required full operation or none at all. Some processes simply could not be operated at half speed, or lower intensity. Further, all hands had to be present for the process to be operated at all. Employment was thus fixed by the size of the production team, apart from clean-up jobs, and the like, so that output could only be changed through varying the intensity of the inputs – the same labour force would have to work harder and faster when demand was strong, but could take it easy in slack times. Growth in demand was accommodated by adding new firms of optimal size – not through the expansion of existing firms. The fixed nature of the production process did not allow for many economies of scale; when these were exhausted, limits to effective size would be reached rapidly, although the optimal size from the point of view of production might not be the same as the best size from the marketing or financial perspective (Robinson, 1931). Once its optimal size was determined, however, there was no economic motive for a firm to expand beyond it.[8]

Moderate changes in demand would be met by changes in the utilization of factors and through changes in price. A sharp fall in demand would result in falling prices, which if substantial and sustained, might force many of the small production establishments out of business. Similarly, large increases in demand would be associated with rising prices and the opening of additional, optimally sized, production establishments, employing the same technology as existing firms. (A single firm might operate several establishments, of course, but the family's managerial resources could not be stretched far.) Moderate declines in demand would be met with falling prices but relatively stable employment and output – there would be little or nothing in the way of Keynesian multiplier effects (which we will explain in a moment). Quite the reverse: the lower prices imply a higher real wage, so, with stable employment, the effect will be higher consumption spending, and induced change in the *opposite* direction. Drastic declines in demand would lead to falling prices and bankruptcies that would or could have successive rounds of repercussions, but the multiplier, in these circumstances, would be a bankruptcy multiplier – not the traditional Keynesian spending multiplier.

The adaptability of prices to changes in demand within an environment of stable output, employment and money wages is extremely important when considering the volatility of the economy in the early period. If, with an increase in demand, prices rose, real wages would fall and, as a consequence, so would consumption. Working-class households in early capitalism have few assets against which to borrow to sustain consumption; their consumption is therefore governed by their real earnings. Consequently, the initial increase in demand would be offset by a subsequent fall in the level of consumption. The same offsetting effect would come into play if demand fell, and brought declining prices. Falling prices with fixed money wages would lead to rising real wages and, hence, increases in household consumption. Therefore, market adjustment is based on an inherent stabilizing mechanism which is grounded in the technology of that era (Nell, 1992, ch. 16).

But no one should get dewy-eyed over the Craft Economy and its price mechanism. It had serious problems. From the firms' point of view, the system's stability was purchased at the price of fluctuations in profit. Firms had to put aside reserves in good years to tide them over in bad. Moreover, work teams controlled the pace of work, and could slow down when they were unhappy with the terms of pay and/or conditions of work offered by employers. In any case, fixed costs were too high a proportion of total current costs. And why should productivity decline with sales; why not maintain productivity and vary employment? Why should the firm pay the same wages for slower work? But to change this required changing the whole mode of operation. The Craft system had to be replaced with Mass Production.

Under Mass Production activities are carried out not so much by teams as through integrated tasks. 'Batch production' is replaced by 'continuous through-put'. Instead of a 'batch' of raw materials, or partly finished products,

55

being carried through the various operations by a work-team, all working simultaneously on the same batch, raw materials are fed in continuously, and move through the different stages from one work-station to the next, so that workers perform operations successively (Chandler, 1990). Both output and employment can be varied with demand – output more nearly in exact proportion than employment, since some labour is overhead – while the overall expansion of production is accomplished through increasing the size of the production establishment. Expansion reaps the benefits of economies of scale, therefore, which in turn leads to larger firms, differently organized than small production teams, and motivated to grow.

The ability of Mass Production to vary employment and output with demand has led to two very important characteristics, distinguishing early from late capitalism: prices could be more stable, predictable and controllable, and, varying employment and output in response to changes in demand has resulted in typical Keynesian spending multiplier consequences. The price adjustment mechanism evident in the early period is not to be found in the later. Following World War II, prices tend only to rise and the inflationary pressures pushing them up are not in general stabilizing. The output and employment adjustments likewise tend to be destabilizing. And strong expansion – or contraction – in output can lead to adjustments in the capital stock, with further multiplier implications for output. Evidently there is a degree of inherent instability, contrasting sharply to the earlier period.

Government, however, tends to play a role as a stabilizer, in contrast to the earlier period, when its activities were generally supposed to be limited to the duties of a 'Night Watchman'.[9] This enhanced role is not only a matter of large and growing size, but also concerns the increasingly complex nature of the activities involved.

FROM KINSHIP TO BUREAUCRACY

When capitalism first appeared on the stage of history it was dressed in the clothes of Mercantilism. Merchants and craftsmen figured as the chief players; businesses were run by the heads of families, and were passed along to the oldest sons, just as fathers had trained their sons in the secrets of the trade or craft for centuries. But while the family was suited to the guild and the craft system, it was not the appropriate vehicle for the development of capital. Competition leads to the development of better products and better methods of production; in turn, these require control over the labour force, control not possible when workers determine the pace and quality of work. But the development of machinery that works labour, in place of machinery that labour works, opens up the possibility of economies of scale – and this changes the nature of competition. For now the firm must invest regularly, expanding with the growth of markets, finding ways to enter new markets, seeking out opportunities and new products. In the Craft Economy growth took place through the creation of new firms, each attaining an optimal size, and then remaining at that level from then on. Under Mass Production firms invest competitively; for if any firm can significantly increase its market share, it can reap economies of scale and then, by undercutting, ruin or threaten to ruin the others. Hence firms will have to be organized in such a way that they can develop and carry out competitive strategies in an almost military fashion. They must be able to expand, take on new ventures, drop old ones, change the nature of their activities, or contract, re-locate, re-position themselves in their markets, and so forth. This requires professional management and bureaucratic organization; it is not something that can be built around the family. But this has large implications.

The change from the family firm to the bureaucratic corporation alters the relationship between capital and the kinship system. In the Craft Economy social classes were classes of families: some families were property owners, owning land or capital, and receiving income from rents or from interest or profit. Others were propertyless, and received income from wages. In between were families in mixed positions. Of course, class lines were never perfectly precise. The status of any given family depended on what kind of property, or what mix of kinds, it held, compared to others. Nevertheless, the main outlines were clear and the principal criteria of division relatively simple. No longer. In Mass Society kinship relations have been progressively reduced from the extended family to the nuclear unit, and the accelerators of modern life, like those of modern physics, split even that. Social position now depends more on corporate rank than on ownership of property or family background. Family, of course, helps; in particular, it helps to get into the right schools and into the right initial positions. But from then on performance counts most, and you have to rise to the top.

In the Craft Economy the players in the competitive game were relatively simple: households and family firms. In Mass Society households are breaking up and firms have swollen into giant and complex bureaucracies. The players have changed and the rules of the game are different. The Invisible Hand no longer beckons.

TECHNICAL CHANGE AND
TRANSFORMATIONAL GROWTH

At the heart of transformational growth is the claim that the function of the market is to generate competitive pressures to innovate and to assemble the financial resources to invest in innovations. Allocation of existing resources is of secondary importance; moreover, in practice, competition often generates waste, offsetting allocative efficiency. To make a huge generalization – in the manner of textbooks – one could argue that innovation, driven by competition, is what distinguishes the capitalist West since the Renaissance – broadly, Europe and North America – from all other economic systems, past and present. Such a sweeping claim needs many qualifications – but no more than the equally sweeping claim that markets, always and everywhere, allocate scarce resources efficiently. And it has the additional advantage of being nearer the truth!

The introduction of new products and new processes of production normally opens up new fields of competition. The new products will usually displace some older ways of doing things – the automobile (and before it, the bicycle) displaced the horse and buggy, more or less rapidly transforming whole areas of the social landscape. Firms will compete in developing, redesigning, producing and marketing the new product, introducing variations of it into all sections of society. As a new item catches on, complementary products and associated processes of production will spring up, and the system will move into a long upswing, as more and more sectors of the social order are transformed. This upswing need not be steady; it may be highly variable and irregular, but the long-term trend will be consistently up, until the new goods have saturated the available markets. Moreover, this general expansive tendency will itself help to engender further technical progress. If markets are developing strongly, and competition for the best form of the product is heated, then innovation will be in the wind. Business will encourage and underwrite inventors and innovators; new ideas will be put to the market test. So technical progress promotes sales and market growth, and such growth in turn supports technical innovation.

On the other hand, when a period of transformational growth has finished, when the markets are saturated (when the automobile has come to the end of the road, so to speak), sales will tend to slump across the board. There will be nothing to give impetus to a broad expansion, a general redevelopment of the style of life. So technical change in the largest sense provides a stimulus to sales, and its cessation brings a tendency to slump in sales.

A very important effect can be seen here. When employment and output can be changed in a relatively flexible manner, changes in sales, up or down, bring about further changes in the same direction. Suppose there is a new product being introduced – the automobile in 1905, the television in 1948 – and dozens of companies are competing for what they hope will eventually be a huge market. They will have to build factories and sales outlets; they will need raw materials and equipment; they will have to hire distributors, advertising and showrooms. All this activity means *additional* employment in construction, in the manufacturing of equipment, in the production of raw materials and in advertising and distribution. These secondary industries will have to expand employment to increase their output. The people so hired will in turn spend their incomes, generating further activity in the production of consumer goods. (So there will be additional hiring in consumer goods, which means still more spending, and so on, ad infinitum. Although an 'infinite' process, theoretically speaking, the effects diminish quite rapidly – so, in practice, only the first couple of 'rounds' count. In short, an increase in activity, in spending, generates a *further* increase in spending.

Of course new products displace old – automobiles wiped out the horse and buggy. Won't additional sales of automobiles be offset by declining activity in the horse and buggy trades? It's true that carriage-makers, wheelwrights, saddlers, grooms, curriers, harness-makers and many other trades gradually found themselves out of work. Some no doubt found new employment in related areas of the new automobile industry. But the lesson is that the total impact of a new area of activity has to be considered the new investment plus its secondary effects *minus* the portion of the earlier kind of activity that is displaced, plus secondary effects. The net increase will be this difference.

THE MULTIPLIER

In the Craft Economy, employment tends to be relatively difficult to vary. As long as sales are strong enough to cover running costs, output should be produced, even if weakness in the market leads to falling prices. Workers cannot easily be laid off, since the full complement is needed to run the shop. (Think of early mills: each work-station must be manned.) Start-up and shut-down costs are high, so it pays to keep running.

Since employment tends to be relatively steady, short of general crises leading to widespread closures and bankruptcies, money wages will not be so immediately affected by weakness (or strength) in the market. Prices will tend to vary more readily than money wages. Hence, as we have seen, when markets are weak, prices will fall, but money wages will hold steady or fall more slowly. Hence real wages will rise. But this means that household consumption will tend to rise. Thus, as we saw earlier, a *weakness* in the market, say, due to a collapse of exports, or a slowdown in investment, will tend to generate an offsetting *increase* in consumption spending. This is an automatic stabilizing effect, brought about by the price mechanism.

However, under Mass Production, this no longer holds. Modern industrial processes can be started up and shut down easily; extra shifts can be added and taken off. Workers can be laid off or put on short time. When workers are laid off, their household spending drops, leading to weaker markets elsewhere, and very likely, more layoffs. Again the process will work through various stages, as the effect is multiplied. In this case, as we will see in more detail later, an initial fluctuation in exports or investment will lead, not to *offsetting* changes in consumption, but to changes that *compound* the initial shock.

Let's take a closer look at how these 'further increases' in spending work themselves out. Start by supposing that investment increases, so sales rise, so employment rises, which means that household consumer spending goes up, and therefore sales are further increased – leading to another increase in output and employment. How long does this go on? How many times is this supposed to be repeated?

59

At each stage as new sales are made, inventories are reduced, and of the revenue received, a certain portion is 'set aside', to meet capital costs and pay dividends, while the rest is used to pay the costs of producing replacements for the depleted inventory. These costs of production will consist mainly of wages – two-thirds or more. (Other costs will be materials, heating and lighting, electrical power or other energy.) Wages, of course, are also passed along as consumer spending. So, if we neglect the other costs, at each stage, capital charges – gross profits – are withdrawn, and variable costs – wages – are passed along. The wages are then spent, creating further sales, the revenue of which is split into gross profits, which are withdrawn, and wages, which are passed along again.

That's how it works: an increase in net spending – exports, for instance, or government spending or investment – means higher sales; the revenue at each stage is split into profits withdrawn and wages passed along; the passed along wages are then spent, creating a further stage of new or additional sales, and so on. (Notice that we have completely neglected to mention household savings, about which we hear so much in the press and in popular economics. The reason is that household savings are just not very important; business net saving is more than twice as much, and business *gross* saving, which includes capital consumption allowances, is more than four times as much.) So, we see how the process works, but how many stages will there be? What will be the total amount of new sales generated?

Theoretically, one could say there would be an infinite number of 'stages'; but actually, the effect will wear down quite quickly. The capital charges being withdrawn (the markup) will be on average about half the revenue, so that, after a few rounds, the impact on sales would be indistinguishable from any number of other normal and expected fluctuations, the very thing businesses carry inventory to meet. At this point there would be no further repercussions.

As for how large the final impact would be, a little arithmetic will show that if the capital charges or gross profits withdrawn each time are half the revenue, i.e. if the mark-up is 100 per cent, the total sales will be twice the initial. If the mark-up is 50 per cent, so that the gross profit withdrawn is one-third of total revenue, then (since more is passed along each time) the total sales will be three times the initial. The initial expenditure is 'multiplied'.[10]

THE KEYNESIAN COMPROMISE

But if the market is systematically unstable in this way, it is likely to fail to guarantee full employment of labour and equipment, and, as we shall see, may even tend to establish a pattern of systematic underutilization. In such conditions, neither Smith's nor the modern version of the 'Invisible Hand' would seem warranted. This seems almost obvious, but a very great authority staked out quite the opposite position. Keynes (1936) argued that if the State arranged, through direct stimulation combined with low interest rates, to ensure sufficient investment to achieve full employment, then there could be no grounds to question the traditional theory's account of the allocation of resources. He wrote:

> Our criticism of the accepted classical theory of economics has consisted not so much in finding logical flaws in its analysis as in pointing out that its tacit assumptions are seldom or never satisfied, with the result that it cannot solve the economic problems of the actual world. But if our central controls succeed in establishing an aggregate volume of output corresponding to full employment as nearly as is practicable, the classical theory comes into its own from this point onwards. If we suppose the volume of output to be given, i.e. to be determined by forces outside the classical scheme of thought, then there is no objection to be raised against the classical analysis of the manner in which private self-interest will determine what in particular is produced, in what proportions the factors will be combined to produce it, and how the value of the final product will be distributed between them.
>
> (pp. 378–9)

> To put the point concretely, I see no reason to suppose that the existing system seriously misemploys the factors of production which are in use. There are, of course, errors of foresight . . . When 9,000,000 men are employed out of 10,000,000 willing and able to work, there is no evidence that the labour of these 9,000,000 is misdirected. The complaint against the present system is not that these 9,000,000 men ought to be employed on different tasks, but that tasks should be available for the remaining 1,000,000 men. It is in determining the volume not the direction of actual employment that the existing system has broken down.
>
> (p. 379)

But suppose that government spending guaranteed full employment. Could we then say that the traditional system 'comes back into its own'? Could we say, with Keynes, that there is no reason to think the labour of the 9,000,000 is misdirected? That the only problem is to find employment for the remaining million? In a sense it sounds quite plausible, and, intellectually speaking, it is a neat sort of compromise. But it carries a strong implication – namely that the size of the system can be separated from its makeup, scale from composition.

Yet this is just what the multiplier makes impossible. For actual mistakes in the composition of the system will show up as apparent errors in scale. Suppose that the total level of aggregate demand is the 'full employment' amount, but that the government has stimulated 'too little' consumer demand

and 'too much' investment. To put it another way, in the past 'too much' has gone into building consumption goods factories, and 'too little' into basic capital goods plant. So with the current demand, even though in the aggregate it is the 'full employment' level, there will be excess capacity in consumer goods, but a shortage of capacity in producer goods – in relation to demand. But the shortfall of demand in consumer goods will lead to layoffs and multiplier contraction; workers laid off will have less to spend, so supermarkets and department stores will sell less, and so on. By contrast, the shortage of capacity in producer goods will not lead to more hiring, since labour can't be employed in factories or on equipment that doesn't exist. Of course, the demand pressure will lead to more intense working of present plant, extra shifts, overtime, etc., so there will no doubt be some upward multiplier pressure, as some workers receive increased pay cheques. However, the downward pressure will predominate; and, as a result, the demand for producer goods will be cut back – for why should firms in the consumer goods sector build more capacity when they already have too much? Hence demand for both consumer goods and producer goods will be cut back, which means that the scale of the economy's operation will be reduced as a consequence of *mistaken proportions*. Scale and composition can't be separated in the way Keynes seems to have thought. It is not enough to ensure the right amount of aggregate demand; it must also come in the right proportions.

So the Keynesian compromise is unacceptable. The system evidently fails to provide full employment, but whether this is because of a failure to generate the required volume or the correct proportions of demand – or both! – cannot be determined without further study. What we can say, however, is that 'the price mechanism' does not bring about an optimal allocation of resources. Unused or underutilized resources have not been optimally allocated, and if they remain un-or-underutilized the system is not self-correcting. Consequently neither Smith's nor the later, modern, version of the Invisible Hand can be accepted.

INFLATION

It is more or less universally believed that inflation is caused by demand pressure, yet surprisingly, in all the post-World War II inflations, both in the US and in Western Europe, demand lay well below capacity. Perhaps equally surprising, in the few cases – West Germany in the late 1960s – where demand seriously pressed on capacity for a prolonged period, there was much less inflation than at other times when demand was manifestly weaker. Inflation is often described as 'too much money chasing too few goods'; but if demand is less than capacity, the goods in circulation can easily be increased. Why raise prices and bring on threats of government action, antagonistic responses from customers, and competitive bids by rivals? Just bring back laid-off workers and run an extra shift.

In manufacturing, an increase in demand is usually met by an increase in production, with prices kept pretty much the same. To be sure, in particular cases prices will often be temporarily raised, but businesses will want to be careful not to antagonize regular customers, and will not want to drive away or discourage potential new ones. Higher prices will make it hard to enter new markets; trying to charge different customers different prices will create antagonism. Hence, even when current supplies are short, companies will prefer to take orders and expand production, rather than ration by raising prices. Moreover – and this is the inner economic meaning of the system of Mass Production – it will generally be possible to increase output. Sometimes, when production is already near capacity level, it may not be possible to increase it without an increase in costs. In such cases increased production will have to be accompanied by rising prices. But whenever current production is well below capacity, an increase in demand can be met (after a delay that depends on the time production takes) with an increase in supply at the current going price.

The above applies to manufacturing, but it is not true for all categories of prices, and this gives us the clue to the real relationship between demand and inflation. Prices of primary products, that is, roughly, agricultural goods, raw materials and oil (when not controlled by a cartel), tend to be sensitive to variations in demand. It is often harder to vary primary output quickly; also the cost structure of primary industries tends to be different – a much larger proportion of costs are fixed. So when aggregate demand rises – a business boom – primary products may rise in price. These products are raw materials and basic foodstuffs; their higher prices will appear as higher costs to the rest of the system, so that other prices will start rising, reflecting the new level of costs, and setting off a wage–price spiral. This last can take on an independent existence – prices go up, so workers demand higher wages, which means costs are up again, so business raises prices further. Hence a rise in demand, even though it falls well short of capacity, can set off an inflation through its effects on the prices of primary products. But the answer, surely, is not to prevent expansions. It is to prevent the prices of primary products from responding so readily. More about this later.

BALANCING SALES AND CAPACITY

Now we come to quite a difficult point. The normal working of the system as a whole leads to two outcomes: more income, meaning more demand, as just explained, and more plant capacity, that is, more building of factories. Factories are built because it is expected that the goods they can produce will find a market at a profitable price, and the activity of building them generates incomes which are spent, thereby generating more incomes, and so on. Can we expect these two processes, the building of factories and the generating of spendable incomes, to neatly balance out, so that the additional demand created will always just employ the newly produced capacity? Or will they sometimes balance and sometimes not, with demand falling above and below capacity?

If the economy is really self-adjusting, we would expect the two processes to balance; if it can't adjust itself, then we would expect failures going both ways, above and below the balancing point. In fact, we find neither of these. Since World War II, aggregate demand has only reached the full capacity level twice, *twice* in more than 40 years, and both times during wartime. Aggregate demand systematically falls below capacity; the economy normally operates in conditions of excess capacity, or demand shortage. Not only that: 'full capacity' itself is a very imprecise notion, as shown by the fact that it is very easy for the economy to operate *above* full capacity, if demand is strong enough and sustained enough to push it there! This was spectacularly demonstrated in World War II, when the economy grew at more than twice the full capacity growth rate, and operated for more than two years at 30 to 50 per cent above capacity. It also ran a few points above capacity during both the Korean and the Vietnam Wars. Full capacity doesn't mean that it's impossible to produce more.

So what does it mean, then? And why will business build capacity that it does not use? If they are carrying excess capacity, why doesn't business move to get rid of it; after all, it's expensive and by definition, unnecessary.

PRODUCTIVE CAPACITY IN MASS PRODUCTION

These questions go to the heart of the matter, which is the way the system of Mass Production works. For this system, vintage World War I, but reaching its peak in World War II, rested on a fundamental innovation in the way goods and services were produced that distinguishes it from everything that preceded it since the dawn of history. Under Mass Production *more is cheaper*; Mass Production rests on economies of scale. Bigger is better; hence the pressures of competition will lead firms to overbuild. Each firm wants plant capacity sufficient to support its strategy in the market – but only some firms will win. The rest, the losers in the scramble for markets, will certainly be carrying excess capacity. But if they can get big enough orders, or run their orders all at the same time, their large capacity will give them low unit costs – and the rest of the time they can shut down. The cost of carrying excess capacity is only the capital cost; labour costs are incurred only when the plant is actually operated. By contrast, in most prior systems of production – Craft-based systems – the bulk of current costs were fixed in real terms. Work teams had to be kept together and kept working all the time, even when sales were depressed. Excess capacity meant that the establishment was too big – the work teams were too large or there were too many of them. By contrast, in Mass Production, capacity size (and therefore the potential for economies of scale) depends on the dimensions of the plant and equipment, not of the work teams.

These observations will help us to see the answers to the questions posed above. 'Full capacity' does not necessarily limit production, because there will frequently, perhaps even normally, be as yet unrealized economies of scale in Mass Production technologies. These will become attainable under heavy demand pressure, provided it is certain that the heavy demand will last, because they will normally be achievable only at a cost, and after some experimentation with reorganizing the production system. Excess capacity is common, indeed the normal condition of the economy, because the carrying costs are relatively low, while it provides the only way of achieving economies of scale sufficient to underwrite a competitive marketing strategy, should favourable conditions emerge.

Hence the modern system does not do what Smith claimed – it does not produce the largest possible output and employment. But it doesn't produce the best allocation, either; it doesn't live up to the textbook claims. For if there are unemployed resources, then prices don't measure opportunity costs. They can't, for there are no opportunity costs associated with unemployed resources. Neither the older nor the modern version of the doctrine of the Invisible Hand can be sustained.

THE PRICE MECHANISM

But surely, it will be objected, this can't be right. Each and every individual business, faced with the costs of equipment and resources on the market, has to adjust its uses of such things so as to make sure that their 'contribution' to the business is worth what has to be paid for them. A business has to plan its production – and sales, for that matter. It knows it will have to have machinery, warehousing, certain kinds of skilled labour, energy, etc. And it knows how much these will cost. A business will use more or less of a resource, or use the resource this way or that, until it is clear that the contribution (to the revenue of the firm) of a unit of each resource just equals or exceeds its price. Otherwise it wouldn't be worth using it. So prices, it seems, *must* measure 'productive contributions'. (An optimal 'productive contribution', what the use of a resource adds to the revenue stream of a firm, will be the largest contribution the resource can make; hence it will be just greater than what could be made by using the resource some other way – which is what is meant by the 'opportunity cost'. The use that has been made is optimal because it is just better than the best alternative; the price ideally lies on the margin between the current productive contribution and that of the best alternative use.) And if they do, then the use of resources must be optimal; so the price system must function as an Invisible Hand. How can this be reconciled with the normal demand shortage characteristic of a Keynesian world?

If we think about it carefully it's not so difficult. The shortfall of demand results from the normal day-to-day *working* of the system; the adjustment of resource use, so that productive contributions are brought into line with prices, takes place in *planning*, in the design of the production process of each business. So, in a sense, the price adjustment is purely notional. For such price relations to become real, these plans must be put into practice, which means that the production processes must be actually built. When this happens then the price relations will indeed become real, but they will also be overridden by the consequences of the system's actual working – which as we have seen results in normal excess capacity (shortage of demand). For building production processes is simply investment, which brings about results through the multiplier and the other associated reactions, together making up the system's mode of normal operation.

In other words, in planning and designing its plant and equipment, each business will try to ensure that the resources it proposes to acquire will be used efficiently. This is the more urgent because it must compete in the market for scarce customers; it must keep costs down and quality up. But when it actually comes to building and then running its factories, the results will reflect the way the economy works, the effects of businesses interacting, as well as what was planned. And this means that, overall, resources will not be used efficiently, since there will be systematic underutilization – wasted capacity. Such excess capacity, in turn, puts further pressure on the firms to cut costs, and in so far as these are wage costs, this further reduces overall demand, thereby making the *aggregate* problem worse. We see here a bizarre but important interaction: wastage at the level of the whole leads to efficiency at the level of the individual unit.

NORMAL EXCESS CAPACITY AND RESERVE LABOUR

The existence of generalized excess capacity has far-reaching consequences. Indeed, it explains many of the most characteristic features of the modern economy. Firms are everywhere burdened with an extra cost – and with the knowledge that they could substantially reduce their running costs if they could only get enough orders to justify running flat out (possibly after some initial reorganization). Hence competition for demand will be intense; costs will be cut in order to justify price cuts to compete for markets. In other words, the burden of excess capacity provides a constant stimulus to technical improvement and cost-cutting.

But cost-cutting just exacerbates the problem. For aggregate demand depends on the total impact, direct and indirect, of decisions to buy. Purchase of a final good sets up direct demand for the labour to produce it, and indirect demand for raw materials, tools, and the labour and raw materials and tools to produce raw materials and tools, and so on, ad infinitum. Cost-cutting and technological improvement *reduce the indirect impact* – the multiplier effects – of any given purchase. Moreover, cost-cutting usually means increased productivity, which is to say, increased potential output. So, on both counts, this *widens* the gap between capacity and demand, which in turn just intensifies the competitive pressure to cut costs and raise productivity.

The gap between capacity and normal demand, then, is not a defect of the system, nor is it an indication of an accident or a breakdown. It is the result of the normal mode of operation of the economy. As such it partly accounts for one of modern capitalism's most notable features, namely its technological dynamism. This dynamism was noticeably – even notoriously – absent in the planned economics of the now-defunct Soviet system, where, as we shall see later, demand pressure tended to be excessive. Anything produced would be absorbed by the market, almost regardless of quality, and no one could be penalized for cost-overruns, since the only effective penalty, shutting them down, would remove badly needed capacity from production. But those economies did use labour and resources fully, whereas in Western economies resources are not being fully utilized.

This leads us to a further, closely associated, feature of the Western system. Productive potential cannot be considered really available unless there is also the potential labour force available to work it when it is needed. Over the history of capitalism, along with excess capacity, the system has regularly generated a pool of redundant labour, ready and able to work when called upon. This has happened in several ways. Innovations in methods of production ruin old industries, who can no longer compete, and replace them with new, more productive factories, employing less labour. New products displace old, putting the old producer's factories out of business, releasing labour, while the new products normally require less labour per unit of output. Labour shortages, when and if they occur, lead to rising money wages, which, in turn, stimulates innovation in ways to economize on labour.

But historically the major supply of new industrial labour has been workers displaced from agriculture. With mechanization, new fertilizers, new and improved seeds, over the years the productivity of both labour and land in agriculture has risen more rapidly than growth in general, while demand for agricultural products, on the whole, has risen less rapidly. The result has been a decline in both the percentage of employed workers, and in the absolute numbers, in agriculture. But there aren't many farmers left, and even fewer farm-labourers. So a new supply of reserve labour has had to be found – and it is turning out to be just as American as apple pie. That's right – it's Mom!

TECHNICAL PROGRESS AND THE BUSINESS CYCLE

Demand and productivity are related in contradictory ways. On the one hand high demand provides a strong stimulus to increasing productivity – it means, for example, that it would be worthwhile to undertake a possibly costly reorganization; it means that it will pay to push the system hard, to remove slack, tighten up discipline, and above all to work, not hard, but *smart*. So strong demand tends to generate rapid rises in productivity. But then another effect comes into play: rises in productivity tend to weaken demand, by reducing the indirect or multiplier effects of spending. Even worse, a rise in productivity is an alternative, in a sense, to investment. If the productive capacity of existing facilities can be increased by reorganization of equipment and rethinking procedures, then why build a new one? Building new plants increases the demand for labour; renovating existing plants may be done largely by the existing labour force. Building new plants generates demand for all kinds of supplies and equipment, construction materials, heavy engineering, earth-moving machinery and everything from heating systems to new windows and flooring to doorknobs and typewriters. Renovation may just involve closing down the plant while the existing labour force moves things around and installs some new parts – or, more likely, a new computer-driven control system – which will enable it to run faster, or make longer and more flexible production runs. Building new plants increases aggregate demand while adding to capacity; renovation increases capacity, but adds little to aggregate demand.

So heavy demand leads to rising productivity, which in turn weakens demand, by reducing the multiplier, and slowing down or delaying investment spending.[11] (Rapid growth also tends to bid up the interest rate, another factor that tends to weaken investment.) Thus after a time demand will tend to fall off, and excess capacity and unemployment will rise to dangerous levels. This will lead to serious pressure for scrapping and reorganization, leading to pressures encouraging innovation. When innovation brings new methods of production and new products, old factories become obsolescent, and new factories will have to be built – it won't be enough just to renovate. At this point an investment boom will begin, and demand will rise. Thus a cyclical pattern can be seen here: demand will rise in an investment boom, lead to rising productivity, which (in conjunction with rising financial costs) will dampen demand by weakening the multiplier and curtailing investment, leading to a downswing and slump, intensifying the pressure to innovate, and the innovations, when they develop sufficiently, will set off another investment boom.

Notice that this cycle proceeds without any necessity to reach full capacity in the boom. It is common in business cycle theory to argue that the upswing proceeds until it hits the 'ceiling' of full capacity, bringing the boom to a halt, and setting off the downturn. (The argument goes like this: when the ceiling is reached demand stops growing; when demand stops growing, investment to build new capacity is no longer needed, so investment spending falls off sharply – and demand falls, starting the downswing.) In practice, however, business cycle peaks rarely reach full capacity. But, as we have seen, even if they did, the argument would not work, for 'full capacity' as normally defined is not a ceiling, in the sense of a level of output that can't be exceeded. In the analysis just presented here, however, the peak of the cycle can still lie below full capacity and/or full employment of labour. The turning point is created by the deflationary impact of rising productivity on demand. And this is in accordance with the way things have actually been during the whole post-War era – the downswing normally begins well before anything like full capacity or full employment is reached.

There is an important implication: if the economy normally operates with varying degrees of excess capacity and excess labour – unemployment – then the market system does not allocate scarce resources. Prices don't and can't reflect relative scarcities, because resources – means of production – aren't scarce. If anything is scarce it's demand! Markets are certainly important and they certainly perform socially significant functions, but what they are and what they do is not something we can discover from the textbooks. If there is an 'invisible hand' we will have to find it for ourselves, and watch it carefully, through special lenses, to see what it does. And we had better brace ourselves; there are those who claim that, far from ensuring the general welfare, it nowadays picks the pockets of the poor!

3

INSTITUTIONS
Market incentives and the general good

There is the story of the American tourist in Oxford who is taken to see the various Colleges. After a long day, visit after visit, he's seen them all. 'OK, enough of that,' he says, 'now let's see the University.'

The point of the story is not simply that he's already seen it; nor is it, as is often said at this point, that the University consists of the Colleges 'taken together'; it is rather that the University manifests itself in the Colleges, and exists as certain relationships which define both the Colleges and the functions and activities of their members. The Colleges, in one sense, can be seen, because they are embodied in buildings; the University, however, defines the Colleges and is constituted in and through their relationships and practices. When you see the Colleges, you also necessarily see the University, even though it is invisible.

More generally, the University consists not only of its present faculty, students, staff and administrators, but also of all its past and future members, in the above categories and others, perhaps discontinued or yet to be defined. Alumni know this well. Many can be heard to claim that the true nature of, for example, one great University or another is being subverted by the *present* group of faculty/students or even administrators. What is this 'true nature'? Claims about true natures, or the 'spirit of the country' are often dismissed as meaningless; but they are no more meaningless than claims that certain Presidents betrayed or fulfilled the heritage of the nation, that Hitler or Churchill betrayed or fulfilled the destiny of Germany or England. Or that Republicans tend to be more conservative and business-oriented than Democrats. To say that such claims are meaningless is to say that there is no such thing as the spirit of a party or a nation, that an institution has no ethos, no soul, no natural orientation. Of course you can't see its intentions, or touch or measure them. Institutional intent is not something that can be subjected to scientific scrutiny – but it certainly can be the subject of scholarly study. And it is frequently the basis of political choice. We will need to understand the intent of various economic institutions to explain the market more fully.

INSTITUTIONS

We saw earlier that a society survives because it can reproduce itself, and we modelled this in miniature in the relations between Robinson and Friday. Now this must be extended to a larger scale, to encompass the basic arrangements by which a society maintains itself and replaces its members as they age and die. As we shall see, this involves various kinds of *exchanges*, but it does not necessarily involve the market, certainly not a fully developed market. Feudal societies, for example, rested on a class system that provided a complex division of labour, produced a surplus, and engaged in both exchange and transfers. But markets were limited and partial. Many exchanges and transfers were made in kind, although records were normally kept in terms of money of account. Yet when markets developed, they helped to transform the feudal economy. Our question is, how do markets relate to the basic institutions by means of which the social order maintains itself? What role, if any, does the Invisible Hand play?

At the most basic level we have two kinds of institutions essential for social reproduction: those that produce the goods that support the system, and those that socialize the people that run it, and clearly they are interdependent. The first produces basic goods and services – food, clothing, shelter, tools etc. – and the second, socialization and training, as carried out in families, churches and schools. Production institutions need appropriately trained personnel to replace those who retire or die; socialization institutions need goods and services in order to function.

Such institutions, then, can be said to have goals and purposes, even character, distinct from those of the actual people who currently staff them. This is not meant in a metaphorical sense. A producing institution, in the smallest sense, is just a job or a socially defined role running or operating or accomplishing some clearly defined task that has to be done on a regular basis, in order for things to function smoothly. In a larger sense it is a *system* of jobs or social roles, interlocked to accomplish some socially useful or socially desired result on a regular basis, as for instance, a farm, a business corporation or a government department. The desired results define the producing roles.

The same applies to socializing institutions. The position of 'schoolteacher' carries certain duties and privileges, related to the purpose of imparting education; when someone takes on such a position, they implicitly and sometimes explicitly undertake to carry out those duties – regardless, for example, of the fact that they may be uninterested in the activities in question, and have taken the position for their own private reasons (e.g. to be near their girlfriend, to have a job while waiting for a better position in advertising, etc.) The exact duties, of course, depend on the particular situation, but the general concept of the role 'teacher' implies a generalized natural intent to educate. Similarly, a farmer has a natural intent to grow crops, but particular

71

kinds of farmers will grow different crops, or husband animals, or even put soil in the 'bank', etc.

Systems of 'production roles' make up producing institutions – institutions that turn out results which then figure in the activities of other institutions. A firm makes steel, which then is used in making machinery, the machinery is used by another firm which makes coke, which is used in steel-making, and so on. Socializing institutions are likewise composed of roles. Consider a university: it is an organization of teachers and students, where these roles are interlocked in a particular way. A high school is a different organization of teachers and students, defining the content of the roles differently. Both produce graduates, trained at different levels, but ready to take on various roles, chiefly in firms, but some graduates go back into teaching. In turn, both universities and high schools fit into the overall system of social re-production, along with elementary schools, corporations, small businesses, farms, government institutions and every other system that provides jobs and draws on other enterprises for materials and inputs – or for consumption goods for its jobholders. (Not all producing roles are jobs, of course: 'father' and 'mother' bring up and socialize children, but are not paid for this. Yet turning out a new generation is certainly part of the reproduction of the social system.) The particular producing system specifies what kind of teacher, farmer, worker, etc., we are considering, and the overall system determines what the particular producing systems will be able to do.

So the institutions of reproduction – the jobs and roles that make up society's world of work, that make things run – are defined by the results they are supposed to bring about. At least these objectives provide the targets; technology – the way we are able to do things – defines the specific activities in the jobs and roles. This helps to make clear an obvious, yet subtle, point: these definitions of roles, the duties of the various jobs, are independent of the actual people who will carry out the tasks. The activities to be carried out in particular roles depend on the objectives of the institution, together with the technology and division of labour. These activities, in turn, call for skills of different kinds, general social skills, specific operating skills, managerial and human relations skills, and so on. These are demands for trained human abilities. Jobs and social roles thus create a set of *demands* for skills and talents; the socialization processes – family, churches, schools – will then turn out the corresponding *supply* of people appropriately prepared and trained.

Families produce children and begin their 'socialization', the process of fitting them for their likely, or sometimes predestined, roles in society.[1] Families are only the beginning; churches, schools, and training programmes provide formal instruction and shaping; peer groups, fraternities, brotherhoods and the like impart the informal code. In short, socialization institutions shape people and provide them with the skills society needs – and sometimes also prevent them from becoming 'overqualified' for the types of jobs/roles they are likely to move into. Traditionally, of course, socialization was carried out by the extended family, in conjunction with organized religion. This was possible so long as the skills the children needed in their lives were ones the parents could impart. What parents today can teach their kids to use the latest software – or even to programme the VCR? Education has become more and more the prerogative of specialized institutions and the state.

Another way of understanding the distinction between producing and socializing roles: there are in general two ways of referring to people, two ways of saying what people are. We can refer to them by the social roles they have undertaken – 'engineer', 'doctor', 'lawyer', 'businessperson', 'mother', 'cabdriver', 'student', 'musician', 'artist', 'writer', etc. (Roles that are also jobs carry some form of income, others do not, or may not.) Or we can refer to people by descriptions that derive from their origins, background, genetic makeup or education and socialization – for example, Negro, Caucasian, Ivy Leaguer, European, upper class, working class, redneck, college grad, etc.

The essence of a class society lies in the relationship between these two: families and socialization institutions provide appropriately prepared people for roles that enable them to support families that will socialize people for the same (kinds of) roles. In this way, the roles of society will be appropriately manned, while the next generation is properly prepared. Some families provide people prepared for leadership and elite roles, other families provide workers and followers. Two (or more) classes of families can thus be reproduced from generation to generation.

In turn, when they move into the roles for which they have been prepared, the products of socialization will perform activities that will provide the goods and services to support the institutions of socialization – the families, schools, churches, etc. And, of course, they will produce the goods and services that need to be exchanged among the producing activities, as explained in an earlier chapter. As we saw then, such production systems, when run efficiently, can be made to produce a surplus, which can support luxuries, develop the arts, or, all too often, underwrite wars.

In what follows we shall be concerned primarily with the first kind of description – roles – but later we will return to consider the second, and the relationship between the two, as well. This will have some significant implications for social theory, particularly for individualism, the doctrine that social wholes are constituted by the agreements of individual agents.

COMPONENTS AND THE WHOLE

But, to go back to our example, the university is not, and could not be, a 'compact' made between the current students, faculty and administrators; it exists independently of them, and more importantly, it defines what students, faculty and administrators must be and do, though of course, in practice, at any given time, those filling such roles might strongly influence the character, not only of their own roles, but of the whole system. But the current population filling the roles that make up the system will inherit and be the custodians of its traditions; if they try to change these too dramatically or without good reasons, they will be deemed reckless or even blasphemous. And their claims to speak for the institution may be rejected.

As all graduates know all too well, the university has to support itself; it has material needs which have to be met on a regular basis. In general, for an institution to exist, it has to have a way of supporting and perpetuating itself. This means that it must have a normal way of working, a normal way for it to meet its material needs. But this further implies that at any given time it can be working well or badly; its working can be criticized, and ways of improving it can be proposed.

The institution as a whole – the university – is thus at its core an invisible set of relationships, defining and constituting a number of components – the Colleges, and/or the students, faculties and administrators – which require material support on a regular basis. This gives rise to a normal pattern of activity which can be carried out well or badly, and therefore can be the subject of policy proposals.

But policies which make the whole work better may create hardships at times for one or more components, or may benefit one part at the expense of another. The component parts of major social institutions – ones that are designed to produce some kind of results, like Universities, business enterprises or cities – have a degree of independence, and as a consequence have independent although supposedly subordinate interests, which may clash with those of other components, and/or with the good of the whole. The interests of the students may clash with those of the faculty, the interests of the police with those of the firemen, to say nothing of possible clashes between workers and management or between one division of the company and another – or we may find that what is best for students may not be best for the university as a whole, what is best for the uniformed services may not be best for the city, i.e. what is best for one of the parts, or even for all of the parts, may not be best for the whole.[2]

Different kinds of conflicts may arise. Consider students; a black student's interests as a black might conflict with those of the university. A woman student might find a conflict between her feminism and the needs or policies of the college. That is not the kind of conflict at issue here; the social definitions of blacks and women are given from outside the university. By contrast, the role of a 'student' or 'faculty member' is defined by the university system itself. What we shall call the 'component roles' are defined by the specific larger system of which they are a part. Persons can only come to hold those roles through some kind of appointment or recognition process – being admitted as a student, appointed as a teacher, passing the bar to become a lawyer. The role implies certain duties or normal activities, and these can be carried out well or badly. To do well, and therefore to have the resources to do well, will be in the interest of those holding such positions, independently of the working of the whole system. It is the possibility of conflict between the interests of whole and part, internal to the system, that is interesting here.

To continue with the example, students, as people, as products of a reproduction and socialization process, have identities based on their origins; they come from families, have nationalities, racial religious and cultural identities, come from some geographical area, went to certain schools, and so forth. It is easy to see how conflicts could arise between the interests flowing from such identities and the interests of the university. But the role of a student is defined by the university system itself, the role of a nurse by the hospital/medical system, just as the role of a carburettor is defined by the internal combustion engine. How is it possible that genuine, legitimate, real interests of students or nurses can conflict with those of the university or the hospital as a whole? (Indeed, especially during the 1960s, many administrators held that, in principle, they could not.)

To repeat: what concerns us are specific producing or professional service institutions – hospitals, schools, cities and other governing bodies, corporations, business firms and the like. Or the medical or legal professions. These are arrangements of agents with various skills and abilities, cooperating to bring about some clearly defined results or end products. In the course of this cooperation the agents will normally have some autonomy in determining the exact ways and times they carry out their tasks or assignments. The benefits of the end result will normally exceed the costs of bringing it about, which is to say that there is a surplus. All the agents will participate in the benefits, at least to the extent of meeting the minimal costs required to ensure their continued participation (which, of course, could involve the costs of coercing them). As for sharing the surplus, what some get others don't – here is the basis for conflict between the parties, and between any or all of them and the whole. The university's revenue can go to student aid or to faculty salaries – or to new buildings or be ploughed back into endowment. The interests of the components are real and serious – students need financial aid, teachers need better salaries, in each case in order to perform their assigned functions better. Their interests arise directly from their respective roles, not from any extraneous identities. But it could be that the performance of the whole would be improved more by some other use of funds, even though the claims of students and teachers are both valid, e.g. adding to the library. Moreover, it is very likely that it will be difficult to make exact comparisons, or even to gauge accurately the impact of any strategy on the performance of the whole. So it will come down to judgement calls, which will also permit each part to confuse the issue by dressing its particular concerns in the garb of the general interest.

A producing or professional institution defines the roles its components play; they are to be cogs in a machine, as it were. Doctors are defined by the medical profession, lawyers by the legal. To be a teacher is to be licensed and hold a job in a school system. But doctors, notoriously, are driven by what Veblen used to call 'pecuniary interests'; appendectomies and hysterectomies no doubt often tend to improve the health of those on whom they are performed; but all too frequently – and with much greater certainty – they provide down payments on Jaguars for those who perform them.

Thus for producing institutions, each defined by the specific results it seeks to obtain, systematic conflicts of interest are possible not only between the component parts, but also between such parts and the interests of the whole. If we now consider the economy as a whole, we can evidently treat it as a producing institution – its product is the GNP – and the various components are the different industries that make up the business world and the income groups and social classes that make up households and the labour force. Clearly the interests of the various groups can clash with one another and with the good of the whole system.

INDIVIDUAL INTERESTS AND THE GENERAL GOOD

But there is a major difference between this case and the examples considered earlier. In those examples there was no reason to suppose that policies or strategies for seeking the good of the whole would be based on different principles than those for pursuing the interests of a part. Students should work hard, should not go too heavily into debt, and should not try to do too many things at once; so for the university as a whole. Nurses, doctors and hospitals should plan ahead, not overcommit, keep up with new developments in medical technology, and so on. There seems to be no reason to suspect that the strategies for achieving the good of the whole will be any different from those for enhancing the interests of a component.

By contrast, in the next chapter we will examine a set of paradoxes, in each of which actions undertaken by 'components' of economic systems are systematically frustrated. These paradoxes, it will be argued, show that the pursuit of the good of the production system as a whole, since the advent of Mass Production, must be based on different principles than those that govern the strategies for furthering the interests of individual units. In improving the positions of individual units the principles to be followed are those of the marketplace – maximize subject to the given constraints, keep a sharp eye on alternatives, remember opportunity costs, stay within your budget, calculate the risks. In short, don't overextend yourself. Not so for the system as a whole; at the level of the whole, the constraints are not binding, or do not bind in the same way. As we have seen there are two basic strategies, austerity and expansion. But austerity intensifies competition and promotes the *market*; only expansion promotes the development of the system of production. The problem for the system as a whole is that it faces a chronic shortage of demand, so the danger is of too little, rather than too much spending.

To see the implications, let's first discuss the market, then the system of production as a whole, paying particular attention to the 'natural intent' embodied in that system, and then we will look at the relationship between the market and the production system. Markets develop as a medium of exchange attains general acceptance. A wide variety of goods and services are valued in this medium, and begin to circulate against it. At this point competition begins to iron out differentials, establishing market-wide prices and uniform standards for goods and services. The market depends crucially on the existence of money.

So markets provide a responsive forum for the expression, coordination and compromising of the interests of individual units. It takes the efforts of individuals pursuing their interests and forms from them the economic analogue to what Rousseau called the 'will of all'. This is the resultant, the vector product, of the competing interests of the various individuals or units, each trying to further its own interests as far as possible, usually subject to a condition to the effect that there at least be no damage to the interests of those others who are strong enough to retaliate. The function of the market, its raison d'etre, is to collect together the competing interests of all the concerned individuals and coordinate them, allowing each to be fulfilled as much as possible, subject to the others. The market arranges for the conflicts of competing interest to be settled not only according to rules, but in the process it also harnesses enough energy to expand or improve the output of the system.

But the market outcome is *not*, per se, the general good of the system; it is a general compromise or consensus formed by the market out of the particular interests of the various components, acting in their particular capacities. This cannot, in principle, be the economic analogue of the general will, which would have to be formed from agents acting not in their particular capacities, but as representatives of the system as a whole, planning for the good of the system as a whole. In the marketplace, no one can afford to do this. If an agent planned a market strategy on the basis of what is good for the system as a whole, ignoring its own interests, competitors would very likely be able to move in and take over its market position. Only if its own interest and the general good coincided, could a competitive individual unit afford to pursue the general good. To put it another way, units that pursue the general good instead of their own interests will be eliminated by competitors maximizing their own private advantage. Pursuit of the general good is an inferior strategy, one that will systematically lose out.

But what is the 'general good'? And is it right to speak of '*the*' general good, as if it were unique? We have so far referred to the proper or better working of the system as a whole, but surely this is unacceptably vague. Yet there need be no mystery; the general good of a system indeed arises from its proper working, meaning working the way it was intended – leaving aside criticism of the system's basic purposes,[3] and assuming that the initial design was the best available. There may be more than one way the system can 'work properly', so there may be more than one 'general good', or, better, more than one way of realizing the general good. But the idea itself is simple enough, at least in relation to productive institutions. Productive capacity is meant to be used, and skills to be exercised – otherwise the capacity would not have been installed, nor the skills acquired. The system must be run so as to fulfil the purposes for which it was designed. If it doesn't then, *prima facie*, it is not working well. Simple and obvious criteria are built into the system. But to understand them, we first have to understand what the system is supposed to accomplish.

PRODUCTION AS A SYSTEM
OF NATURAL INTENT

A producing institution or system or role is defined by the result it is supposed to bring about. The medical system is supposed to bring about health, teachers are supposed to induce learning, policemen public safety. Borrowing a leaf from Aristotle an objective of this sort can be described as the 'Natural Intent' of its respective system. It is the point of the system's operation, the objective towards the realization of which all component activities contribute. (These component activities – and the roles of their performers – can also each be said to have a defining Natural Intent, namely, their normal objectives, which will be subsidiary to the Intent of the system as a whole.)

However, while this idea of natural intent is suggestive, it may suggest both too much and too little. Taking the latter, for example, at most a system's natural intent only indicates the general direction in which policy should move. Moreover, an appeal to natural intent is unlikely to be able to discriminate between competing policies, both of which move in the right direction. But as an example of the former, there may be many ways to realize the natural intent of a role or larger institution. The general good of a system is realized when all its components work harmoniously together, cooperating in the achievement of its natural intent. But, again, there may be *many* ways such harmony could be brought about, and some may be better than others for certain components, or may achieve certain of the aims more readily or more fully. So there is room for disagreement about the general good, as well as over the interpretation and exact meaning of the natural intent.

The system of producing institutions functions as a whole, since the outputs of many activities serve as inputs to others, or as support for performers of activities. Hence the system taken as a whole has to be coordinated; the outputs must be properly designed to serve as inputs, and they must be delivered in the right amounts at the right times. So the whole is the integrated working of all production activities taken together, and working according to certain constitutive rules, those of the capitalist mode of production. And the product of this system is the world we live in; its natural intent therefore is to produce – and maintain, reproduce – the world we live in. (Just to complicate things, we have to recognize that, in the modern world, science and engineering and some businesses are devoted to *changing* – hopefully, improving – various aspects of the world.) This is obviously a very general statement of intent, allowing plenty of room for disagreement over interpretation.

We therefore have three levels: jobs and producing roles, which are components of institutions and producing organizations, which, in turn, are components of the system as a whole, the capitalist production system. At each level we can define the natural intent of the role or institution, and we can set it in the context of its component–composite relations with the other levels of organization. There is thus a system of natural intents, a web of duties, obligations, expectations and privileges defined by the interdependencies of the various producing roles and institutions. Disagreements cannot be arbitrary; an interpretation of what a particular institution should do at any given time must be referred to the whole network of its interdependent obligations and interests. There may not be a single decisive answer, but there will certainly be limits.

Moreover, these interdependencies between producing activities define a pattern of exchanges; the outputs of some are the inputs of others – steel and fibreglass go into automobiles – or support the consumption of jobholders. Given the pattern of duties and expectations, normal conditions can be defined as those holding when duties are carried out and expectations fulfilled. In these conditions there will be normal flows of revenue needed to sustain activities at the proper levels. Such flows, in turn, define normal prices and outputs, normal wages, rents and profits, and so on.

THE MARKET AND THE CLASS SYSTEM

With this framework we can now explore the role of the market. In earlier times, under feudalism, for example, people were born into a status that ensured their socialization and prepared them for a well-defined set of roles later in life – with infrequent exceptions they could not depart from their pre-ordained scenario. For most people options were few, innovations rare, and fear figured prominently among the chief motivating factors. The courts interpreted, and military power enforced, obedience and loyalty. This surely worked well enough; these societies lasted for countless generations.

Traditional society administered itself through kings and nobles, who had a monopoly on military force. They appropriated the surplus produced by serfs and peasants through feudal dues and taxes, and provided protection and public order in return. (In the towns merchants and craftsmen struggled to free themselves from the power of the nobility.) This was a class society. Noble families passed on titles and estates from one generation to the next; peasant and serf families passed on particular holdings of land. In the towns craftsmen passed on skills and merchants their businesses. The Church imparted morals and a sense of duty, leading the members of each class to accept and appreciate their station in life.

But feudalism was a system without much flexibility. It could not easily adapt to innovations. Yet conditions changed, technical knowledge grew, and both agriculture and industry became more complex, as did the problems of governance. Gunpowder and other developments shifted the balance of military power from defence – the impregnable fortresses of the nobility – to attack by large armies with guns and artillery. The towns had the skills to produce the armaments. And skills were more and more necessary. Heredity became less and less effective as a way to select people for positions. Enterprises needed frequent reorganizing, but manors and guilds, once established, were fixed for all time.

The market provided an answer; manorial rights could be bought from the lords, the privileges of the guild could be purchased by paying off the members. Guilds became firms, and manors, farms. Each was run, not in accord with traditional duties and obligations, but in order to make a profit on the capital invested. Laws had to be changed to make this possible. Adam Smith campaigned for an end to the monopolies and special patents granted to certain industries and enterprises. Open competition had to be established; the play of the market would allocate people to the roles, jobs and positions for which they were best suited. (This was not a new idea: see Appendix.) Those enterprises that proved themselves most efficient would take over the business of the rest; thus competition would provide the best sources of supply. Workers who shirked, teachers who failed to inspire, managers who failed to supervise, would automatically be punished – their enterprises would begin to lose out, and seeing this, their superiors would discipline or dismiss them. The market, in short, was able to provide an effective system of rewards and penalties to ensure that agents carry out the activities required by their jobs or roles, and that enterprises likewise perform up to standard.[4]

Early capitalism ran on profits rather than feudal rents and dues, but it also rested on two classes of families – Proprietors and Labourers. They were different in each sector. A simple table will illustrate the system (see Table 1). The three sectors are listed vertically, the two classes of families are arranged horizontally. Each cell comprises a set of families operating in a sector. Those families tend to produce the next generation of Proprietors and Labourers, respectively, for that sector, allowing for various kinds of 'normal' mobility.

In this early period of capitalism, the era of family firms and family farms, a clearly defined class system operated. In Agriculture, the Nobility and the

Table 1

	Proprietors	*Labourers*
Agriculture:	Gentry	Peasants
Manufacturing:	Factory-owners	Workers
Services:	Professionals	Clerks
	Shopkeepers	Shop assistants

Gentry comprised the P-families, while serfs, metayers, cottagers, and landless labourers, made up the L-families. Manufacturing had the Factory-owners and the Workers, and in Services, there were the Professional and the Clerks, and the Shopkeepers and their Assistants. Each new generation was 'produced' by families, aided, of course, by churches and schools. But families passed on skills, property and social position to their children, fitting them for the corresponding roles. P-families handed down property and control over the production institutions – the son of the nobleman succeeded to the title, the son of the Factory-owner inherited the firm. L-families passed on skills and the secrets of the trade. In some cases, this included claims to particular positions in production. P- and L-families did not normally inter-marry; the children of each produced, in turn, new P- and L-families, respectively.

The working class received wages that covered little more than their bare needs – and workers could afford little education and had little hope of advancement. But they were kept in line by the fear of dismissal, since their wages were the only source of support for themselves and their families. The middle and upper classes, however, faced quite different prospects. Their education prepared them for careers starting at the bottom and advancing through promotion; they could reach the pinnacle of fame and fortune. They did not so greatly fear loss of a job; instead their motivation came through the prospects of promotion and pay rises – monetary and status incentives. And these same incentives applied to entire enterprises, in their competition with others for the best position in their markets. Money became the measure of success. With this, however, came new problems, among them 'boundless theft in limited professions', to quote Shakespeare, in *Timon*. And the market determined the distribution of money.

In feudalism and early capitalism, P- and L-families tended to remain in the same sectors, even in the same branch of business. But as capitalism developed Agriculture shrank, Manufacturing expanded, and Services changed character. Hence families changed sectors, and many formerly L-families became P-families. The class system gradually became more fluid. The application of science to production led to the emergence of a new class of professionals – engineers, managers, executives, educational professionals, psychologists, etc. A middle class developed and expanded, and at the same time class lines became blurred.

In early capitalism Proprietorship and the handing down of skills and trades were vested in the kinship system. That is what it means to say that it was a class society. But as capitalism developed this connection gradually unravelled. The kinship system was not an efficient vehicle for either capital or labour. Workers could not pass along skills in conditions of rapid technical change – the skills of the fathers would be outdated. To achieve economies of scale firms had to grow to a size beyond the capacity of a family to manage. Moreover, family disputes could threaten the viability of an enterprise. Hence capital created its own forms. The modern corporation, together with financial institutions such as holding companies, mutual funds and trusts, provided more appropriate arrangements for holding wealth and exercising control, and passing both along. Technical and vocational schools came to provide the means for training new generations of workers.

THE ECONOMY

Now we are able to see what the economy is, and why it waited for the end of the Middle Ages to make its appearance in history. The economy is the relationship between the system of social re-production and the market. The system of re-production defines a network of activities striving to realize their natural intents. In the feudal era and earlier, priests or the Church inculcated a sense of duty, the courts interpreted reciprocal duties and privileges, and such duties and obligations were enforced by military and police power. The incentives to perform the duties of a position were moral exhortation, backed by fear.

'You'll catch more flies with honey than with vinegar', the old saying goes. The market provides an alternative: monetary incentives, which it arranges so as to achieve the objectives defined by the production system.[5] The activities of the production system are interdependent; the outputs of some serve as inputs to others, and still others serve as consumer goods supporting workers and their families. When spelled out in detail, this interdependence implies a pattern of trades and revenue payments (for example, what Smith and Ricardo called 'natural prices'). But many of the necessary activities – and not only low-status ones – are arduous or unpleasant. The incentives of the marketplace encourage the realization of this pattern of trades and revenues. The working of the economy is the interaction of the two. It was only with the breakdown of the feudal order of fealty, duty and privilege that market relations could emerge as the system for ensuring that roles were carried out properly and enterprises performed their functions correctly, that is to say, for achieving the general good.

The breakdown of feudal relationships – the system of fealty and bondage – was the emergence of freedom. In this sense the growth of the market is also the rise of liberty. Artisans became increasingly free to move about and set up shop; they could no longer be bound by guild regulations or by the rules laid down by the nobility. Agricultural workers were freed from bondage to the land; they could move to the towns and learn a trade. Restrictions on entry into occupations were gradually lifted – or were eroded by the pressures of the market. This was the growth of what has been called 'negative liberty'. The expansion of material wealth, on the other hand, provided a great increase in opportunities – an important aspect of 'positive liberty'. But along with these development went the breakdown of community; with the increase in wealth came an increase in poverty and destitution. Market relationships may be free; they are also harsh. 'Free to choose' also means 'free to lose'.[6]

So the market generates the incentives that will lead to the realization of the 'general good', the proper working of the system of social re-production. Furthermore, the market, by encouraging innovation, provides incentives to *improve* the normal working of the system, that is, to increase the general good. In doing so it advances the cause of freedom, but it does so at the price of eroding community.

Two caveats should be entered, however: First, the market will not, cannot, reliably bring the system closer to realizing the general good if it is unstable. That is, it must adjust in such a way that small deviations from the proper position – equilibrium – will be corrected. In the Craft Economy, the price mechanism seems to work this way (although the banking and financial system is quite unstable in this period), but in the era of Mass Production, adjustment through the multiplier-accelerator means that the system is decidedly unstable, calling for government counter-cyclical actions.

Second, market incentives encourage development of *private* activities. Profits are an incentive to investment and innovation. Making a good more cheaply will enable a producer to capture a wider market, thereby bringing the good to more consumers. Everyone benefits. Improvements mean better goods, benefiting consumers and enabling the firm to capture more of the market. However, profit must be appropriated. In the case of public goods and services it is often impossible or difficult to levy charges. Worse, privatizing a public good may set up the *wrong* incentives, e.g. if firms are paid a fixed fee to run a public service, the incentive is to minimize the costs of providing the service, so they are to provide the minimum amount possible. The market is seldom helpful and often damaging to public goods. On the other hand, as we shall see in later chapters, economic development tends to raise the proportion of public goods (and private goods with a public aspect) in relation to GNP.

TRANSFORMATIONAL GROWTH

In the early stages of capitalism, when enterprises operated craft technologies, and the world was young, the market's incentives probably worked quite well. To be sure, as Timon laments, the drive for money can overwhelm loyalty and decency, and as Hegel and Marx argued, it can lead to alienated and distorted social patterns. Nevertheless, these powerful incentives helped to create a world of unprecedented innovation and development. New sources of energy were tapped, new methods of agriculture, mining and manufacturing were brought into play, and rise of new classes threw the social order into upheaval. Urbanization on an unprecedented scale transformed both city and countryside. The new classes demanded representation in the councils of state, and the new industries and cities presented new problems for governments. Revolutionary upheaval brought the modern nation-state into focus.

But with the advent of Mass Production even more far-reaching changes came; for one thing, innovation proceeded at a more rapid pace, leading to changes in skill requirements. Whole technologies began to be replaced. Activities were removed from the home and re-positioned in industry. Domestic skills like sewing, canning and preserving were reduced to hobbies. Centralized mass meat packing displaced local butchers. Trades and crafts were displaced by new and progressively changing industries. Families could no longer pass the secrets of the trade along to their children. Nor could they necessarily even educate them adequately. The family, for millennia the bedrock of the social order, began to be stripped of its age-old functions. The extended family reduced itself to the nuclear unit. Family firms grew into corporations; kinship was no longer an appropriate system for structuring business and property relationships.

These changes led to new demands on the state. Urban concentrations of population required more elaborate police and local government. The shrinking of the extended family to the nuclear posed problems for the aged, who could no longer count on family to provide for them. The rapid pace of technological change required education outside the family; the state had to provide schooling. And the industrialization of activities previously carried out locally or in the home required regulation to prevent fraud and protect public health. The result was a pronounced growth in the ratio of government spending (including transfers) to GNP: in 1900 in most advanced countries this ratio stood at about 5 per cent, but by 1950 it had risen to the neighbourhood of 40 per cent! (Near 30 per cent in the US.)

But Mass Production brought another dramatic change, as fundamental as any so far considered. The market outcomes which in early capitalism tended to realize at least some of the intentions of the roles and enterprises in the production system, began to conflict with the harmonious working of the system as a whole. This conflict between the sum of the market actions of the various agents and the harmonious coordination of natural intent, of course, forms the basis of the paradoxes, to be explored in a moment, and showed itself vividly in the form of depressions.

The paradoxes, it will be remembered, were said to arise from the fact that the principles which govern the working of individual units do not similarly govern the whole. Now we can see the problem at a deeper level. The principles which govern the individual unit are those of the marketplace, and the results are market results. But the needs and requirements of the whole arise from the system of natural intent – they are not market generated at all. The paradoxes consist in the fact that certain apparently normal patterns of market incentives will lead to movement of the whole in exactly the wrong direction. Attempts to move to a position of the whole which is desired by everyone, when undertaken through similar individual actions carried out by everyone, actually lead to a movement of the whole in a direction away from that desired. Conversely, the paradox might be said to lie in the fact that the movement of the whole required to achieve its natural intent would have to run in a direction contrary to the incentives of the market. In these circumstances, the desired position will have to be achieved through actions carried out, not by individuals, but at the level of the system, i.e. by government.

IMPLICATIONS

The 'general good', then, can be defined, though very likely it will not be unique. But it will be quite distinct from the 'will of all', the sum or outcome of the various decisions taken individually by the agents of the system. Thus the general good may be achieved or realized consistently with a number of different configurations of the 'will of all', that is, with the economic welfare of the components of the system. Hence it makes sense for the holders of component roles to fight one another, even though they are all still trying to achieve the general good. Students may fight with faculty even though both quite genuinely seek the best for the University. Moreover, the general good could conceivably be advanced, even though the overall economic welfare of the component parts declined.

Market incentives drive the decisions of the component agents; the outcome of market processes is the economic analogue of the 'will of all'. In earlier eras, this could be presumed to be close to the general good, and the two could be presumed to move in the same direction. That is, market incentives and market outcomes tended to move the system in the direction of the general good – as far as the production system was concerned. (Social justice is another matter.) The market increased output and both generated and financed innovations on an unprecedented scale.

But in the modern era, as the paradoxes we will now explore show us, this can no longer be presumed. The market system is unstable, and even more problematically, as we shall see, it cannot handle the problems created by the growing volume of public goods.

APPENDIX: COMPARATIVE ADVANTAGE IN PLATO

The economy was defined above as the relation between the market and the system of production. In early societies the market had not yet emerged, so there could be no economic system in our sense. Yet this does not preclude analytical study of the production system, as the following example shows.

During Socrates' cross-examination of Thrasymachus, he rather carefully examines examples of the various crafts and professions – physician, ship's captain, etc., showing that each has as its natural object the interest of the subject on which it is exercised. His purpose at this point is to show that each profession or craft serves the interest of the weaker, rather than the stronger, so refuting Thrasymachus, but an implication, not drawn until later, is that corresponding to each natural object are certain specific skills which are therefore peculiar to each craft or profession. Then in beginning his reply to Glaucon and Adeimantus, he sketches the rudiments of social organization (pp. 54–7 in Cornford). Here he suggests the advantages of the division of labour partly in terms of the 'right time' for the work, but the argument chiefly rests upon the claim that 'innate differences' naturally fit men for different occupations. And he concludes 'that more things will be produced and the work be more easily and better done, when every man is set free from all other occupations to do, at the right time, the one thing for which he is naturally fitted'.

If 'naturally' in this last quote also has the sense of 'best' – doing what you are relatively best at – then this is a statement of the Ricardian doctrine of 'comparative advantage'. That this might be a reasonable interpretation is suggested by an argument recounted a few paragraphs earlier. There Socrates asks whether each of the 'four or five men' (forming the absolute minimum social organization) should farm and build houses and weave and make shoes, or whether each should specialize and 'share' (trade?) with the others? Adeimantus replies that 'the first plan', i.e. 'sharing', might be 'easier'. And a little later we are told that 'if a farmer is to have a good plough ... and other tools, he will not make them himself'. Thus specialization on the basis of innate differences which naturally fit one for certain occupations is presented as the basis of social organization. This is pretty close to the Ricardian position.

To get the fully fledged Ricardo, however, what Cornford translates as 'sharing' must also have the sense of 'trading', and 'naturally fitting' must have the sense of 'best fit'. Moreover, it would strengthen the case if Adeimantus' reply – 'might be easier' – were more definite, even if it were nothing more than 'would work better'.

This may well be plausible since, when he comes to discuss the virtues in the state, Socrates remarks 'when we first began to establish our commonwealth ... we ... laid down, as a universal principle, that everyone ought to perform the one function in the community for which his nature best suited him'. Now this statement (this translation) very clearly suggests comparative advantage, and the following two pages contain passages confirming this – although the comment that the cobbler and carpenter could interchange their positions without occasioning great harm to the community would seem to undercut the idea. But one cannot be too sure; the passage clearly implies the *presumption* that such interchange, or one man doing both, would be harmful, but then goes on to explain that the real harm would come from mixing different kinds of work. Cobblers and carpenters, according to this view, do the same *kind* of work and thus rely on the same innate abilities and so would have the same type of education. No doubt this example is wrong, but it may well be correct that there are jobs of sufficient similarity, though yielding quite different products, that the principle of comparative advantage would be indifferent between them.

So did Plato present the first statement of the Law of Comparative Advantage? Did he state that even if one person can do both types of work better than another, it pays for each to specialize in what he is best at, and for them to share/trade the proceeds of their efforts? This does seem to be implied, although it may not have been stated altogether explicitly.

Part II

RUNNING THE SYSTEM: CAPITAL, LABOUR AND THE STATE

In the modern economy, the system as a whole operates in such a way that what happens may be contrary to what the individual components intended. As a result a number of apparent 'working paradoxes' can be identified. These are circumstances in which a group of individual agents undertakes a course of action in the reasonable expectation of a particular result, but the working of the system brings about a diametrically opposite conclusion. This poses problems for control and direction of the system, particularly since the movements may be quite unstable.

The policy orientation of the system can benefit either capital or labour (or the general populace). Austerity tends to strengthen the position of capital, in particular, financial capital, whereas expansion to full employment will tend to benefit labour and the general public. But austerity has become the favoured policy in recent years. Yet a coherent policy of expansion can be defined which would benefit the population in general.

4

THE PARADOXES OF INDIVIDUALISM

Economics is meant to be a learned and dignified subject, neither light-hearted, nor given to philosophical speculation, let alone playfulness or humour. Economists are hard-headed – and some may be hard-hearted, too! The subject, after all, is the nature and consequences of making money, a serious business with little room for sentiment. Hard, cold calculations, backed by facts, form the basis of discourse. Writing should be precise, informative and unencumbered by metaphors, or alliterative turns of phrase. Economics is the science of cold cash.

In such a science there can be no room for paradoxes. Unfortunately, the economy is full of them, perhaps an indication that the world and the science of cold cash may be at odds.

There are certain acceptable paradoxes in economics which do not raise serious problems. The conventional wisdom tends, of course, to underplay any element of paradox. But these acceptable paradoxes are well understood, and discussions can be found between the lines of most normal textbooks. Banking, for example, is known to rest on a systematic confidence trick. Why do bankers dress conservatively, speak in measured tones and utter only the safest platitudes? Why do banks occupy office space in large buildings with white pillars, high ceilings and Georgian windows? Because they borrow short and lend long, and anyone doing that needs every possible scrap of respectability that can be mustered. To say nothing of luck.

This sort of observation tends to belie the aura of dignity, the measured scientific pose, cultivated by the conventional wisdom. But, however entertaining the exposé, this is not what is at issue here. We are concerned now with working paradoxes, paradoxes built into the system. In the sense considered here, a 'working paradox' exists when individual households and/or businesses, acting individually, decide upon a course of action, so that everyone is pursuing the same end, but the working of the system is such that the outcome is more or less the exact opposite of what everyone desired or intended. The effects of the system counter-act the actions of the individual agents.

As a first approximation, these paradoxes arise because of the differences between the requirements for the smooth working of the economy *as a whole* and the self-interested decisions called for by the economic situation of individual units. The capitalist system as a whole responds to energy, to vitality, by creating additional income and resources in response to demand. But individual units cannot create additional resources; their circumstances are given, they have to take the world as they find it, and make the best they can of it. Individuals must take the world as given and economize, but the economy as a whole can create the world it needs as it goes its way. We will explore this further shortly.

Let us start with an easy example, sometimes called the 'paradox of thrift'. A war threatens, international disorder looms, and in the face of a menacing future, households, acting individually, decide to build up reserve funds. Everyone therefore increases the proportion of income which they save. The result? Since *saving more* means *spending less*, consumption demand falls, which means that consumer sales will be down; hence production will have to be slowed, and economic activity will decline in general. This is bad enough, but there is worse to come. For the total decline will be *greater* than the initial drop in purchases for consumption, because the initial decline in sales leads to contraction among the suppliers of consumer goods, which leads, in turn, to further contraction. At each stage the decline in sales leads to lay-offs of shop assistants. Their incomes are cut, so they will spend less, leading to lower sales in the places they normally shop, who will similarly lay off shop assistants. With such generalized declines in sales, factories will cut back production and lay off workers, who will, of course, then have to contract their spending. There will be a sequence of contractions; each drop in sales leads to declining purchases from suppliers, and therefore to declining sales for suppliers of suppliers, and so on. It was shown earlier that this sequences converges and sums to a definite amount. Such a contraction can be expected to adversely influence spending for investment purposes. So with activity and income down, overall savings will certainly be no greater and, if investment is adversely affected, will be less than if no effort had been made to increase saving.

Let's look more closely. Each individual household or business tries to increase their reserve holdings by withdrawing a higher proportion of their income or revenue. So each is spending less; hence overall demand is less, and so realized sales revenue will be down. Firms will therefore lay off some workers, put others on short time, and otherwise take measures to cut back expenses. But this further reduces demand, and, consequently, sales revenue, leading to still further measures to cut expenses. And so on. The result, then, is that a higher proportion of a lower income is saved; if the proportional fall in income is larger than the percentage increase in the saving ratio, the absolute amount of saving will actually decline. Everyone tries to save more, and ends up saving less. That is what we mean by a real paradox, 'real' because it is embedded in the way the world works.

Notice carefully what the paradox depends on: the individual households or firms wish to build up their reserves; but they can do this only by saving more. But to save more they must consume less; they can only have more reserves if they have less of something else. The individual units are constrained by their given resources; they must take the conditions of the world as they find them. By contrast, the system as a whole reacts to demand. When sales change, the system responds with a further change in the same direction. Sales drop, and the activity level of the economy as a whole drops by an even greater magnitude, thereby changing the given circumstances of the individual units. The paradox therefore arises from the interaction between the individual unit and the economy as a whole.

For future reference we should note the philosophical implication: such paradoxes are *prima facie* evidence that society is *not* simply an aggregate of individuals, or – put more dramatically – the whole is more than (or at least different from) the sum of its parts.

MORE PARADOXES

A variant of this paradox concerns debt. It is dangerous for individual house-holds and firms to run up too much indebtedness in relation to their earnings. A time may come, therefore, when circumstances seem propitious for reducing the burden by paying some of it off. Firms will cut back on their investment spending and households will hold off on purchases of big-ticket items, and both will pay off loans. Expenditure will be down; hence sales revenues will be down and the funds that formerly were spent on capital goods and consumer durables now end up in idle accounts in banks. The banks, of course, will want to loan these out again, and it might be thought that this would drive down the interest rate. This won't happen, however, because the contraction caused by the reduction in spending will shrink income just enough that the new lower level of saving will reduce new bank deposits by just the amount that loan repayments have increased them. So nothing will happen to the interest rate. The net effect of everyone trying to repay loans is to bring aggregate incomes down just enough to leave the ratio of indebtedness to income unchanged. Everyone trying to get out of debt just makes everyone worse off, but leaves indebtedness ratios unchanged.

A very important point in political theory, to which we have already alluded, lies half-concealed here. The individual decision-maker operates at the level where the conditions of the social order are given; the decisions are therefore self-regarding only. They are taken from the perspective of the individual firm or household, and are designed to achieve its particular purposes. The aggregate of such decisions is strongly analogous to what Rousseau called the 'will-of-all', a partial and imperfect construction which he opposed to the 'general will': – 'general, not in its origins only, but in its objects, applicable to all as well as operated by all' (1950, p. 196). The market tends to form the 'will-of-all'. By contrast, the 'general will' must take as its object the condition of the economy as a whole, and this must be 'willed' – to use the eighteenth-century terminology – by all economic agents acting together *with the condition of the aggregate, not their individual goals, as their intention.* The state of the whole system brought about by the will-of-all can only be an accident, resulting from the interaction of the aggregate of actions taken in pursuit of individual goals, in given circumstances. The paradox above and the ones we shall now examine show quite clearly the difference between these two levels of decision-making – and the significance of this for economic policy will prove momentous.

The paradox of thrift has a parallel in the related paradox of wages. Following the preceding example, consider each business acting individually, in circumstances where slack has emerged in the labour market. Lower wages mean lower costs, and therefore, with prices the same, higher profits. (We'll consider the case where the lower wages permits prices to be cut in a moment.) Each will take action to cut down wages, perhaps eliminating overtime pay, trimming benefits, combining grades, even, if the slack is great enough, directly assaulting hourly rates. As a result money wages will fall throughout the economy, and with prices remaining firm, the proportion of revenue designated as profits will rise. But businesses will not be any better off, and may be in worse shape than before. For the decline in money wages, with prices firm, means a similar decline in the purchasing power available to the households of working people; they will therefore buy fewer items, since their dollars don't reach as far. (And because their incomes are lower in real terms, it will be harder and more expensive for them to borrow.) So, if fewer items are bought, fewer will be sold, and fewer salespeople will be needed; fewer goods will have to be produced, so factories will run at a slower pace, and workers will be put on short time or laid off. This will lower consumer purchasing power still further, leading to further contractions. As before, such sequences of contractions will converge to a definite sum. The general slowdown in consumer sales, and the consequent emergence of excess capacity in manufacturing, mean that the construction of new production facilities can be postponed. Hence investment spending will very likely be cut back.

All in all, it's an unfortunate picture. Each firm does what comes naturally to it, namely cuts its wage costs in order to increase its profitability, and the overall result is necessarily a decline in employment and output, accompanied by no increase or, worst of all and quite probable, an actual decline in profits.

But if money wages fall, won't competition force firms to cut prices? This depends on how competitive markets are, and, even when they are competitive, on the unspoken rules and conventions governing pricing. Businesspeople generally oppose 'cutthroat competition' and 'spoiling the market'. There are good reasons for this. Consider what happens in a general deflation. With *both* prices and money wages falling, the real wage, that is, the purchasing power of household incomes, will remain more or less the same. So there wouldn't have to be any cutback on purchases by households;

the same number of consumer goods would be sold, and there would be no need to cut production. Employment and output would be unaffected. But, since profits would be no greater, the whole operation would have been in vain. Yet not without effect, for a decline of both prices and wages means a rise in the value of money, and therefore a gain for lenders at the expense of borrowers. To put it another way, if both prices and wages decline, the burden of debts fixed in monetary terms rises. Fixed charges for debt servicing will now require a higher percentage of the profit margin. A substantial fall in prices and wages can significantly increase the risk of bankruptcy for businesses that have a large amount of debt. Bankruptcies, however, can set off a chain reaction, affecting a broad range of businesses. This can very well lead to a general decline in investment spending, followed by an overall slump. Deflation is not good for business.

(There is a fairy tale told in many textbooks about deflation causing a rise in the real value of cash balances, supposedly then causing a rise in the spending of those with large holdings of cash. But as we've just seen, deflation increases the burden of debt, and since debt considerably outweighs the relevant holdings of cash, very few economists take this alleged effect very seriously as a practical matter.)

All in all, then, lowering money wages appears to be clearly to the advantage of each individual firm, and if markets are competitive, cutting prices in the wake of lower wages may also seem to be a good strategy. But when everyone pursues these strategies, it is likely that everyone will lose.

Now let's turn the argument around, and consider the effects of high wages. Clearly high wages are a disadvantage for every individual employer; an increase in wages is an additional expense, at best a nuisance, a cost which must be passed along as far as possible in higher prices – at the risk of losing goodwill if not customers – and at worst, a cost which has to be absorbed if prices can't be raised. First suppose that prices can be raised, so that the cost of higher wages can be passed along. This will lead to cost–push inflation, a wage–price spiral, which is an inconvenience to everyone. But it does also mean that the value of money will be lower, so that the burden of debt will be reduced. This will encourage investment and expansion. We saw earlier that deflation leads to slumps; the opposite corollary is that inflation brings expansion. (Notice that inflation is not necessarily due to excess demand, any more than deflation is due to demand deficiency. In each case what happens depends on market conditions and the pricing policies of firms.)

Next consider the case where prices cannot be raised, or cannot be raised by the full amount of the wage increase. In such conditions the real purchasing power of households will have increased; they can therefore buy more, so consumer sales will rise, and business revenue will be up. Production will have to increase, so employment will expand, leading to a further increase in household incomes. The generally higher level of activity will encourage investment, which will further intensify the pressures for expansion. High wages, or increased wages, are bound to lead firms to consider ways of replacing labour with mechanized or automated systems, thereby increasing productivity; worker resistance to changes will be offset by their increased take-home pay. Moreover, substitution of equipment for labour requires investment, and therefore acts as still another stimulant to expansion. Thus high and/or rising wages are good for the system as a whole, because they lead through household spending to higher output and employment, and through incentives to business and labour to pressure for higher productivity and investment. But, of course, for any individual firm, high wages or increased wages, must be considered a misfortune.[1]

Just as an aside, it is worth remarking that this point is relevant to understanding American economic history. An important school of thought – Charles and Mary Beard, Frederick Jackson Turner – held that the fertile and free land on the frontier set a high level of the living standard, below which wages in the cities of the Eastern seaboard could not fall. If Eastern wages fell too low, labour would up stakes and move Westward. Hence wages were kept high in the East, and the fertility of the frontier meant there was a good market there. So high wages meant a large and active market; but it also put the pressure on Yankee ingenuity to invent and invest in labour-saving machinery. The result was continuous pressure for rapid growth. High wages, dictated by the frontier, were an important key to the American success story.

INDIVIDUALS AND WHOLES IN THE MARKET

Now we come to a very difficult idea – not that the preceding ones have been all that easy. It is a different sort of paradox. It doesn't involve the actions or choices of individuals, or the working of the system as a whole. Instead it concerns the economic characteristics of individuals as compared to the characteristics of the system. The paradox is this: Individual firms are in constant competition for sales (and households for jobs, too); they have to be as efficient as possible in order to compete in price, and also in quality. This is so because aggregate demand is normally less than aggregate capacity; there is, in a sense, a scarcity of demand, and this scarcity puts pressure on businesses to scramble for the available markets. So individual firms – and households – are as efficient and cost-conscious as possible, and those who are not will tend to lose out in the race. But the very feature of the system responsible for this – the shortage of demand in relation to capacity – implies *that the system as a whole is inefficient and wasteful.* Each individual producer plans to use its resources fully and optimally, but the economy in the aggregate always has excess capacity and wastes resources.

By way of contrast, consider a centrally planned economy, or a large multi-unit bureaucracy. (The US Department of Defense together with its suppliers, making up the 'military–industrial complex', tends to behave in ways that are similar to those of a planned economy.) The level of output in such a system is typically constrained, not by demand, but by resources. In a centrally planned economy demand tends to exceed productive capacity, partly because wages tend to be high (relative to consumer goods capacity), but chiefly because enterprises are subject to few restraints in undertaking construction of new facilities and ordering equipment. Investment regularly tends to run ahead of itself, creating demand pressure. (In the military–industrial complex lobbying has tended keep demand high.) With excess demand the normal condition, shortages will be endemic, and sales very easy. There is no competition for markets; anything produced can be sold; quality need only meet minimum standards. Cost overruns are not significant; the important point is to produce, to meet or surpass the quotas. But the implication is that the economy as a whole uses its resources fully, according to plan, and hence (if the planning is well-managed) efficiently, although no individual enterprise will be cost-conscious or motivated to produce quality goods efficiently.

In short, a free market/free enterprise system tends to generate technical progress and promotes the efficient use of resources by each individual enterprise, but wastes resources at the level of the system as a whole, while a centrally planned economy uses resources fully and efficiently at the macro level, but generates incentives to wasteful operation at the level of the individual enterprise.

THE FALLACY OF INDIVIDUALISM

In short, the modern economy, taken as a whole, does not work the same as an individual or a business firm. The economy as a whole is not, and never has been, not even in the Craft era, analogous to its individual component units. But it has become increasingly unlike them as the system of industrial capitalism has developed. The system as a whole obeys different laws, and this arises from the fact that it confronts the world in an altogether different way, compared to one of its component parts.

An individual, a family, or a business must take the world as given. Resources, social standing or position, technology, means of production – all these are given, or if they are not, the resources to develop or improve them are given. The economic problem for an individual is to make the most of what is available; this requires choice and calculation, efficient use of what is given. An individual or a family can rise in station; a business can expand or improve its market position. To do so, however, it must make the best use of whatever resources it can obtain. It must save in order to invest and expand. By contrast, for the system as a whole nothing is given; the world is *produced* by the system. Everything, even what we normally consider 'nature', is produced by the economic system; the world is man-made. Obviously everything at the Princeton Club is man-made; the tables and chairs, the linen and the silver service. The wine was pressed, fermented, aged and bottled; the fish were stocked, then harvested; the cattle were bred, fed, given shots of hormones and antibiotics, fattened and slaughtered. Even the vegetables, especially the tomatoes, are products of an industry, 'unnatural'. (But 'organic' food is also produced, just with more attention to health and nutrition.)

Here in the Catskills, where this is being written, it may seem a little odd to declare that everything in sight is man-made, but a little reflection shows it to be true, though in a slightly different sense. As I look out my window, the trees I see were all planted – the primeval forest was cut two centuries or more ago. The hillside has been shaped and seeded to prevent erosion. Flowers have been planted or selectively cultivated to provide colour all summer long. The streambed was dynamited, blasted and bull-dozed by the Navy in the 1920s to prevent flooding and the washing out of the little road that runs alongside. The big maples were selected and cultivated for syrup, and the trees alongside the road have all been trimmed and shaped to protect the electrical wires. The deer population is regularly counted and controlled, the stream is stocked with fish, the forest is periodically cut – 'harvested' – and underbrush is cleared every year. At Harvard the gene-splicers have even patented a better mouse! But there is a darker side, too, the unintentional impact on the environment – the chemical wastes in the water supplies, the forests denuded by acid rain, the algae-choked lakes and ponds, the changed weather and wind patterns, 'Chernobyl' rain . . . Nature has ways of her own; the world is not wholly our creation, nor is it our heart's desire. But the world we see and touch and feel, the world we live in, is, for better or worse – and till death us do part – the product of our economy.

In short, for an individual the world is given, for the system as a whole the world is produced. For the individual it is a constant, for the system it is a variable. For the individual the world as we know it constitutes the starting point, the input into the problems of life; for the system as a whole the world is the conclusion, the output of the life process.

How does the system work? How is the world produced? Of course, by the normal processes of everyday life, including in that the processes of modern industrial society – for not so many centuries ago, the world was not man-made, at least not to anything like the same extent. The rivers and streams, the forests and mountains, the skies and the climate were all beyond the reach of the hand of man. Even the earth and its fertility could only be marginally influenced. Animals could be domesticated, but breeding was limited, slow and uncertain. Distances determined the pattern of life; communication depended on personal contact or on intermediaries delivering messages. The conditions of life could be modified, but the time and space framework of the world was given, and the social system had to fit into it.

No longer. Modern transportation and communications have freed the social system from the natural framework of time and space. Industrial processes have put the energy of the most powerful natural processes at the disposal of modern production, while the information revolution has vastly increased the precision of our control over these processes.

But perhaps most important for our purposes here, the system as a whole works on different principles from those that govern individuals. For an individual to improve his station it is necessary to act efficiently, to make optimal economic choices. In order to expand it will be necessary to save; in order to increase activity in one area there will have to be cutbacks in others. But to improve the world, to expand the economic system as a whole, it is not necessary or even helpful to husband resources, to save or to act efficiently. This certainly doesn't mean we should be inefficient; it's just that efficiency is less important than vitality. The system responds to energy; if resources are thrown into a project, more resources are created. But if resources are withheld, and conserved, they will wither and die. Muscles unused atrophy, but used, increase in size and strength; so with the resources of the economy. The system, in a famous metaphor drawn by Keynes from the Bible, is like the Widow's Cruse – the more you draw out of it, the more there is still in it. So there is no need to have cutbacks in order to increase activity; it is not necessary to save first, in order to invest later. Activity will increase vitality; investment will generate savings; effort will bring reward. But by the same token, inaction will breed stultification, passivity will engender depression. If the system is not actively expanding, it will tend to collapse. It is *inherently dynamic*; unlike an individual household or business, it cannot remain quiescent at a stable level – it must either expand or contract.

PARADOXES AND POLICY

Arguments which depend on the assumption that the system as a whole works like one of its parts are thus totally and crucially wrong. Yet all versions of the familiar overspending complaints – governments or consumers are spending too much, bankrupting the country – rest on this largely unexamined, common-sense premiss. 'Overspending' matters only because it is assumed that increased consumption implies reduced investment; but if both can increase, or if a rise in consumption tends to encourage additional investment – by demonstrating that new markets are available – then the problem disappears. Similarly excessive government spending, creating a deficit, supposedly matters, because it absorbs the savings required for private investment. But if investment can generate savings, the deficit cannot be important. The matter is complicated, of course, by the alleged role of the rate of interest, a technical matter that permits bankers and other psuedo-experts both to pose as scientists, and to issue satisfying warnings of doom if other people do not mend their profligate ways. But, of course, if investment spending does expand the economy, and thereby increases savings, there need be no dire effect upon the rate of interest – the supply of loanable funds will adjust to the demand! All the learned technical talk turns out to be smoke and mirrors, reflecting nothing.

Deficits

Next let us turn to a somewhat different set of problems, this time concerned with the discussion of policy questions: econobabble again. Paradox can be found in the contrast between what the individual units want and what the working of the whole produces, given the presumption that the whole and the individual units must work in the same way. So long as we assume that the system as a whole operates in much the same way as its parts do, then certain policies will seem incomprehensible. How can any sensible person advocate running up huge government deficits? No firm or household could go on doing that year after year. Much the same can be said about a general run-up of wages, about certain kinds of taxes and about protection. Let's look more closely.

Start with deficits: clearly an individual business or household cannot continue borrowing indefinitely. There will have to come a point when the question of repayment will arise; before that, almost certainly, questions will arise as to the good sense of the strategy being followed: what is the point of all this borrowing? Is it going to lead to greater earning power? Businesses normally – and often wisely – borrow to invest; households, likewise, to pay for schooling, or to buy a home or a car. But such borrowing has to be shown to meet well-accepted criteria. Sensible ratios of indebtedness to earning power have been established, on the basis of which reasonable schedules of repayment can be constructed. Getting into debt, in other words, has to be clearly related to the prospects for eventually getting out, even if, in some cases, the debts will be rolled over.

Many of the public's concerns over budget deficits simply result from transferring this perspective to the national level. Examples include the claims that deficits will be a burden on future generations, the total debt may become too large to ever repay – and no plans for repayment are ever discussed, and the allowable limits of borrowing have never been spelled out. Moreover, it often seems, and is usually assumed, that the borrowed funds are used for *unproductive* purposes, essentially to finance consumption, military spending or welfare payments. They are not used to enhance the country's ability to repay.

This last assumption is just not true; a great deal of government spending is *capital expenditure*, for which borrowing is entirely appropriate on any grounds. Indeed, for similar projects in the private sector, it would be considered the most appropriate form of financing. The construction of dams, highways, bridges, public buildings, the re-equipping of veterans' hospitals, of research centres, the facilities for space exploration, for military testing, reclamation projects, the management of forests and public lands, and many,

many other government projects are both productive in the perfectly reasonable sense that they contribute to enhancing the national income, and long term, in the sense that the benefits are received over a long stretch of time, while the construction and purchasing bills have to be paid more or less immediately. Much government spending is investment in a perfectly normal sense, and it is just as reasonable to finance it by borrowing as it is for a corporation to issue bonds.

Keynesian deficits do not necessarily imply a reduction of the government's net worth. A Keynesian deficit exists when the *flow* of current tax revenue is less than the *flow* of current expenditure, regardless, for example, of any changes in the valuation of assets. To judge changes in net worth it would be necessary to adjust the value of government assets, in the light of current economic events. But the budget is not drawn up in accordance with standard accounting practices. If it were, most of the deficits of the post-War era would disappear. (Just think what happened to the value of federal lands when the price of oil went up.) Instead, the deficit refers to spending pumped into the economy in excess of what is pulled out in the form of taxes. (Actually, the official deficit is not a fully accurate expression of this, either, but the adjustments can be made easily enough.)[2]

Government spending, whether for construction, equipment or payments of wages, leads to increases in sales, and therefore to additional activity; by contrast, taxes draw money out of circulation. If it's paid to the government in taxes, it can't be spent on consumption. Thus when the government spends more than it withdraws from the economy, it provides a net stimulus to sales.[3]

Nothing like this can happen with individual units; if individuals are in deficit, then they are in potential trouble – they will have to borrow and repay later, or cut back their activity now. The government can always tax or it can borrow – and it does not need to plan to repay – and finally it could also decide to create money to pay for its activities. These options are not available to private individuals.

'Creating money' tends to be described in the business press and public discussions as 'running the printing presses overtime', by implication to pay for the wasteful squandering of our substance. Surely, it is held, this will just result in inflation, inflicting costs and inconvenience on everyone. Nothing could be more ridiculous – once the working of the system as a whole is understood. The extra demand by the government – spending in excess of tax withdrawals – creates additional output. If additional money is created, the new money will exactly swap for the new output. So there is no inflationary pressure on prices whatsoever. (Money, by the way, is not created by 'printing' any longer; the Federal Reserve creates a bank balance for the Treasury.) Money creation will have a further effect, however; it will tend to lower interest rates. To finance a deficit by money creation is therefore doubly expansionary.

Critics complain at this point that money creation is inflationary in the long run – the newly produced goods will be consumed, but the money will remain in circulation, so next year the same output plus normal growth will find itself exchanging against the normal money supply, plus growth, *plus the money created to finance the deficit.* This is not how things work; the 'money supply' – a much abused concept – does not exchange for output. Money circulates through financial channels with a variable velocity; when there is more available, it tends to move more slowly, when less, faster. And of course it responds strongly to demand. Money is drawn from the financial reservoir to make payments for goods and services; depending on the pattern and velocity of circulation, the same money can finance a number of payments. In short, if the money supply is increased by government activity, velocity will adjust so that the stream of finance will properly lubricate the movement of output.

Alternatively, the new output could be put into circulation through borrowing: in this scenario the government borrows funds equal to the savings (retained earnings) that will be created by the expansionary pressure generated by its spending. In other words, since the government deficit must be matched by an equivalent private sector surplus, the government stimulates the private financial sector to provide the funds.

What about 'crowding out'? Why doesn't all this borrowing force up interest rates, reducing investment and household spending on consumer durables? For the same reason that the creation of money doesn't push up prices: output expands in response to the additional demand represented by the deficit. The government is buying more from the private sector, and therefore paying more to it, than it is withdrawing from businesses and households in taxes. There is a net injection of purchasing power. This increase in new sales revenue requires a higher output, which means more employment, which in turn translates into higher sales of consumer goods to the households of the newly employed – and when the total of the additional earnings from all this extra activity is calculated, it adds up to exactly the amount that has to be borrowed. (If it added up to less, there would still be a stimulus to expand output and employment, that is, there would still be more spending being pumped in than was being withdrawn in taxes plus borrowing.) So the spending of the borrowed money generates the funds that will finance the loan, and the normal working of the financial system provides the 'bridge'.

In short, if the question of the deficit is approached on the assumption that the government's relation to the economy is the same as that of a household or any other individual unit, then the problems become incomprehensible. Once we see that the government interacts with the economy on the level of the *whole*, matters are easy to understand. Moreover, we can also see that there are two wholly different kinds of taxation – taxes that fall on activity and taxes that fall on withdrawals. Contrary to the conclusions that follow from considering individual cases, taxes on profits do not reduce activity, since retained earnings are already a withdrawal. Here again is a paradox: any burden on profits and certainly a tax, will cause an individual businessman to recalculate whether it is worth investing in a project. If there are two otherwise equally profitable projects, only one of which is taxed, it is the other that will get the nod. But when all profits, arising from any and every project, are taxed equally, (and less than 100 per cent) no useful recalculation can be made; some profit is better than none. Since profits are a withdrawal, no spending is reduced. (Retained earnings per unit of sales are less, of course, but since total withdrawals must equal total injections, the lower ratio of retained funds must be just offset by a higher level of activity.) Contrast this with taxes on wages; such taxes reduce consumption spending, since households must finance their regular spending from income. After all they have no significant assets to put up as security for loans, especially for consumption loans. Thus, paradoxically, a tax on profits is expansionary, a tax on wages, depressive, for the economy as a whole.

Free trade

All these points are subject to an important qualification: they hold for a *closed* economy. If a significant part of a country's output is traded, and/or its capital held trans-nationally, then these points no longer hold – for a very simple reason: the country is not the *whole*. If it is a part of a trading system, then *the system is the whole*. The country will be a 'part', a unit, and consequently will behave in accordance with the principles governing the activity of parts.

This can be seen by considering a paradox at the level of the nation, where it is understood to be an individual unit engaged with others in international trade. 'Free trade', has, for ages, been considered the bedrock of rational international economic policy. Protection, it has been argued, is narrow, selfish, irrational, and nothing more than the expression of particularistic special interests. The mark of an educated, public-spirited citizen – the *pons asinorum* of civilized discourse in economics – has been the willingness to support free trade and resist special pleading for tariff protection. To put it another way, if anything has been believed to express the 'general will' in economics, it must be the doctrine of free trade; equally certainly, protection has been seen as the expression of partial wills.

In fact, just the reverse is true. Each nation is an individual unit with regard to the world system, but each is also an operating system in itself. If each tries to achieve equilibrium at the level where it just pays its way, where its imports are just balanced by its exports, then the level of world demand will be set by those countries with the *least desirable exports*. For each country will have to restrain its imports to the level of its exports. This will be done by cutting the domestic activity – that is, by deliberately engineering an appropriate level of unemployment, making people sufficiently poor that they cannot afford to buy more than the amount of imported goods covered by the country's exports. But this has a further implication: if one country cuts its imports, other countries will not be selling as much to them. Hence the economically stronger countries will now also have to cut back their imports, since their exports are down, due to the cutbacks in the weaker countries. Thus the weaker countries will now sell even less, and so will have to make further cuts – and so on. Each round, however, provided certain important conditions are met, the cuts will be smaller, so the whole sequence will tend to converge to a definite level of total demand and trade, but a level far below the potential of the system. (If the conditions just mentioned are not met, however, the cuts may not get smaller, and the sequence won't converge – the system will just shrink until trade disappears altogether, and countries consume only domestically produced goods.) Free trade, therefore, involves substantial unemployment and waste.

On the other hand, protection and/or negotiated import restrictions permit a country to reduce its *propensity* to import – and therefore to run its economy at a higher level of output and employment. Its imports will still be limited by its ability to export, but it will run up against that limit at a higher level of aggregate employment. Protection operates differently at the level of the individual and at the level of the aggregate.

THE MEANING OF THE PARADOXES

The paradoxes arise because the whole works differently from the parts. This also helps to provide a preliminary answer to the question that arose at that famous banquet. Our leaders are accustomed to thinking in terms of the strategies appropriate to individual units, and are led, as it were, by the invisible hand of custom and philosophy, to assume that the aggregate works on the same principles. The results are disastrous for understanding – and for policy.

For the paradoxes show something else, as well. When incentives lead individual units to act, and their actions lead to the expected result overall, as in the Craft Economy, then we can argue that the market will tend to bring about the general good. Market incentives will lead agents to act as they should, and, indeed, to improve on the way things are done. But when incentives lead everyone towards a certain line of action, and the overall result is the opposite, then the market is not going to realize the general good. There will have to be deliberate, conscious direction of the economy. The general good will depend on policy.

5

ALTERNATIVES
Austerity vs. full employment

'Austerity has no political colour anymore', a remark widely attributed to a European Socialist leader during the 1970s, certainly fitted the mood of those Reunion evenings. Sunlit parties on the banks of the river and the generous socialism of youth were both far in the past; nostalgia and conservatism were served with cigars. Austerity, it was agreed, simply made sense; economic science, of course, could be dragged in to support it, but surely it is *obvious*, just plain common sense. We have been on a binge – that's why we have deficits – and we've got to come off it now that 1980s are over, tighten our belts. Which we certainly have done, or rather, our leaders have done it for us. The slow growth and weak recovery of the late 1980s gave way first to recession, then to depression – by many measures the worst slump of the post-War era, not only in the US but also for the UK and other European countries. In the US policies that might have reversed the downhill slide were never put into play – apart from an anaemic reliance on lowering interest rates, 'trying to push on a string'. When recovery finally came it was the weakest boom of the entire post-War era – and it was given the least help by policy. Austerity ruled.

The elements of an austerity programme are quite simple. Push wages down; tighten credit up; cut deficits, as far as possible by reducing spending rather than raising taxes – but if taxes are necessary, use sales taxes or value added taxes, regressive taxes. Nothing should be done which could possibly impair the 'incentives' of business or the rich. Deregulation should give the market as much free play as possible; social programmes should be cut back; and, most of all, a sizeable amount of unemployment should be allowed to emerge and should be tolerated (but only the minimum welfare spending to support the unemployed should be permitted.)

This is what common sense calls for? When recession is on the horizon? There's no political colour here? Well, of course, my classmates averred, it *looks* very conservative, a Reagan–Thatcher sort of thing, updated by Gingrich, but in actual fact it's nothing more than what is necessary to get the economy on its feet again. Simple realism. We have to tighten our belts – another brandy, please – rein in our desires and make do with less.

'We' helped ourselves to a plateful of scepticism. Just who would have the privilege of being the first to tighten their belts? The biggest companies? The banks? Or perhaps the top managers – their salaries could be cut first, since they were already so well paid? And a given percentage cut would count for more absolutely. That way the wages of ordinary workers could be cut later, only if absolutely necessary. Cut back the yuppies and stop the drain of dollars on BMWs. Such an idea, it seemed, was neither in accord with common sense, nor with economic science. In fact, unlike a normal austerity programme, it had political colour. The wrong colour. And it certainly was not the way things were happening.

Quite the reverse, in fact. Austerity during the Reagan–Bush era made the rich richer and the poor poorer – both before and after taxes. In 1969 the lowest-paid fifth of the population got 5.6 per cent of domestic income (some surveys show less), falling a little during the Nixon and Ford years, but collapsing under Reagan to 3.6 per cent in 1993. By contrast the top fifth went from 43 per cent to 49 per cent in the same period. And these figures do not consider capital gains, which are concentrated at the top. Another calculation showed that the top 1 per cent of the population received 8.1 per cent of income in 1981, but 14.7 per cent in 1986! The top 5 per cent went from 16.6 per cent of income in 1969 to 21 per cent in 1993. According to still another computation, between 1977 and 1987 the average family income, in real terms, of the lowest 10 per cent declined 10.5 per cent, while that of the top 10 per cent rose 24.4 per cent! Of course, while the Reagan years had high unemployment, it was not full-scale austerity – wages were held down, credit was tight, and civilian government spending felt the axe, but military spending rose, and with some lightening of taxes – at the upper levels – this created sizeable deficits. True believers in austerity would like to cut social programmes enough to fund military spending without deficits.

Reflecting on the evening later, I decided that I had not taken the right approach. Where the burden of austerity falls is important, and it usually falls on the poorest and weakest – not surprising, given our view of the market as an arena for conflict – but the prior question is still, why austerity at all? There's no easy appeal to the interests of business, for austerity hurts sales and profits in general, and drives many firms under. Austerity is hard on business. Why not opt for a 'full employment policy'? That was the consensus in most advanced economies at the end of World War II. The US Full Employment Act of 1946 set forth the goal and provided some of the powers and policies needed to achieve it.[1]

A 'Full Employment policy' usually guarantees strong sales and high capacity utilization through government stimulus, and provides government support for development of technology and innovation, and helps to arrange 'partnership' with organized labour to manage the effects of innovation on jobs. Truman, Kennedy, Johnson – even Eisenhower and Nixon – all developed programmes of this kind. The UK and the countries of Western Europe went even further, setting up Ministries of Technology, as well as bringing organized labour into formal arrangements with the government. Countries committed themselves to 'counter-cyclical' policy – they recognized the potential for aggregate instability, and mobilized monetary and fiscal policies to counteract it.[2] They adopted an aggressive, interventionist stance – governments were the shepherds, and fiscal and monetary policies were their sheep-dogs, herding the business sheep to where they belonged in the marketplace. Given what we have seen of the paradoxes, a full employment approach would seem to be the natural response. Why has it been abandoned virtually everywhere in the advanced world? Why is it opposed by business everywhere today, and why has austerity, a policy of creating recessions instead of curing them, been so widely hailed as the choice of wisdom?

WHY AUSTERITY?

It is often thought self-evident that austerity programmes are necessary to 'combat inflation'. Only by curtailing demand, creating unemployment, curbing credit and restraining the money supply, it is universally agreed, can we prevent the wild gyrations of upward spiralling prices. Runaway inflation is the great danger, and some belt-tightening, even a considerable squeeze, is little enough to pay for financial peace of mind.

But we have already seen that (contrary to general belief) post-War inflation has usually not been caused by excessive demand. Even at the height of the Korean and Vietnam Wars, there were substantial unemployed resources; demand pressure never approached the levels experienced during World War II. And the strongest inflation came during the 1970s in periods of serious unemployment. Indeed, at that time inflation and unemployment appeared to rise and fall together – leading observers to coin the phrase 'stagflation'! Trying to control or stop inflation by curtailing demand is like using a hammer to drive a screw – it will work, after a fashion, if the hammer is heavy enough or the screw small enough, but it will cause a lot of damage, and, considering the availability of screwdrivers, it's certainly inefficient.

Almost equally widespread is the belief that only through austerity can we restrain imports sufficiently to keep from running a foreign trade deficit. To keep up the value of our currency it is necessary to prevent the trade deficit from growing too large. Austerity packages built around this reasoning are normally prescribed by the IMF for countries in balance of payments difficulties. Again we've seen that while austerity can enable one country to improve its balance of payments, generalized austerity not only need not improve everyone's, it may not improve anyone's.

Econobabble takes austerity for granted; it thinks it is just common sense. Obviously, we should tighten our belts – women and children first, of course – which should improve profits, which in turn will increase savings, leading, naturally, to more investment, especially in securities and financial instruments, the benefits of which will eventually trickle down to everyone.

Every link in this argument is fallacious: belt-tightening may raise profit margins, but it contracts sales, so the *amount* of profits is likely to decline. So savings need not increase. Even if savings did increase, this would not lead to a rise in real investment; we saw this in connection with the paradoxes. Financial investment tends to be speculation; it often attracts funds away from useful purposes. An increase in financial activity does not lead to an increase in factory-building or job creation. So the preferred policy stance is advocated for reasons that are demonstrably unsound; worse, policy-makers in general believe that what is true of the part applies also to the whole, and consequently do not even pose the problems correctly. Our rulers literally do not know what they are doing.

AGAINST AUSTERITY

Austerity, taken simply as economic policy, and judged in terms of its effects on people's welfare, must be considered an almost unmitigated disaster. On the whole, its impact on inflation and on the balance of payments has fallen short of expectations. But it has been extremely costly in two ways – in terms of opportunity costs, it has meant the sacrifice of output we could have enjoyed, and in real terms it has meant a great deal of needless human suffering. These points deserve a close look.

First, inflation. Inflation in modern capitalism is for the most part cost-inflation, including under that term what we earlier called 'cost-shifting' inflation. This has to be so, since the system normally runs with a margin of reserve capacity, a margin that is compounded by the sluggishness of investment, turning it into excess capacity. So demand pressure does not bid up prices – it will simply lead to increased employment and production. The same holds for claims that inflation is a monetary phenomenon – 'too much money chasing too few goods'. If there is too much money, then all that has to be done is to produce more goods. In general, and contrary to much conventional wisdom, *production is elastic*; output can always be increased. To put it another way, industrial capitalism always operates well below full capacity. (A contrary view, widely shared by conventional economists, arises from a mistaken identification of the levels of output at which prices begin to rise with the levels at which production ceases to be elastic. Prices rise for many reasons, only some of which have to do with capacity constraints.) It is demand, not supply, that is scarce in modern economies; hence we should look for the causes of inflation in cost conditions, not in demand pressure.

There is a grain of good sense in the conventional view that demand causes inflation, however. In Mass Production economies excess capacity always exists in consumer goods and in capital goods, that is, in industrial production. But it is not always present, in the short term, in the primary sector of raw materials and agricultural products. A sudden increase in demand could very well catch producers at a point where they were unable to raise production immediately; in this situation prices might be temporarily bid up. Yet primary goods enter into the production of practically all manufactured goods; these industries will therefore experience a rise in costs, and will pass this along in higher prices. In the same way, a collapse of demand could catch primary producers with large and expensive inventories (expensive in terms of spoilage and storage costs) which they would eventually have to dump. Thus the rise and fall of demand, especially when the changes are sudden and sharp, can lead to generalized changes in prices, even though prices of manufactures are insensitive to demand.[3]

Yet such price variations are essentially temporary, and, in principle, could be mitigated by 'buffer stocks' managed by international agencies – were there any such agencies with the powers and expertise to undertake the job! The idea is simple enough. 'Buffer stocks' are inventories of raw materials and agricultural products which are run down to keep prices steady when demand is exceptionally heavy, and built up when demand is short or supply unusually large. Their purpose is precisely to prevent price fluctuations, so that producing countries will know their income reliably, and purchasers can estimate their prospective outlays. In other words, in the one case where demand pressure might cause prices to rise (and raw materials increases would then appear as cost increases in the rest of the economy), it could easily be prevented by a very standard sort of market intervention, one practised in one form or another by most countries in their domestic agricultural markets. But it has not proved possible to reach the international consensus necessary to set up appropriate agencies.

Of course, if you depress an economy enough, it won't be possible, at least for weaker firms, to pass along cost increases, and non-union or weakly organized labour will find it harder to win wage settlements that keep up with the cost of living. In other words, inflation can be broken by forcing the weakest to bear the burden of cost increases – and depressing the economy makes this easier. So inflation can be brought to an end by creating a recession that's strong enough and long enough. Alexander the Great brought his fever down by jumping into a freezing river. His fever ended; so did his life.

Austerity works no better, perhaps even worse, as a cure for balance of payments difficulties. First, while it can lead to some short term improvement by bringing about a reduction in imports, it does this at the expense of growth. Creating a recession not only reduces imports, it also cuts into investment; new technology, however, is introduced by investment. Modernization of plant and equipment will therefore be cut back, and the country's ability to compete will in the long run be reduced. The short term improvement takes place at the expense of long term competitiveness.

This is made all the worse by the fact that even the short term improvement is only possible if the effects of the recession are localized in a single country. If all countries are trying to improve their balance of payments or control inflation by pursuing austerity policies at the same time, then each country's reductions in imports will be accompanied by reductions in its exports, reflecting the cutting of imports in other countries. The result will be a general contraction, leading to a downward spiral that could only end either with the virtual elimination of international trade or at a level of output so low that only absolutely necessary and largely bilateral trade takes place, financed by specific agreements. Of course, once such a downward trend begins, austerity policies will run into increasing opposition, and they will eventually be reversed; we never see the full results. But what we do see is disaster enough.

Ordinary inflation is a general nuisance, requiring constant running to stay in place – and the weak tend to lose out in the race. Very few inflations are neutral; most end up bringing about some kind of redistribution, and the inflation may be good or bad depending on how you judge the change. Hyperinflation is potentially disastrous; whole classes and sectors may be wiped out financially. But not even hyperinflation is as bad as serious unemployment – the disastrous phase of hyperinflation comes when output and employment are disrupted! In any inflation, however serious, that has not reached this point there is no loss of output, no collapse of investment, and no one starves, although the weakest are likely to go short. In a moderate inflation, no one ends up malnourished, or misses out on an education. No needed public or private investment fails to be undertaken. But *all* of these things happen regularly in even moderate recessions.

Econobabblers advocate austerity as the answer to hard times. In times of recession we hear the refrain that now we must conserve, make do with less, tighten our belts. No time to be extravagant. And this is certainly true for individuals, perhaps for all individuals. But it is *not* true for the system as a whole. A recession implies unused and underutilized productive capacity, together with unemployed and underemployed labour. In other words, for the system as a whole, output can be expanded in any direction, without sacrifice in any other. There are no tradeoffs; we can have more of something, even more of everything, without less of anything. Everyone will be better off if everyone spends more. Yet this is very hard for people to understand in times of distress; psychologically, it makes much more sense to think in terms of cutting back. But cutting back only makes things worse.

More specifically, society incurs two different kinds of costs when it goes through a recession. First and foremost is the opportunity cost of lost output: had demand been stronger, employment would have been greater and output larger. Consumption could have been higher, and more investment could have been undertaken; moreover the higher consumption would have provided business with a greater stimulus to invest, so factories would have been modernized, raising productivity.

Corresponding to the lost opportunities for additional output there is the second category of losses: the real costs of making do with less. There are two kinds of costs, moral and economic, and two categories, human and physical–institutional. In the human category, making do with less means children being malnourished, and undereducated; it means homeless people, drug-ridden streets, battered wives, anger and frustration, and social violence. These are moral costs; but they have an economic aspect, too. Undereducated and malnourished children from anger-ridden or broken homes will be much less likely to grow up to be productive citizens; they are statistically quite likely, in fact, to grow up to be burdens on society – unemployable, criminal, or both. Consumption and public expenditure is in part an investment in what economists often call 'human capital', the ability of the population to engage in productive labour. If we make do with less, either in our private or in our public consumption, we fail to invest in human capital, and our labour force will be less productive in the future.

The same holds for physical plant and equipment, and for the development of organizations. If we cut back, we fail to modernize, we do not install the newest and most productive technology. Economically, then, our plant and equipment will not be competitive with the best; our organization will not function as smoothly as it could. Our products will not be as well-designed or as well-made as they could have been. The moral dimension here is perhaps not as compelling, but it is significant, all the same: it means that work will be harder and less efficient, and perhaps less safe, than it could have been, had modernizing investment taken place. Life will have fewer possibilities and more dangers.

So there are both opportunity costs and real costs to an austerity programme, which in any case, cannot deliver the goods it promises. Of course, as we saw earlier, there are other reasons for supporting austerity; it may not provide prosperity for the many, but it can help deliver power to the few. This is not what we want. What alternatives are there?

ARE THERE ALTERNATIVES?

Some of my classmates' wives, uncontaminated by experience in business, instinctively understand that you can't make the country rich by making its people poor. Yet that is exactly what the austerity programme tries to do. In a way it is honest; it recognizes quite clearly the conflict of interest between people and business. And it chooses business. But it misses a point: business and ordinary people share a common interest in a high level of activity and employment. Under a full employment policy, business will have high sales and large profits (though lower *profit margins*, since labour will be able to push up wages), while people will have jobs and enjoy high wages. Both benefit. By contrast, partisans of austerity admit that initially people will suffer (many businesses will, too), but advance the 'trickle-down' theory – in the long run, if we have depressed wages enough, raising profit margins enough, firms will invest, so that, eventually, everyone will benefit. Yet if we depress wages we constrict the market; if sales prospects are poor, why should firms invest? Depressing wages also eliminates a major incentive to innovate – since labour is cheap, why invest in labour-saving (productivity increasing) technology?

Consider Sweden. (But don't they all want to commit suicide? asked one of my questioners; no, recently the average life expectancy of women there, suicides included, was over 80, of men, 74 – both a few years higher than the comparable figures for the US.) During the late 1980s, unemployment in Sweden ran at about 1.5 per cent, everyone got a five week paid vacation, health care was free, and 80 per cent of adult women worked – benefiting from a generous maternity *and paternity* leave programme. Recently inflation has run about 5.5 per cent, but wages have risen faster. The public sector employs about one-third of the labour force, and income distribution is highly egalitarian. There are no pockets of poverty, but there are no wealthy pockets, either. In the last decade the economy has made a largely successful effort to move away from 'rust-belt' industries to high-tech, while at the same time imposing strong environmental and conservation rules. Sweden represents the best of social democracy – a market economy planned and managed by a strong popular party representing the working class. But aren't people fed up? Bored? Isn't the new government about to scrap all this? No; one party has been in power virtually since the mid-1930s. It is surely 'time for a change', and changes there will be. But the *system* is not going to change, only the management.[4]

Sweden, it should be noted, is also a small and very homogeneous society, in which political conflict can be contained and limited. Agreement on values can be reached. Moreover, people feel an obligation to others; they are all part of the same family, in a sense. None of this holds true in the US Nevertheless, even though it is a very different society, the Swedish case may suggest some ways that a market economy can be managed for the public good.

In contrast to the 'trickle-down' approach, we have the theory of 'cumulative causation', to adopt the phrase of Nicholas Kaldor, the famous British economist, which in turn leads to transformational growth. The system and the individual face different conditions. For the individual, high consumption now must come at the expense of high consumption later – 'you can't get something for nothing', 'there are no free lunches'. To consume more now is to save less, hence to accumulate less, so there will be less to consume in the future. Saving is the key to growth, for individuals. But not for the system as a whole. Saving is simply not spending; saving is a withdrawal from the stream of circulation. Consumption is demand, and demand is the key to production; investment occurs only when there is an expectation of further pressure on the facilities of production, or when there is pressure to innovate to keep up with the competition. Without such pressure there is no reason to invest. Hence high current demand is required to provide business with a stimulus to invest, and it is chiefly through such investment that technical progress takes place. Thus high consumption and high public spending not only mean investment in human beings, making for a more productive, healthier, better educated labour force; they also stimulate investment in physical plant and equipment, bringing technical improvements and better organization. High current spending not only does not take place at the expense of high spending later; it is a prerequisite for high consumption at a later date. Spending begets spending; the system moves cumulatively in a given direction. If we set it on an upward path, we initiate a virtuous cycle, if we allow it to sink into a recession, we set off a vicious spiral.

And how can policy set in motion the chain of events leading to prosperity? Designing policy is a complicated matter, which requires careful empirical work – a few percentage points difference in an interest rate or a tax can be the difference between prosperity and bankruptcy for whole sectors of the economy. We can only sketch some basic ideas here. But it will be enough to show that even in today's conditions, a full employment programme is feasible. However, we will also see that such a programme requires government to exercise a great deal of control over markets and business decisions – far more than was necessary a few decades ago. Moreover, such a programme involves government deeply in business and market processes. But what exactly are the aims and ambitions of these government agencies? Whom do they represent? What are their motivations? Can they be trusted? We will see that these are serious questions. They may provide a clue to some of the deeper reasons for the popularity of austerity.

A PROGRAM FOR RECOVERY AND EXPANSION

First, this is a programme for the Whole. That is, these are policies for a nation that is self-sufficient, or insulated from the pressures of trade by a system of Protection coupled with bilateral agreements. But if it is a part of a trading system, then it cannot act like a Whole, and it may not be able to undertake at least some of these policies. If nations are part of an international market, then the programme must be carried out at the level of the world as a whole.

Second, these policies must be legislated with an eye to the general good, and must be carried out by well-trained and dedicated civil servants, acting in pursuit of the general good. Neither legislators, nor the executive branch, are to expect to profit in monetary terms from their policy decisions. Nor can civil servants expect to profit individually in any way from the policies they manage. No one making interest rate decisions can be involved in money markets; no one making taxing decisions can have a position in the shares of firms that will be affected. Spending must be decided and contracts awarded by agents who have no material interests at stake. Regulations must be imposed by impartial arbiters. Otherwise – in each of these cases – the policy-makers will simply turn out to be one more special interest. No one will direct the system towards the general good. But the paradoxes have shown that when actions are undertaken by a collection of special interests the outcome is likely to be the opposite of that desired.[5]

Needless to say, these conditions have never been met. Aristotle, after all, described the 'sub-lunary sphere' as the scene of corruption and decay. But in Keynes's time the British Civil Service had a well-deserved reputation for incorruptibility. In the US the New Deal attracted men and women with high ideals, as did government during and immediately after World War II. So while a good approximation may be the best one could hope for, it was possible to achieve that in the early post-War period. However, in later years, especially in the US, the election process cost so much that the political parties fell increasingly under the influence of corporate money. As we shall see, it has become more difficult than ever to insulate the world of policy-making from the pressures of the market.

We can start from the present – the mid-90s, and the weakest recovery on record. Times are still slack, unemployment is high by earlier standards, so the first thing is to begin spending – increased spending by the government.[6] The government budget must provide a strong stimulus. Remember, government deficits do not 'crowd out' private borrowing in the capital market for investment purposes, because the deficit spending leads to an expansion of employment, output and incomes, providing an increase in business and household savings exactly equal to the increased demand for loanable funds. That is how the multiplier works. So there need be no upward pressure on interest rates. (In technical economics it is sometimes argued that the higher level of activity itself leads to upward pressure on interest rates, due to an increased 'transactions demand' for money. But the higher level of activity also stimulates the commercial banking system to generate more money and 'near monies', so the supply adapts to the demand, without any need for interest rates to rise.)

Deficit spending does have one great drawback, however. It leads over time to substantial government debt, the interest payments on which constitute large transfers every year from the general taxpayers to the wealthy. This will be particularly significant in times of high interest rates. As interest payments over time, they constitute a substantial redistribution of income, and this reduces the stimulative effect, since the wealthy spend a lower percentage of their income. This could eventually come to offset the stimulus of the deficit. But the way to deal with this is to tax withdrawals, that is, retained earnings and savings, idle funds and idle wealth. (Tax IRAs?! No, that is not what this means. Political realism requires that pension funds and sacred cows both be exempted. The idea is to tax the largest withdrawals, namely business retained earnings and capital consumption allowances.) Let's consider this more closely.

A deficit means that the government is spending more than it is taking in, and it implies that the private sector is taking in more than it is spending.

114

(That is why there are funds to be borrowed; remember, government spending plus private investment equals taxes plus total household and business saving.) This is the effect we want, but without the long term redistribution. So, instead of borrowing the idle private funds, the government could tax them! As long as they are idle or being used for financial speculation, they would be subject to tax. This would encourage private business to put such funds to productive use, i.e. invest them in plant and equipment. Since such a tax would fall only on idle funds, far from discouraging investment it would actually stimulate it – put the funds to work, and avoid the tax. This is the 'stick' corresponding to the 'carrot' of the investment tax credit. (Of course, it will require defining 'idle' funds, and 'financial speculation', as opposed to 'productive investment', but just such distinctions are essential to any successful investment policy.)[7]

Government spending is badly needed on the social infrastructure, and private spending is needed to rebuild and modernize our decaying manufacturing sector. Deficit spending and fiscal incentives are a beginning, but more is needed. Most obviously, given the large build-up of debt by US households and firms in recent years, a policy of easy money would be a help. But, as the early 1990s have shown once again, just driving down interest rates is not enough. And it's not just that 'you can't push on a string', though that particular bit of economic folk wisdom was apparently forgotten. As well, it seems that, given the present state of the banking system, lower interest rates will mean lower earnings in difficult times, so that easy money could easily lead to an intensified financial crisis. Interest rates will have to be kept steady at a reasonably low level but one the banking system can manage. To promote investment, then, would require selective subsidies, including tax breaks, for special categories of loans – for modernization of plant and equipment, for product development, for education and job training, to take a few obvious examples.

Yet fiscal and monetary incentives alone cannot stimulate investment; there has to be a growing market. New capacity is built either because there are new customers to be served, or because new technological developments have made the old plant obsolete. We have already seen that part of the problem for the US arises from the fact that the major markets for consumer durables have ceased to grow rapidly. But a substantial part of the population is still either in poverty or just above it, and lacks the basic amenities of life. There is plenty of room to create a substantial market; but purchasing power not only has to be channelled to this group, they also have to be enabled to earn enough to pay their way on a long term basis. We need a programme of long term assistance, designed to enable the poorer levels of the population to become self-supporting, able to form families, and buy houses, stocking them with consumer durables. Moreover, if they are provided with this, we can expect business to follow suit by investing in the construction of capacity to supply this new group of consumers.

After World War II a gigantic new market was created by the US GI Bill of Rights, which provided servicemen with high school, if they didn't have it, job training or a college education as long as they could keep their grades up, home mortgages at a low rate, other loans, pensions and insurance, and free medical care. In other words it subsidized them in setting up their household, and provided them with the investment in education that would give them the earning power to support their families. Families were insured against medical and other disasters, guaranteed support for their old age, and turned loose on the market to keep up with the Joneses. Nearly twelve million men came out of World War II, and every one was set up to buy a car, a home, household appliances and the whole works. By contrast, in the 1930s, a large number of the corresponding young men were unemployed, and many more were unable to set up households or establish families. And in the 1970s, the War on Poverty was lost – Poverty won – while the Vietnam Vets, who were far fewer, and far less popular, were given a lower level of benefits.

How can we re-establish this kind of growing market? One way would be to revive the Poverty Program, building in a set of educational grants. Another would be to re-establish the draft, not just for the Armed Services, but for National Service, including such US programmes as the Peace Corps and Vista, a Teachers' Corps and an Environmental Corps, and then provide the equivalent of the GI Bill to everyone who does, say, two or three years of such service. Such National Service would undertake socially useful projects, and would, as well, enhance both the self-esteem and the skills of those participating, very possibly helping to reduce crime. Given the present inadequate high schools, almost certainly these service programmes would have to provide remedial education to many, which might go a long way towards lifting the general level of literacy. But all these programmes would help to provide opportunities, reduce poverty, and increase the markets for household goods.

Another proposal which deserves careful consideration, because it has other desirable effects, would be to increase both the coverage and level of the minimum wage. Raising the minimum wage can be expected to unleash howls of protest from business, especially from many small businesses. (And it might be difficult to enforce in some circumstances.) But protests should be resisted; if a business cannot be made profitable enough to pay its workers a decent wage then perhaps it should not continue to operate. Cruel? Well, perhaps it is, although it is just borrowing a Schumpeterian leaf from Thatcher and Reagan. But why should we protect *declining* unprofitable businesses? Infant industries, yes; established enterprises that can no longer make it are another story. Many simple – and some complex – manufacturing processes can be done more cheaply in other parts of the world – South Korea, Mexico, Brazil. Many industries – textiles, for example – are done better or more cheaply abroad. Many retail outlets in the US are so old fashioned that they need some real pressure to modernize. But the US is still the leading technological innovator in the world, and the leading hi-tech producer of capital goods. And that is what we should be doing; we should concentrate on hi-tech, research and development, and especially hi-tech production of advanced or innovative capital goods – the equipment that the Koreans, Mexicans and Brazilians will use to produce their manufactured goods. Being forced to pay high wages will help US industry shift resources towards our strong points.

High wages also normally provide an incentive to innovate, especially to introduce labour saving, productivity enhancing reorganization and equipment. (Wage pressure alone is not enough, of course; demand has to be strong and it is certainly better if the market is still growing.) Such innovation usually requires investment, so high wages tend to stimulate investment, which, in turn, expands the market further. Rising wages, in other words, (if the rise is not too extreme) can set off a process of cumulative causation – a virtuous chain of expansion leading to innovation leading to further expansion. Of course, finding just the right increase of the wage may be quite tricky.

Controlling inflation: yardstick firms

Surely, it will be objected, businesses faced with rising money wages will just pass the increase along in higher prices? A rise in money wages will simply set off a cost-inflation, starting a wage–price spiral that will inconvenience everyone and bring none of the benefits described above. To prevent this, it will be necessary to develop a policy for controlling or containing prices, and this policy will have to work with the forces of the market, not against them.

Well-tried and workable policies include various kinds of administrative controls, which require a well-paid and trained staff, and need to be supple-mented by a set of tax rewards for keeping prices steady and penalties for increasing them. Designing an appropriate, flexible, not-too-oppressive administrative structure is no easy job, although there are good precedents from wartime experience. Even more important are the tax rewards and penal-ties; if they are properly designed they could be handled easily by the present administrative system. The principle is straightforward; businesses would be entitled to a tax credit for not raising prices, but would face a surcharge if they did. The details become very complicated – how to calculate the average price, over the year, on all the different product lines; how to make allowances for quality changes; how to allow for cost changes – suppose you raise price, but by less than your costs rose, do you still pay the penalty, or do you pay a lesser penalty? These are difficult but not insoluble problems, and they have mostly been faced before.

To make the forces of the market work for price stability means harnessing competition. There is also a fund of experience here, in the history of TVA, the Tennessee Valley Authority, which for many years produced and marketed electricity at a 'yardstick' price, a price which privately owned utilities had to match. This experience literally could be generalized, in the following way.

The government could buy into representative private firms in every strategically major industry, taking an important position, though not necessarily controlling, in a large number of the two or three thousand largest firms. Given the commanding importance of these companies it is easy to argue that the public interest requires a public presence in their deliberations. Government directors would be well-trained and experienced. They would be career executives, devoted to the public interest. The government position in these firms would be maintained for one to two decades, after which it would be sold out, and government interest would shift to other firms. No major firms would have a government presence all the time, but all major firms would have a government presence some of the time.

And where will the money for this come from? A good question – but easily answered. It's already there; in fact a great part of it is already invested in the companies in question. But the ownership rights have not been mobilized. The assets of public employee retirement systems at the end of 1991 were over a trillion dollars; private pensions, Social Security and 401k plans add up to a little less than another trillion.[8] Roughly two trillion, and at the end of 1991, Standard and Poor's Statistical Service estimated the total market value of stocks listed at $3.7 trillion. Instead of managing these funds according to the present criteria – which have permitted wholesale raiding of pension funds by employers, for purposes of speculation, with disastrous results – they should be used to establish the control over key corporations needed to set up a working partnership between Government, representatives of workers and consumers, and business.

These firms – or rather, their appropriate divisions – would become the yardstick firms of their respective industries. They would be guaranteed government support, but they would not be allowed to make more than the normal profits required for debt-servicing and to underwrite research and development and basic investment. They would practise model labour relations, setting standards for workplace safety, paying high wages, innovating and introducing the best-practice technologies, while keeping prices down, and responding to wage increases by improving productivity. These firms could be managed by an independent board, modelled along the lines of the Federal Reserve, but having representation from organized labour and consumer groups as well. By keeping prices down, and reacting to wage increases by reorganizing and raising productivity, these firms would set a competitive level of prices that other firms in the respective industries would be forced to meet. On the other hand if a cost increase could not be offset by a combination of productivity increases and tax breaks, then, following sound business practice, such firms would raise their prices. In other words, they would provide a flexible and knowledgeable way of responding to changes in costs and other aspects of the business environment.

Exit and speculation taxes

Even if the US were self-sufficient, as it no longer is, with modern technologies, such a programme could lead businesses to re-locate abroad. Production facilities can be located in countries with lower wages, but still managed in detail from the home office. To slow down or prevent capital flight, exit taxes can be imposed on large companies, to be used for re-training workers and helping the community which the firm has abandoned to rebuild. A company that has been located in a certain place must pay these taxes, if it closes down and leaves. If it 'downsizes' by more than a certain percentage in any given year, it must pay a lower variant of the tax. If the reason is bankruptcy, then the tax will be added to the debts which the bankruptcy must manage. Such taxes won't prevent capital mobility, but they will slow it down, and mitigate its impact on communities and workers.

World trade and the US deficit

Finally, an expansionist programme has to have a way of dealing with the imbalances in international payments that may emerge at higher levels of activity. Domestic expansion requires either that the international economy is also expanding, or that the domestic economy can be insulated from international pressures. Technically this is not so difficult. Policies that would prevent international stagnation are not hard to define. For example, the burden of adjustment must not fall exclusively on the deficit (economically weaker) nations – for if it does, the result will be an international (multiplier) contraction, as we already saw. So, the surplus nations have to bear at least part of the burden. One suggestion is to impose a penalty on surpluses – a tax that must be paid into an international fund which will be used to make low interest loans for development purposes to deficit nations. This could be accompanied by the requirement that some percentage of surpluses be deposited with the IMF, again to be used for loans to deficit nations. These deposits should also be subject to considerable penalties for withdrawal unless some long period of notice has been given. Such policies would help greatly, but, to put them into place requires that the rich and powerful agree to reduce their powers!

A policy with perhaps more chance of success is 'managed trade'. By agreement, deficit nations should be allowed to impose temporary tariffs, provided they guarantee that such tariffs, which lower the *propensity* to import, will be offset for as long as they stay in place, by domestic expansion, so that the total volume of imports will be at least as great as it would have been under austerity. To put it more simply: a tariff cuts back the percentage of domestic income that will be spent on imports. This hurts other nations, and they are inclined to retaliate with tariffs of their own. To prevent this, the tariff-imposing nations agree to *expand*, which means that though they are spending a lower percentage on imports, their total national income is higher – offsetting the effect of the tariffs, through higher volume. Such a policy is an alternative to adjustment by contraction.

Austerity vs. Expansion

In short, a package of policies can be designed which will control the market and put it in the service of the public interest. An expansionist policy can be designed that will control inflation, encourage accumulation and innovation, and stimulate productivity growth, thereby cooking up a bigger pie for society to divide. Everyone benefits, it seems, but it requires that government intervenes actively in markets, and exercises a significant degree of control over business practices. This may help to explain why, for more than two decades, austerity has been the favoured policy of sound opinion. Austerity is the watchword of the World Bank and the IMF. Expansion can be permitted, indeed, it may be politically necessary at times, especially election times, but the sane and prudent course, the choice of business and sound finance, is always austerity. Yet austerity never has and never could have delivered the goods, while an expansionary policy, if carried out successfully, leaves everyone better off.

The hidden agenda

Yet perhaps this is too hasty. Besides their supposed beneficial effects on inflation and the balance of payments, austerity programmes are commended for other reasons, too, and these may be the real basis for their popularity in business circles. For example, high unemployment and the increased likelihood of lay-offs certainly helps business maintain labour discipline. When sales are strong and labour is badly needed to maintain high levels of production, strikes and slowdowns are costly; labour is in a strong position. But when sales are slow, and inventories are high, so that production is not urgent, labour has no ground to stand on. In general, austerity forces people to think more about profit and loss, and less about environmental and social issues. In boom times, popular democracy will force business to curb pollution, restrict the dumping of dangerous wastes, improve unsafe working conditions, and the like, but in hard times no one wants to risk driving business over the edge and making things even worse.

In short, austerity has helped to banish the spectre of the 1960s – no more unbridled challenges to corporate authority, or angry demands for regulation and social accountability, perhaps most important, no more mass refusals of talented youth to start the scramble up the corporate ladder, preferring instead to 'turn on, tune in and drop out'. In times of austerity the college-minded look to business school; everyone is glad of a job – if they are lucky enough to get one!

Table 2

	Production	*Finance*	*Labour*
Austerity	–	+	–
Expansion	+	–	+

The timing has also been important. At the end of the 1960s the advanced world, especially the US reached a point at which the growth of the major markets for consumer durables began to slow down. Essentially, the markets for automobiles, electronics and household appliances had become saturated, in the sense that they would henceforth grow only at approximately the rate of new household formation. But these markets were just taking off in the Newly Industrializing Countries; it therefore became imperative to shift production facilities and sales efforts to the NICs, which the developing computer technologies made possible in a hitherto undreamed of way – production in Korea or Singapore could still be controlled in detail from Detroit. But firms could not take full advantage of these possibilities if they were hampered by all sorts of regulations concerning the movement of capital, or required to take account of the impact of their decisions to shift capital on the communities of which they have been a part. Austerity in the advanced world served to facilitate the movement of capital to the NICs and the consequent restructuring of production. Austerity strengthens market incentives and improves the position of capital.

Austerity promotes control; it strengthens authority and weakens labour. Expansion undermines authority; by creating prosperity it provides the weak and the powerless, the underdogs, with the resources to stand up to the system. Austerity supports the center, weakens the periphery, creates dependency and intensifies competition. It promotes innovation and cost-cutting, weeding out the weak and rewarding the strong, who therefore favour it. Austerity removes the state and popular forces from the marketplace; expansion both requires and promotes control over business by labour and popular sentiment.

Perhaps equally important, austerity favours finance over production. Austerity raises the earnings of finance at the expense of production capital; at the same time it weakens the position of the latter, by simultaneously shrinking their markets and raising their costs. A simple table (see Table 2) will help us to compare the policies. We consider the impact of each of the two policies on businesses in the 'real' economy, producing and marketing goods and services, businesses in the financial sector, and finally, on labour.

From this it would seem that a policy of Expansion is clearly superior, and so it is from the point of view of the public. But this is not *at all* how it appears to business. For Expansion improves the bargaining position of labour, and not just over wages. After a long period of full employment, labour is likely to bargain to increase job safety, reduce pollution, re-design jobs to make them less repetitive, and generally improve the quality of life. What labour gains in these respects, restricting management powers, businesses of all kinds lose. Consumers and citizens may likewise be emboldened to demand regulation of dangerous or unsavoury business practices. Hence Austerity, by weakening labour, promotes the interests of both kinds of capital, whereas Expansion, by strengthening labour does both kinds of capital a disservice. From the point of view of business, austerity is indispensable in maintaining the freedom of business to do what it pleases with its assets.

ALTERNATING POLICIES: THE POLITICAL BUSINESS CYCLE

Alternating between these two policy stances, (tending to emphasize full employment in the early period and austerity in the later), has provided modern capitalism with an unparalleled measure of stability – not without costs in terms of heightened uncertainty and blighted lives, to be sure. But the *system* has worked without a breakdown for half a century. A period of expansion generates prosperity, builds capacity, expands markets and benefits all groups. Then austerity re-establishes the dominance of capital, intensifies competition, weeds out the weak and unproductive, undercuts regulation and reverses reform, finally weakening labour enough to set the stage for another expansion. To the extent that timing can be managed, expansionary policies will be set in motion so as to have an impact prior to an election, while austerity will be put in place when elections are a safe distance in the future.

We can now see another part of the answer to our initial question: our leaders *do not have to know how the system works*! They represent constituencies respectively calling for austerity or expansion, and their job is to promote one or the other. They do not have to transcend the limited vision of the parts they represent – since the whole responds to either programme, and is benefited in different ways by both. Consequently, so long as the policies alternate, the system can be run without being understood!

WHY IS AUSTERITY THE POPULAR CHOICE?

We still haven't answered the question with which we began, why austerity has become the favoured policy orientation. We started from a remark about 'Socialist austerity', which would seem on the face of it, to be a contradiction in terms. Far from it; most major European Socialist parties adopted a favourable attitude towards austerity during the 1980s, in spite of the fact that a coherent expansionary policy, suited to the era, can be developed. Expansion and full employment would seem to be the natural goals of popular – 'pro-people' – political parties. Business certainly has good reasons to support austerity, and it may make sense for austerity and expansion to alternate. But econobabble has it all wrong – austerity is anything but common sense. So why is it so widely favoured?

One part of the answer may lie in the growing weakness of labour. The new technologies and the shift of production processing to overseas and low wage areas has eliminated many unionized, high-wage jobs. In the early period labour was strong enough to establish full employment as the goal and in many countries as the norm, so that austerity had to be justified by special circumstances. But with the decline of organized labour and the weakening of its bargaining strength, it became easier for business to promote austerity.

Another set of pressures arises from the international economy. Over the post-War period tariffs and barriers to trade have been lowered. Furthermore, technological interdependence appears to have increased. Trade is more important; traded goods and services make up a higher percentage of GNP in most nations now than even a decade ago. This may increase productivity, but it also increases vulnerability. For each country is responsible for maintaining, and defending, the appropriate value of its currency. To do this its Central Bank will build up a stock of hard currency and gold reserves. But these have to be defended – and the international economy is dangerous!

Consider any country, A, and its trading partners, B. Suppose the country A decides to expand, while its trading partners, B, adopt austerity. Then A will draw in imports, because it is expanding, while its exports will suffer, since its trading partners are going into recession. Hence A' s balance of payments will deteriorate. As a result doubts will arise about the value of its currency, which will begin to fall. Speculators will move against it; A' s Central Bank will have to spend its reserves defending A' s currency. B, however, will experience just the opposite; its imports will decline and its exports rise. It will therefore experience an inflow of currency, and its reserves will rise.[9] On the other hand, suppose A adopted an austerity approach, while its trading partners, B, expanded. Then A will see its imports fall and its exports rise, and it will be the currencies of B that will find themselves in trouble. Hence, austerity is the best strategy in a world of flexible exchange rates and currency speculation.

This is surely an important piece of the puzzle. But it would explain a *reluctant* adoption of austerity, something a government was forced to do. It cannot account for an *embrace*, and that appears to be what we see in some very unlikely quarters. Not full-scale austerity, but a moderate version, or at the very least, a partial austerity, has been supported by many Democrats, leading voices in the Labour Party in England, among the French and Spanish Socialists, the Italian Democratic Party of the left (successor to the Communist Party), and, of course, among reformers throughout Eastern Europe. Moreover, what is asserted is not just that austerity may be needed on occasion, but rather that it is the right approach to managing the economy.

So we must look further, into the nature of government itself. A full employment policy, particularly one for today, requires extensive and detailed government control over markets and business. We saw earlier that these policies had to be carried out by agents who had no personal or material interest in the outcomes. And we also noted that this was very unlikely to be the case. As a result, government agencies are likely to act in pursuit of special interests. But if they do, they are as likely to make things worse, as better – perhaps more likely. Government, we often hear today, is part of the problem, not part of the solution. To understand this, we have to look next at how markets interact with morals, first in everyday life, then in politics.

Part III

PRIVATE MARKETS AND PUBLIC MORALS

The conventional wisdom tends to contrast markets with bureaucracy, but not only does the market not work the way the textbooks tell us, it turns out, in practice, surprisingly, to be the province of bureaucrats. Yet it is certainly true that market forces are dynamic, while bureaucracies can be stultifying. The clash between the two is central to understanding the ways of the world. But there is a deeper dimension. The market has its own 'morality', its own code. But it is Machiavellian, a code based on expediency and accommodation. By contrast, the traditional code governing household cooperation, and extending to professions and in some areas to public life, is a genuine ethics. These two codes give conflicting guidance, but the conflict is itself a significant source of the innovative dynamism of capitalism.

The market cannot be governed solely by the Machiavellian code. At the centre of the market, as at the centre of politics, as Hobbes correctly saw, there must be a regulatory power that is governed by the traditional code. For the two codes are in competition, and the Machiavellian code is better suited to the struggle, and is effectively aided by many aspects of economic development. In a kind of Gresham's Law of Morality, the bad code tends to drive out the good. Over time, organized activity in pursuit of high purposes tends to degenerate into a self-interested scramble for advantage. Such a scramble will be limited and governed by the 'Articles of Peace'; yet these will be ineffective unless enforced, and the enforcer must be *disinterested*. In practice, this enforcer must be the State. Unfortunately, the tendency for activity of high purpose to degenerate affects the State as well.

6

MARKETS, BUREAUCRACY
AND MACHIAVELLI

My old friend from Oxford days always tended to bubble with schemes and enthusiasm, but never more so than when he appeared in my SoHo loft with a mock-up copy of his new political board game, Class Struggle. We could educate the American public and become rich at the same time! People *know*, instinctively, that what is good for General Motors is unlikely to be good for America, people know that Big Business robs the poor to help the rich, that Uncle Sam taxes the middle class but not the corporate class, that Big Business tolerates small business until its ideas are fully developed – and then steals them. But they can't act on their own best intuitions, because the media and the educators, especially economists and political scientists, confuse them. Academic flunkies fill their heads with free markets and efficiency, pluralism and voter choice, until they forget that when money talks, democracy walks. So let's give them a helping hand, a board game, fun to play, that will remind people of what they already know!

Class struggle? Capital versus labour? Surplus value? And we were going to make money? Enthusiasm is great, but so is realism. Where did this 'we' come from, anyhow?

SELLING CLASS STRUGGLE

In the end the jargon went out, the jokes went in, and 'we' took the plunge, right into the deep waters of the debt-driven marketplace. The game was fun, and the Chance Cards funny as well as pointed. A serious, but good-natured indictment of a system that plundered abroad, created homelessness and despair at home, while overworking its own managers to the point where stress was the chronic condition of executive life. The initial publicity was great, *Live At Five*, page six of the *Post*, the *New York Times Book Review* – seemingly endless media attention. And a big order from Bloomingdale's! My loft turned back into the warehouse it once had been and it seemed we couldn't keep up with the orders. That was the euphoric period.

Next came realism. We had over-ordered. Too many games, far too many. One member of our board of directors, pursuing riches as much as political reform, had mortgaged his house to put up the money. And then we discovered – not only did we have too many games, they were defective as well! The boards didn't fold properly, and the printing was blurred.

But, paradoxically, this was our salvation. We couldn't have paid for our overly large order; our sales were too slow, but much more significantly, we were having trouble *collecting* – and from respectable businesses, too, not just from small specialized companies like our favourite deadbeat, 'Do Something For Jesus'. The factory was about to sue us for $95,000 – and we had nothing. Now we had a countersuit.

And we had learned how to behave. If you couldn't pay or didn't want to, you stalled. And made excuses, or, if necessary, just lied – but only to those who didn't have the clout to hurt you. And when you were up against the wall – or at least needed extra time – you sued.

CLASS STRUGGLE AS A BUSINESS

No one could be trusted in the games world; we learned that very quickly. But it wasn't necessarily because they were dishonest or disreputable or unpleasant. We liked some of the people who did some of the worst things to us. They were just doing their jobs, following company policy. They were not supposed to pay up quickly, and they were supposed to pay the biggest and most important suppliers first. So we got paid last. During most of the time we handled our own distribution we had between one hundred and one hundred and fifty thousand dollars of receivables over three months old. (1970s dollars: multiply by two or more for today's figures.) The interest cost was staggering for a small outfit. As for buyers, they would string us along, assuring us of a large order, making sure we would reserve games for them – and then they might or might not actually sign an order. But it would always be last minute – we were small fry. The same with distributors – they would agree to handle us, verbally; and then they might or might not. But if they did, the fee would turn out to be unpleasantly large, making it only marginally worthwhile. The handling of foreign rights required an agent, who in turn contracted us to Simon & Schuster. Between them, they took a third; we actually made the contacts and did most of the negotiating. They gave us 'credibility'.

And, in fact, that is just what they did. Wherever we turned we were the little fish, and the big fish just played with us. If it was useful to them, they gave us a break; if not . . . we had better get out of their way. We needed protection, just as Al Capone's clients did; and we got it, just as his did.

THE WAYS OF THE WORLD

This wasn't quite what any of us had expected. We knew business was competitive and most of us had read about the Robber Barons, but this was tougher and more cutthroat than we had ever dreamed. And the rules were not what we expected. Not that we had believed the textbooks, but even we sceptics were surprised at how radically wrong they were. Consider what they tell you – or sometimes just take for granted – about the world of small, competitive businesses:

- You can sell all you can make at the going price, or if your product is differentiated (ours was) you can always sell more by cutting price.
- The market's demand is definite, ascertainable and a well-defined function of price.
- You can borrow all you want at the going rate of interest.
- It is reasonable to assume that all buyers and all sellers in the market are well-informed.
- Making a sale is the same thing as getting paid.
- Production costs are the chief costs; selling and distribution costs are secondary.
- Unit production costs increase as output increases, at least after a point; to produce more it will be necessary to raise price.
- Prices vary quite a lot, as demand curves shift about, but output and employment are relatively stable in the short run; both prices and output shift in the longer term, but employment and productive capacity are normally fully utilized.
- Price competition is the main form of competition; strong competition eliminates profits beyond those necessary to meet fixed costs.
- An important objective of the firm is to find its optimum size.
- The market, working largely through price movements, tends to bring about the full use and optimal allocation of scarce resources.

Not only are none of these true; they are almost the opposite of the truth,[1] and studying them too much is likely to render one unfit for the experience of the real world of business. Those who have been taught that tigers are pussycats who need to be petted, will not do well in the jungle. Based on our experience, and on the study of the behaviour of corporate business:

- Business firms try to grow, sometimes faster, sometimes more slowly, but there is no such thing as an 'optimum size', once and for all. The problem instead is to choose the optimum rate of growth.
- Competition comes in many forms, in growth, in product design, in advertising and marketing, in the race for patents and/or franchises on new technology. But it very seldom shows up as price competition.
- Prices once fixed, tend to be quite stable. Output and employment fluctuate widely; productive capacity is often idle for considerable periods, and seldom works flat out for three shifts, even when demand is strong.
- Production costs are a surprisingly small proportion of total supplier's costs, and a mere fraction of final price. In round figures, production *and*

129

handling cost us $3.00, warehousing, shipping, distribution, advertising, came to another $2.00 or more, then salaries, rents and miscellaneous office expenses plus interest costs, all had to come out of our profit margin of less than $1.25. The price to the customer, of course, was $12.50; the final distributor, the stores, marked games up 100 per cent. That was business.

- Unit production costs are always lower the larger the production runs; production costs never increase with larger orders; neither do distribution or handling costs. In general, unit supplier's costs are lower the larger the volume.

- Lower prices on the part of a supplier do not necessarily increase sales; we improved our selling position by *raising* our price – our initial price of $9.95 for a board game of our physical size meant that it would be an item of too little value to take up the amount of shelf space it required! As for customers, professionals and high income shoppers tend to suspect the quality of games significantly cheaper than similar items. You can't automatically sell more by cutting price; nor does the market set the price for you. It's a matter of finding the right price, which means carving out a niche in the market. There isn't a 'demand curve' out there waiting to be discovered; customers, buyers, distributors and salespeople alike are very, very ignorant – and often misinformed – about the characteristics of the things they are dealing in. (One buyer boasted that he *only* knew the colour, size and weight of the games he dealt in – colour attracted customers, weight confirmed that the item was substantial, not flimsy, and size in relation to price determined whether it deserved shelf space.)

- Finally, you most certainly cannot borrow all you want – or need – at the going or any other rate. We couldn't borrow what we needed at one point at any price, from anyone. Banks and financial institutions generally, including factors, have rules about creditworthiness, and if you don't meet them, you're out the door. We were too small, we had only one product, and we didn't have enough experience; we couldn't borrow even offering real estate as collateral! Even though we had sold over one hundred thousand games! (and were later to sell another hundred thousand).

THE CONVENTIONAL WISDOM:
MARKETS VS. BUREAUCRACIES

The conventional story of the marketplace doesn't tell it like it is. In fact just about everything is wrong. But it is not a matter of deliberate deception or ideology – although the implications of the free market story are surely welcome in conservative (and some liberal) quarters. The textbooks tell their story for two reasons. First, once upon a time, the story was more or less true, at least as regards small firms, flexible prices, diminishing returns, and competition. In the era of the Craft Economy, the story is not so far from the mark. Second, the assumptions of small size, flexible prices, diminishing returns, etc., are necessary to permit the Rational Choice model to be treated *descriptively*. That is, the rational agent cannot affect prices, cannot shift any of the constraints, and so can only adjust output. Hence the model can predict. Otherwise, the rational agent could decide to use the implications of the optimizing model to change some of the 'givens'.

The textbooks develop a contrast between market allocation and bureaucratic or command allocation. Free enterprise economies work through the market, communist and socialist economies operate by plan and command, carried out by bureaucracies. Most advanced industrial economies, especially in Europe, are described as 'mixed', with a large market area being complemented by a significant planned sector (in the US the military is the bureaucratically administered sector.) Even communist countries, however, were in practice 'mixed', since a large part of agriculture and services were organized by the market. No economy turns out to be purely market or purely bureaucratic, so the question then is, what is the mix, and which industries are organized by the market, and which bureaucratically?

The burden of the argument is the familiar claim that markets are efficient, bureaucracies slow and wasteful. In relation to our previous discussion: austerity will help to promote competition and encourage – or force! – the development of markets. By contrast, an expansionary, full employment policy requires the development of bureaucracy. So does regulation. Where the important and dynamic sectors are assigned to the market, growth will be rapid, technical progress impressive, and prosperity will flower; where these fall under the sway of bureaucrats, life will be listless and grey, youth wasted waiting in the queue, shortages will be endemic, and the goods when they finally get home won't work. The conventional explanation for the difference between the technological dynamism of capitalism and the lacklustre quality so evident in the recently collapsed economies of socialism is that the former runs through the market, while the latter was governed by bureaucracy. And this feeds into the conventional wisdom that austerity will lead to market miracles, while interventionist policies will get bogged down in red tape.

These doctrines don't fit our experience. For we were *in* the market, up to our ears, but everywhere we turned we were met by bureaucracies. Our agent was a large corporation, our producer a small one, we sold to huge stores and small ones, but whichever, we had to deal with buyers, accounting departments, and managers, all of whom had to report to higher-ups, couldn't make decisions on their own, and were *sure* the cheque was in the mail. Our employees joined a union, and from then on we had to negotiate every move both with the union and with its insurance companies. We had to abide by all sorts of state and federal regulations. We sold games to toy companies, large and small, and we finally sold ourselves to one, too. To a very large one. When we had problems we went to court, or to the government.

131

Everywhere we turned we were involved with a bureaucracy in one way or another.

In short, in our experience, the market is run by bureaucracies; there's no opposition between the two at all. No doubt our bureaucracies are not the same as those in socialist countries – but it is not a question of bureaucracy being somehow displaced by the market. On the contrary; it is everywhere, dragging its feet and tangling everyone in red tape. Whatever the virtues of the market, they do not include freeing us from the bureaucrats. (Try filing an insurance claim some time, or let your credit rating get in trouble.)

Yet there could be no doubt that the market was a dynamic place. We constantly received letters from people with new ideas for games, or for marketing, for putting Class Struggle into computers – or whatever. Innovation was the order of the day, and cutting through red tape, evading regulations – and taxes – and working around the bureaucrats, escaping their scrutiny, were the means. Dynamism and growth were certainly in evidence; not so any tendency to move toward full employment or full use of capacity, let alone to 'optimality'. The best use of scarce resources? We never saw any scarce resources. We couldn't get credit, but the problem was not that credit was in any sense 'scarce'. The only thing that was 'scarce' for us was customers! To get a good price for production we needed a large production run; to get a good deal on handling and distribution we had to have volume. To put it in the terms used earlier: our operation was demand-constrained.

THE NATURE OF MARKET BEHAVIOUR

Machiavelli would have felt quite at home in our market; and in fact he would have been comfortable in any of the Universities I have known. The precepts he proposed for the conduct of states and princes adapt very easily to the operations of CEOs and modern business – including the business of education. The object of business is to increase its profit and expand; the means require well-planned strategic manoeuvres. To succeed it must first ensure its survival, then it must outwit or outflank its rivals – and it must at all times appear appealing, honourable, decent and upright to its customers and suppliers. This is not so different from the circumstances of the city-states of the Renaissance. The object of the Prince was to survive and increase his power; the method entailed the strategic outwitting and outflanking of rivals, using the most efficient means, including force, fraud and murder, if necessary, all the while appearing honourable and upright. We met plenty of fraud, and were confronted on more than one occasion by threats of force – if we didn't pay certain bills by a certain date our manager would be beaten up, our windows broken, etc., and we were advised to make similar threats ourselves, in order to collect from small businesses. And we heard stories of worse, though nobody ever confirmed them. All this in the *toy* business! What would it be like in a bigger, tougher market?

The stakes would be bigger, and the going tougher, but the strategic game would be essentially the same. Markets are arenas in which competing bureaucracies fight it out over power, money, and fame, behaving in much the same way as the *competing bureaucracies* of the city-states of the Renaissance, so well understood by Machiavelli. Deceit, manipulation, playing on human weaknesses, entrapment, making and breaking promises, presenting false fronts, and other Machiavellian strategies all have a part to play. And the object is the creation and acquisition of wealth.

Consider the following commonplace observations – not that these generalizations are always true, but as a practical matter, one ignores them at one's peril:

Advertising and sales campaigns are designed to mislead, or to inform selectively, not to educate; the point is to stimulate people to a particular *action*, namely to purchase the good or service in question, whether they need it or not. (On the back of a certain prepared breakfast cereal can be found a claim that it contains more nutrients 'per serving' than its competitors. But comparing fine print reveals that its serving contains one-and-one half ounces plus milk, the serving of its competitors only one dry ounce.) In short, don't believe ads or salesmen. *Caveat emptor!*

Promises in business, including warranties, delivery dates, quality assurances and promises to pay, are made when they are to the maker's advantage, but if that changes, they tend to be kept only if there are sufficient penalties for breaking them. Get it in writing and have a lawyer ready!

Costs are kept down by shifting the burden of hidden defects to the public, and by minimizing or denying the deleterious effects of pollutants. Dangers in the workplace will be kept hidden, and long term health hazards concealed from workers and the general public alike. Workers will be paid as little as possible, regardless of what they are worth – unless there is a chance they will be bid away – and long term employees will be dismissed or retired when they cease to be useful, regardless of their past service or loyalty. Hearts are warm, but cash is cold.

Of course, it often pays, and even pays well, to produce a good product, to sell it cheaply, and to keep promises even when it is not immediately advantageous to do so. Behaviour that is moral and honourable, or at least which appears to be, can be profitable – and that is the point. It will be done, if at all, because it is profitable, not because it is right. But 'profitable' should never be confused with 'immediately profitable' – a lesson our business schools perhaps still have to learn, although the Japanese have been teaching it to us for a long time.

Conduct in the business world, in short, is Machiavellian, which is to say, realistic, worldly, competitive, shrewd, manipulative and oriented towards the achievement of power and wealth. It is not inherently evil, and certainly not diabolical, although it may use evil or diabolical methods from time to time. But it is realistic; it will choose the most reasonable and cost-effective means to achieve worldly ends. Committing moral outrages tends to be bad business, unless they can be concealed cheaply – in which case they are more likely to be indiscretions than outrages. And some apparent 'outrages' – some Mafia killings? – may be more like 'settling scores', terrible, no doubt, but morally complicated, when looked at more closely. The approach tends to be limited and practical; business competition may be likened to a war, but it is a limited war, fought according to rules and conventions, for limited and precisely defined, worldly ends, namely wealth and power. It will be brutal and deadly at times; perhaps, beneath the surface, most of the time, but there are certain things it will not be. It will not be a crusade, it will not be ideological, or a matter of principle; neither sentiment nor mercy will play a role, but battles will never be fought to the death or the bitter end. There will always be room for compromise, for deals, for bargaining – unless, of course, you're out of chips. Then expect no quarter.

It sounds terrible – yet there is a Faustian bargain here, in the relations between the market, and the Machiavellian behaviour inherent to it, and society's system of natural intent:

> Who art thou, then?
> Part of that Power, not understood
> Which always wills the Bad, and always works the Good
> (Goethe, *Faust*, I)

The market wills the bad, that is, it is always driven by self-interest and greed. But out of the self-interested struggle come innovation and productivity – it works the good. This is not the Invisible Hand of the textbooks, nor even that more reasonable idea of Adam Smith. Scarce resources are not at issue; it is demand – customers, not resources – that is scarce. But, though the quotation overstates the case, the Machiavellian behaviour of the market, appropriately channelled, does bring about an unexpected and socially beneficent result – motivation and innovation, and with these, social change of the sort we have come to think of as progress.

MARKETS AND INNOVATION

Machiavellian behaviour is inherently unsettling to traditional ways, since it only accepts those traditions that serve its interests. If a tradition can be made to pay, it's fine; otherwise, find another way. In the pursuit of wealth the Machiavellian constantly probes for weakness; if the traditional rulers of a city-state are losing their grip, then it may pay to try to oust them – or at least create a threat which they will have to buy off. Today we call it 'greenmail'.[2] And in business, anything is fair game. If George Washington will sell furniture, then we will see him in the ads. If religion can be used to make money, PTLs and Heritage Parks will spring up like mushrooms; an earlier era saw revivalists and Bible salesmen. Commercialism will erode and undermine everything sacred, anything traditional.

But there is more to it. Machiavellian behaviour alone will not change society; it will simply corrupt it and shift the wealth around. Bandits and brigands are not the agents of social change; they destroy and lay waste, but they don't build. The same holds true of those more successful condottieres who become princes – they may redistribute wealth but they don't in the process augment it. For that to happen the Machiavellian pressures have to be channelled into the struggle for markets. But even trading is not enough. The business frame of mind alone will not be enough to undermine and transform traditional society. That frame of mind has to be directed towards the creation of wealth by finding new ways to serve old functions.[3] These new ways will then have to be introduced and set into competition with the old. Wealth creation will then bring about the destruction of older, less effective ways of behaving, as the new displaces the old.

Making money rather than taking money has to become the central aim; building an empire rather than conquering one. This first began in the Renaissance, with the application of urban science to agriculture, vastly increasing the area of cultivable land and its productivity. Not that the Renaissance man was uninterested in taking – in many quarters that was still the principal objective, but a new way of thinking had begun to grow.

They are combined in the Age of Discovery, in which new worlds are conquered, but new products, new crops, and new materials are brought back to revolutionize the life of the old world.

Very early in the history of the modern economy – even before it could be called 'capitalism' – the basic pattern of development was established; the towns took over many of the functions of the 'gynaceas', the women's workshops on the feudal estates, where weaving, sewing, dyeing, cutting and making clothes, milling, baking, making pottery, and many other tasks were performed by the wives and daughters of the serfs. In the towns these tasks could be done more cheaply and better, permitting the women of the estates to specialize in a few quality goods. This is the pattern history would repeat again and again; urban industries taking over and carrying out on a large scale activities traditionally performed in the household, largely by women. In the nineteenth century the canning industry takes over household preserves, patent medicines and later modern pharmaceuticals take over from household remedies and midwives, off-the-rack clothing takes over from household sewing and small-scale tailor shops, hospitals replace home births, and funeral homes make a business of death, completing the cycle.

INCENTIVES AND STRUCTURE

The effectiveness of Machiavellian behaviour in generating innovation and social progress, however, depends on the structure in which it is set. This can be seen by considering a case where such behaviour apparently has largely deleterious effects, namely, in strongly centralized bureaucratic systems, such as centrally planned and managed socialist systems, or the military bureaucracy of the Pentagon.

To understand this we need to contrast such systems with market capitalism – whether run by corporations, or by small business, does not matter in this context. Two features do matter. First, in a capitalist system, in general, working people have two types of commitments, (more than commitments: loyalties) – to their trade, craft or profession, on the one hand, and to the business they work in, on the other. (Of course, there is also family loyalty, which may be combined with one or both, as in the craft handed down from father to son, or the family business, and family loyalty often helps to mediate between the two kinds of commitments.) A commitment to a trade, craft or profession means believing in and adhering to standards of work; a policeman, a fireman, a carpenter or a plumber knows his work and does his job; doing it well earns both self-respect and a reputation in the community. An accountant, a lawyer, a doctor, a banker practises his (more rarely, her) profession according to the code developed over the years, and promulgated by professional associations. The same holds in the academic world. Quality practice and high standards will earn one recognition and honours. These may bring higher income, but they are not merely the means to such income, and indeed, honours are often earned through sacrificing potential pecuniary gains for higher values.[4]

For an essential feature of the system is that the possibility of conflict exists between the opportunities and requirements of successful business and the responsible practice of the craft or profession. The object of business is to make money, the methods are market strategies, and involve Machiavellian behaviour. By contrast, the object of a profession is to do a specific job well. Doctors are supposed to work to bring about good health; lawyers to achieve justice, teachers to impart learning. But all are in business, where competitive pressures require them to make money. Doing the job well may be good for business – but at times or even in general, it may be too expensive or too time-consuming. Which corners will be shaved and how much?

Whatever the line of work – therapist, welder, carpenter, journalist – there are norms and standards; there is a right way to do the job, and there are right ways to behave as a professional or as a worker. Yet each is, at the same time, in business; to continue to work in that trade requires bringing a sufficient revenue. Hence for any line of work, X, it is always possible to say things like, 'I may not be a very good X, but at least I make a lot of money', or 'I may not make much money, but at least I do a good job as an X'. The craft or profession or line of work, X, is separate from the *business* of X-ing.

Not only are the two separate: each acts as a check or balance on the other. Given the requirements of business, the pursuit of craft-defined or professional excellence cannot be carried too far – it will become too expensive, or will come to exceed the demands of the market. On the other hand, too single-minded a pursuit of money will ignore or undermine the standards of the trade, or may lead to behaviour unacceptable by the norms of the professional group or craft association. And innovations may be called for in order to resolve tensions between the two.

'Business is business'; the implication is that making money has its own ethic. It is a genuine ethic – Machiavellian, but nevertheless a code. Efficient business practices depend in all sorts of small ways on a code of honour, a useful ethic, followed for practical reasons, just as the Prince adhered to a code. Businesses regularly undertake tasks for each other, agree to refrain from poaching in each other's territory, handle money and goods for each other, and monitor transactions, supervise activities, and collect information for each other. These arrangements have to be based on trust; many would not be worth while if the principal had always to be looking over the shoulder of the agent. Outright stealing, embezzlement, complete failure to perform, falsifying (as opposed to 'updating' or 'clarifying') records, and the like are unacceptable; such practices are unethical, but, though criminal, unlikely to be prosecuted. On the other hand, even in these activities, the smaller and weaker of the two parties – whether principal or agent – can expect to be squeezed. Just as we were, by our agent from a publisher (who, for legal reasons, shall remain nameless). There is a line, though a fine one, between squeezing and stealing, and that is the line that defines the code of honour in business.

A second feature of the system, and the one that in practice defines the conditions in which business takes place, is that there is competition for a limited set of markets. Demand is scarce; businesses must compete for customers, and this is the problem that establishes the setting in which markets operate. If meeting professional standards is too costly, or results in products or services which fail to find markets, then there will be pressure to change. And if changes don't take place, the upholders of such standards may be eliminated through failing the market test. On the other hand, if professional standards are not met, the market may judge quality to be inadequate, and look elsewhere. In the same way standards of behaviour that are acceptable, even necessary, in the market may be considered outrageous in the family and unethical in the profession. '*Caveat emptor*' should not govern relations between scientists or scholars – but don't sign a business contract until your lawyer has read the fine print.

Now consider socialism (or the Pentagon procurement system). There will, of course, be intense competition for orders, and for special treatment in the plan. But this is not competition based on either costs or quality; it is competition for influence. The plan uses all available resources; consequently resources and therefore goods, will be scarce. Shortages will be endemic, and therefore the market will eagerly absorb production. Once the plan is set, cost overruns will be accommodated, and whatever is produced, within fairly wide limits, will be acceptable; quality will not be a consideration. So there will be no shortage of demand, no competition for customers.

As a result, there is no independent business system in the way that there is in capitalism. Engineers, lawyers, doctors, accountants, and plumbers, carpenters, and construction workers all practise their trades or professions – but they do not have business problems or business incentives. They are employed as a result of the decisions made in the plan; and they will stay employed to a large extent independently of whether they perform well or badly. They cannot make profits or accumulate monetary wealth. Their performance will determine how their colleagues view them, but they will not receive direct rewards or punishment from their customers; there won't be a direct effect on their financial position. The business arena has been dissolved; production is designed for use, not to compete in the market.

Unfortunately, although the business arena has been abolished, Machiavellian behaviour has not; there can still be competition for prosperity and promotion, and the determinants of success will still tend to be strategic behaviour. But now this behaviour will not be isolated in a separate sphere of its own, as in the business world of capitalism. It will take place in the formation of the Plan, in the assessments of results, and in the assignment of tasks, and perhaps with special virulence in the determination of professional status. The scramble for profits is replaced by the scramble for promotion; short-changing by back-stabbing. The consequences are momentous.

Capitalism sets up the possibility of conflict between the requirements of the business system and the honourable practice of a craft or profession. Precisely because there is an arena of business, in which sharp practices and *caveat emptor* are expected to rule, in the professions and in domestic life, the cooperative, ethical code will prevail. Each code has its proper sphere, even though they may conflict in practical decisions. A good contractor mixes enough cement in the concrete . . . cement is expensive, they'll never know until it's too late . . . But such conflicts face both ways; business pressures can corrupt professional practice – more appendectomies mean fur coats for the doctor's wife – but the code of the professions can also limit and check the corruption and sharp practices of business. The tension and conflict between the two makes up a large part of the drama of everyday life. But it also promotes innovation. For when there is a serious conflict – the business will go under if we don't do this, but it is unethical – a new way of doing things must be found.

In socialism – and in large-scale centrally planned bureaucracies – there is no check on Machiavellian behaviour, because it is not provided with a separate sphere of its own. It is acted out in the trades and professions. Those who rise and are honoured in the professions do so because they play the Machiavellian game well, not because they are good at their work, or have advanced their calling. But the rewards they receive are those which should be given for merit in work. There are no purely financial rewards. Keynes once remarked that it was better for men to tyrannize over their bank accounts than over their fellows. This is not possible if there is no financial sphere, and no purely business activity. The result is a disaster, a corruption of the soul of the society.

By contrast, in capitalism business considerations and the standards of one's line of work are distinct, so that each acts as a check on the other. There is an important exception, however. If we exclude certain traditional professions and some new, hi-tech services, the financial sector does not appear to define a distinct line of work, separate from 'business'. The traditional professions of accounting and bookkeeping clearly do have norms and standards separate from business and marketing. Each has a well-defined objective, distinct from making money, which can be achieved through the exercise of certain skills, which must be deployed with integrity. Similarly, new services such as electronic funds transfers, and computer record-keeping are projects distinct from money-making as such, and likewise require skills and integrity. But the managing of money market funds, speculative investing, and even ordinary banking – judging creditworthiness and charging accordingly – are all simply business. They are not professions or lines of work *separate* from business; they *are* business. As are, for the most part, real estate, marketing, insurance, selling and the like. Someone might be a good accountant, even if he or she did not earn much, but how could a money-market manager, or a salesman say, 'At least I do a good job, even if I don't make any money'?

Yet it is precisely this separate delineation of spheres, raising the tension and possible conflicts between the code of a trade or profession and the calling of business, that generates checks and balances, and also innovation and progress. It is absent in a great part of what can roughly be termed the financial sphere. Only the business code rules there – which may help to account for the remarkable levels of fraud and deceit that are uncovered from time to time, as, for example, in the great US Savings and Loan scandal of the 1980s.

This tension and balance between the two codes has been part of the secret of capitalism's fabled success – yet this aspect of the system may be running down. On the one hand, the financial sphere – all market and no morals – is expanding its influence in the system. On the other, the market does not work at all well for collective goods. Market pressure and the Machiavellian code, if dominant, will lead to socially disastrous developments in education, medical care and the media, for example. And the percentage of collective goods in GNP is rising. If there are no market pressures governing the supply of these goods and services, then there will be no conflict between markets and morals in regard to them, no checks and balances. Machiavellian behaviour may then invade the organizations supplying such goods, and codes of honour will implode.

7

MORAL CODES AND
MARKET FORCES

Why is it, said the best thing that ever happened to me, looking up from the paper, that an uneducated Korean can land here, destitute, and in five years be a multi-millionaire, whereas you, who went to P.......n and Oxford and call Senators and billionaires by their first names, can't pay the monthly bills?

I'm a theorist, I replied.

We're broke, she said firmly, holding up four tuition bills.

It's true; after the Class Struggle adventure, I retreated from business and went back to writing articles. But my children continued to grow, and so did the bills.

To make money you have to play the game. It's a tough game, but it has rules; it's confrontation, bluffs, strategy and sudden strikes. Winner take all, or anyway, lots. I could enjoy it, but in small doses. I like solving intricate problems in capital theory. I like to dream up solutions to social and economic issues. Living in a state of permanent wheels and deals takes too much time, as Oscar Wilde said of socialism. On top of it, profits have a way of conflicting with principles.

There's another way of making money, of course, and that is to get a pay rise or a promotion. Being already at the top rank I couldn't be promoted; but a pay rise? Here the market inadvertently came to my rescue. A while ago a large Midwestern university, famous for its football team, decided for reasons best known to itself that I counted as a star. Dollars I had never dreamed of danced in my future. I began to pack, M to cry.

Our house in the Catskills!

Relax. They have houses in the Midwest. Cheap, too, since business has gone to Singapore.

I just love depressed areas!

Two kids in college, two more in boarding school – *we're* a depressed area. What about your students? Your colleagues? Your plans for the Department? She certainly had a point. But . . .

On my way out the door, my employer beckoned. They had always meant to . . . my value to the University could not be expressed . . . Would this help me reconsider?

140

Meanwhile in the Midwest, while making an end run for the money it needed to hire me, my prospective Department got tackled, and in the ensuing pile-up lost the ball. The offer evaporated, leaving only a sticky residue in my conscience. And an unsettling moral lesson: disloyalty pays.

Yet perhaps this is too simple. What, after all, is disloyalty? Is it really 'disloyalty' when concern for family over-rides commitment to colleagues? Did my employers finally react because they realized they had to match a market bid, or because they finally understood my family needs? There is a fine line here, but it is a line between two radically different motivations: family and collegiality, on the one hand, and market pressure, on the other. The interaction is further complicated by the fact that each case – behaviour with family, friends, and colleagues, behaviour in the market – is governed by a code defining the appropriate or correct actions in normal circumstances. But after a century of industrial capitalism it is still not clear which code should apply when, in governing behaviour with respect to work.

THE TWO CODES

Few things are as varied and complex as human codes of morality; to virtually any rule, exceptions and contraries can be found. Of course, luckily, we do not have to consider morality in general – and we are not concerned at all with such 'foundational' questions as whether moral rightness is absolute or relative, whether it should be grounded in religion, intuition, rationality, or expediency. Or sophisticated calculations of utility. Nor need we consider how we 'know' what is right and wrong. Our only concern is with society's ambiguous norms of right and proper behaviour in regard to basic social and economic activities, meaning the work we do as farmers, plumbers, carpenters, auto workers, interior decorators, or whatever.

Broadly speaking from the Middle Ages on, we can identify two codes of behaviour for work, sometimes conflicting, often agreeing, but always giving different reasons. One is based on custom and tradition, and primarily concerns the family, the household, and domestic activities generally. It is based on fairness and mutual help. It has been thought by some also to cover the public sphere – the world of government. Pericles sought to govern Athens by this code – or at least to justify his actions by it. The other is concerned specifically with how we should conduct ourselves outside the household in the world of commerce and the market (but also diplomacy), and tends to be grounded on considerations of strategy. Its most practical expression is found in Machiavelli, its most philosophical in Hobbes. Each code has its natural sphere, but the two clash in the realm of statecraft.

The traditional code, growing out of the reciprocal exchanges of goods and services making up the household, probably had as its base the conditions for effective cooperation. This is the code of hard work and fair play, seeking to give a guy an even break, a second chance if he's really tried hard, doing

141

unto others . . ., offering help and hospitality to those in need, working together. It is a way of life that builds on cooperation, expecting others to reciprocate, and condemning selfishness, greed, sloth and miserliness. The great religions all embody some form of this code; it is the basis of mankind's joint effort to build a world in which we can live in relative peace and comfort.

By contrast, Machiavellian morality, growing out of the struggle for wealth and power, is derived from the Hobbesian conditions for the effective containment of conflict. It concerns competition, not cooperation. It is based on both fear and ambition, and tells us how these can be managed, both in the sense of how they can be circumscribed so as not to establish a perpetual and incommodious state of war of all against all, and how within such constraints, the arts of competitive struggle can be pursued successfully.

The traditional concept of a good life is quiet, static and peaceful; it involves reciprocity and the governance of affairs with wisdom and justice. The Machiavellian conception is explosive, dynamic and grasping, involving self-aggrandizement through cunning and manipulation. The traditional code provides guidance for man to adjust to the world; the Renaissance code adjusts the world to man. Both are more than moral codes; they are conceptions of life, ways of living, of conducting affairs. They are not simply bundles of principles by which to judge what is right and wrong; each is rather a strategy of life in relation to work. They ask the same questions – what are the proper aims and goals? what are the best ways of achieving them? what is the most efficacious course of action, and what is the most justifiable? – but they give different answers, based on different reasons.

COMPETITION BETWEEN THE CODES

Which code will govern what, when? The traditional code has always ruled in the household sphere, in craft work, and by extension in the workplace. It is the code that governs the behaviour of a team of carpenters, office help, factory workers, management; it defines what we mean by 'good teamwork', 'pulling together'. But the goods and services created by teamwork must also be marketed, and the business code governs marketing. Yet production and marketing cannot really be separated – there's no point producing what can't be sold, and nothing can be sold unless it has been or will be properly produced. The two codes are therefore bound to come into conflict wherever they give rise to different approaches.

And then what happens? The easy answer is to call on a version of Gresham's Law – the principle that bad money drives out good. Business morality will drive out the cooperative ethic, commercialism will undermine pride in work. For sharp dealing and corner-cutting will give business practitioners a competitive edge, enabling them to drive out the rest, unless the others emulate them. But if they do, they will, *ipso facto*, have adopted the business ethic, which will therefore have supplanted the cooperative spirit.

This is certainly part of the story, but just as certainly not the whole. For business practices also depend on trust and are often judged by the traditional code. The conflict cuts both ways, and while business has a competitive edge, it also suffers a deficit in status and respect. Remember, a camel can pass through the eye of a needle more easily than a rich man through the gates of heaven.

Yet the traditional code has had its role progressively undermined since the Middle Ages, and has found its authority especially weakened during the present century. This is widely regretted, but it has happened for a thoroughly understandable reason. The sources for our traditional morality – the rights and wrongs we learn at home, on the playground, in school and Sunday School – derive from a largely artisan and agricultural, family-based social order, the traditional society of the West. The traditional code was designed to provide guidance to right and appropriate action in the circumstances of a static world, in which personal identity is built around family, neighbourhood and clan. With the emergence of capitalism we have moved not only into a dynamic expanding world, but one of progressively increasing dynamism, in which the patterns and sources of change are themselves changing. The traditional code is based on the teachings of great religious leaders distilled through the wisdom of centuries, yet it cannot easily handle some of the problems people now face every day: rootlessness, conflicts on the job, over promotions, divorce, work versus family. It teaches us to cope with catastrophe, but not with change; with loss, but not with stress. It is not oriented towards a bureaucratic world.

Consider the Ten Commandments, certainly a pillar of the Judeo-Christian ethic. What kind of practical day-to-day guidance do they offer us? The first three are concerned with the proper observance of religious custom; the next limits the length of the working week – more or less cutting it from 84 to 72 hours! The commands to honour parents and forbid adultery establish the foundations of family life, and the injunctions against false witness and covetousness establish appropriate norms for neighbourliness, while the commands against killing and stealing provide the groundwork for order and property. These are rules for a traditional social order in which work is organized on a family basis. Now consider today's problems: Is advertising 'false witness'? Do nursing homes 'honour thy father and mother'? Are takeover bids 'covetous'? Are design flaws in products, statistically certain to cause fatal accidents, 'killing'? Let's not even consider adultery, or Presidential candidates.

The answers are not obvious; it's not always clear what the questions mean, so far apart are the world-views. But the more serious issue is how, and perhaps whether, the static point of view underlying the entire code can be adapted to a dynamic world. In moral reasoning, 'ought' implies 'can'; nobody can be held responsible for actions that are beyond their power to control or perform. But industrial growth, innovation and technical progress are constantly enlarging the scope of our powers, and institutional innovations are changing the ways we make decisions and altering the loci of power and responsibility. As our powers expand so do our responsibilities; problems we could formerly shrug off as matters over which we had no control, now must be faced – such as the statistical probability of accidental deaths due to product design. Even more difficult, what, and whose, is the moral responsibility when policy measures deliberately increase unemployment – austerity – where this is statistically certain to increase alcoholism and domestic violence, resulting in deaths of wives and children?

Transformational growth extends our powers. It both widens the range and alters the nature of the behaviour to which a code applies. Previously, economic crises were comparable to 'acts of God', over which mankind could have no control. Previously, the causal linkages between economic and social actions were not understood. But now we can control economic crises, even if not very precisely, and we *do* understand the causal links, even if imperfectly. Hence we are responsible. But who are 'we'?

As our decision-making becomes more complex, in particular as decisions are increasingly reached through the working of committees and bureaucracy rather than made by an individual (an individual identifiable apart from any office, that is) the pinpointing of responsiblity becomes more difficult. Even when the injunctions of the code are clear and applicable, to whose behaviour do they apply? To actions of the corporation, as such, or of its officers? Its officers considered as people, or as office-holders, 'just doing their job'? When unemployment rises, who in the government is responsible? How can we hold anyone responsible for the suffering or deaths of people whom they will never know? The causal linkages may be clear, and the predictive reliability of the statistics high, but the decision was made on completely different grounds, e.g. to dampen inflation. The officials would not be doing their jobs if they were to take remote causal connections into account. Or would they? We are faced with a new set of problems in how to apply – or how to extend – the traditional code so that it covers responsibility by and for collective acts.

THE ARTICLES OF PEACE

On the other hand, Machiavellian behaviour appears to lead rather naturally to a code of conduct that sets rational limits to competition and aggression. Hobbes termed this code the 'articles of peace'.

Machiavellian behaviour is a war of all against all. The natural powers of people are such that the weakest, or groups of the weaker, can overthrow the strongest, given favourable circumstances, luck or the advantage of surprise. Competition for wealth, fear, and desire for reputation and status drive the struggle. But if it is carried out with violence, or pursued without limits, it will destroy the wealth of the nation. It must therefore be presided over by a sovereign who will keep it contained within bounds, or it will ruin the prospects of industry, culture, building and trade, leaving the life of man, as Hobbes put it, 'solitary, poor, nasty, brutish and short'.

So invidious or aggressive behaviour has to be controlled, which is to say, the market has to be governed by regulations.[1] The most fundamental form such regulations may take is, in Hobbes's words, 'Do not that to another, which thou wouldest not have done to thyself.' This clearly implies that one should try to keep the peace, that one should not take undue advantage, that one should keep one's promises, and so forth. At first glance, this looks very like the traditional ethic of cooperation. But closer inspection reveals the crucial difference: in the case of each maxim, the reasoning supporting the conclusion proceeds from the danger to one's own interests which could result from a generalization of a certain pattern of activity. Breaking promises, for example, must be ruled out, since one's own protection will at times depend on the good word of those who have sworn to provide assistance. Breaking promises thus cannot be a generally acceptable norm of behaviour; nor can it be good policy in general, since others will not keep their word to you, if you don't keep yours to them, although to lie or break promises might still be good policy on occasion or in certain circumstances.

Consider, as an example, Hobbes' derivation of his fourth law of nature, gratitude: 'that a man which receiveth benefit from another of mere grace, endeavour that he which giveth it, have no reasonable cause to repent him of his good will' – a very modest 'gratitude' indeed! The argument is straight-forward, and utterly based on self-interest, without a shred of altruism. Here is how it runs – with critical questions interspersed. 'For no man giveth, but with intention of good to himself [is he claiming this is a *fact*? or is it a redefinition of intention in giving?] because gift is voluntary: and of all voluntary acts, the object is to every man his own good; [same questions] of which if men see they shall be frustrated, there will be no beginning of benevolence, or trust; [these have to *arise* from the perception of the possibility of self-interested gain] nor consequently of mutual help; nor of reconciliation of one man to another; and therefore they are to remain still in the condition of *war*; which is contrary to the first and fundamental law of nature, which commandeth men to *seek peace*' (p. 99).

In other words, it is not peace which is 'endeavoured' – to use Hobbes's word – but a convenient truce; it is not true trust or honour, which is involved in keeping one's word, but self-interested reciprocal advantage. These are not principles of morality, holding absolutely, and grounded in obligation; they are maxims of convenience, as can be seen from the fact that the arguments supporting them only hold if both or all parties stand to gain from their observance. The strong should not take from the weak, for to do so is to violate the precepts of endeavouring peace; it is wrong in general since no one wants to be attacked, especially when weak, and it is wrong in particular since there may come a time when the once-powerful have been reduced to weakness, and would not want others to take advantage of such a condition. But suppose a powerful agent (person or institution) had good reason, the best grounds imaginable, to believe both that it would never be reduced to such circumstances, and that if it took the other's goods, no one would ever find out? Then why not?

Hobbes and his defenders would reply that the calculation of self-interest, on which 'laws of nature' are based, does not apply directly to any proposed specific act, but rather to the *general maxim* of such types of acts. The purpose is to define and justify general rules of conduct, so special circumstances and particular conditions have to be ruled out; only the general intent and the normal and foreseeable reactions of others can be considered in calculating advantages and disadvantages. Furthermore, the conduct demanded by the laws of nature, especially the fundamental requirement that men should endeavour peace, is itself fully general: to wit, that a man, insofar as others are willing to follow suit, should lay down his 'right to all things, and be contented with so much liberty against other men, as he would allow other men against himself' (p. 85). Thus what is called for is the renunciation of the right to do as one pleases – the right of the strong, in effect. Such a general renunciation precedes and overrides all particular calculations; once made, to rob the weak, for example, would be to go back on one's word, violating the social contract.

There are two problems with this. First, the self-interested calculation of advantages and disadvantages *has* to be concerned with particulars. Gains and losses are particular to time and place; an abstract gain does not offset a concrete loss. It may be true that in general, or in the abstract, self-interest supports a particular maxim of action, but if in this particular case, it does not – even considering the long-run implications, and assuming that violating the maxim would induce others to follow suit – then surely the concrete calculation must prevail. That is indeed the Machiavellian point of view.

Second, why should the renunciation of the right to do as one chooses, called for by the first law of nature, be completely general, holding for all times and places? Alternatively, why can it not be suspended from time to time, when it is convenient or in one's interest, bearing in mind the long term implications and likelihood that others might follow suit? Again, the argument rests on calculations of self-interest, carried out in like circumstances by everyone – why shouldn't everyone make certain exceptions under the same circumstances?

Looked at in this way, it seems clear that a code of conduct can indeed be derived from calculations of self-interest, but it is a practical, realistic code of mutually useful maxims of behaviour, not a moral code. A moral code holds absolutely, either because it follows from religious belief, or because, as with Kantian constructions, it is grounded in reason. Whether or not it is followed, actions must be judged by it. By contrast a self-interested code will be judged by its success and usefulness, a pragmatic judgement.

Further, though a practical self-interest-based code may be to everyone's advantage, there can be no certainty that anyone will actually follow it. This can be seen quite clearly by considering the question of whether or not it is in one's self-interest to obey the code voluntarily, once it has been promulgated and is generally known. Suppose first, that everyone else follows the code, and keeps his word, refuses to prey on the weak, etc. Then if a given agent does not, he can successfully deceive others (since they will be expecting him to keep his word) and he can enjoy free rein in feeding on the helpless. He will in effect, be what economists call a 'free rider'. Suppose on the other hand that others do not hold to the code; then the agent in question would be foolish to do so, and would only endanger himself. Hence, self-interest gives an answer loud and clear: regardless of what others do, it is not advantageous to adhere to an unenforced code of conduct – if they follow it, take advantage and be a free rider; if they don't, protect yourself.

Of course people might act against their immediate self-interest because, in the long run, they wish to be considered or known as a certain *kind* of person, virtuous or honourable, for example. Being deemed to possess certain qualities may be desired simply for itself, or it may confer definite material advantages, such as making one eligible for certain appointments or promotions. However, if one acts virtuously, not because it is right, but because one wishes to appear in a certain light, there is no contradiction at all; it is simply a matter of balancing long run and short run interests. There is still no reason to follow the dictates of the code if it is *certain* that one will not get caught violating it, unless, for example, following the code is judged to be good training. But in that case, to follow the code is advantageous in the short run as well as the long, so even the conflict disappears.

A code of conduct implies obligation; it requires appropriately designated agents to abide by it. Such a code simply cannot be derived from considerations of self-interest alone. To make the Hobbesian articles obligatory something must be added.

REGULATING THE ARENA OF CONFLICT

To give him credit, Hobbes saw that there was a problem, but what he added to his argument was not the force of reason, but the force of arms. For he converted this difficulty into the basis of his argument for a strong commonwealth. 'Covenants, without the sword, are but words.' The force of obligation would arise from an external enforcer, not from the code itself.[2]

Of course, Hobbes, like Machiavelli, was talking about the wars of late feudalism, when armies were ranging over the countryside, laying waste to towns and estates in a struggle to establish secure productive bases. To control this struggle, both saw that a sovereign power was required, capable of restraining destructive power and channelling competitive energies into constructive efforts.

Very much the same applies to markets. Predatory firms ranging over the markets can ruin productive enterprises through hostile takeovers, or cutthroat competition; unscrupulous businesses can damage public health; embezzlers and con men can destroy confidence in the financial system; and mismanagement of – or failure to manage – the currency or the fiscal system can create inflations or depressions that will ruin whole classes. The market system needs to be governed by a reasonable code, to prevent the destruction of productive capacity and constructive energy. A version of the 'articles of peace' will do fine; but just as in Hobbes's world, the articles will have to be enforced by an agency that itself is disinterested.

The great economists saw this very clearly. Walras, for example: to maintain orderly markets – even though his conception of markets was highly abstract – Walras postulated an 'auctioneer', who ran the auction disinterestedly. Keynes had a highly realistic and practical approach to the economy. He assumed a well-trained and dispassionate civil service, carrying out the policies of a liberal government committed to the well-being of the people. As his biographer notes, this accorded well with his own experience – he was at one point a Senior Civil Servant, and he served as an advisor to the Liberal Party. Marshall assumed that agents were all imbued with Victorian morality; they would compete, but moral scruples would keep their actions within the limits of decency. Ricardo held that the Bank of England had to restrain the issue of notes. And in our time Milton Friedman has argued that Central Banks should adopt a simple rule allowing the money supply to grow at the estimated pace of GNP growth.[3] And we will see shortly that the same problem – the need for a code with a disinterested sovereign – arises in the economic relationships between nations; they too need to be regulated by a reasonable compact, enforced by a dominant power.

In the present context, however, the Hobbesian argument provides a justification for the regulation of markets by an outside or non-market authority. As we have just seen, the code cannot enforce itself; calculations of self-interest will incline agents to ignore or break it. So this implies that the agency that does enforce the code cannot be guided by it, or rather, cannot be guided by the foundations that support the code; it cannot base its operations on considerations of self-interest! In other words, enforcement must come through a non-economic agency, armed with sovereign powers and guided by a code based on disinterested fairness – in practice, this will mean the traditional code. The Machiavellian rules of the game, elaborated as the Hobbesian 'articles of peace', presuppose, and rest on, another code of conduct which imposes obligations and duties independently of calculations of self-interest.

This raises practical and intellectual issues. In the modern world, the practical problem is that the traditional code has been progressively weakened and worn. It has been eroded by the shift of the production system out of the household, leading to its transformation into the modern business, which in turn has altered the nature of work and the workplace. And it has been further undermined by the disintegration of the extended, and increasingly even the nuclear, family. The traditional code was designed to govern cooperative behaviour in spheres of activity that no longer exist, at least in their original form. Hence that code has begun to seem irrelevant, celebrating values that no longer have a role to play in our society.

The intellectual issue, of course, is to find a suitable and rationally defensible basis for a modern code of conduct, capable of providing moral guidance in a bureaucratically managed and constantly changing world. Chains of causality are more complicated – what are the implications for responsibility? Many production processes, professional and business practices today bring about effects which are irrelevant by-products, from the point of view of those involved – but which may impact others. These effects may well be significant and predictable, though unintentional. How are they to be controlled? Who will be responsible for what?

THE MARKET AS AN ARENA OF CONFLICT

In the time of Machiavelli and later of Hobbes, there had developed a system of productive estates and towns, each generating a regular, sometimes sizeable surplus; but which were only loosely controlled, if at all, by traditional rulers. This was due in part to the development of new areas of cultivation, sometimes by free peasantry, but also to the emergence of new classes and new sources of economic and military power in the towns. At the same time there existed a large class of feudal families, based on older estates, whose education, and inclination, was chiefly military, and who were highly desirous of claiming the new surpluses, to enable them to increase their armed escorts. These feudal families, with their armed retainers, and underlings, competed for influence, for control of estates and towns, for control of trade routes and in the display of magnificence when they were successful in establishing themselves. Machiavelli advised them on how to conduct themselves so as to maintain and expand their influence; Hobbes derived the rules of the game and demonstrated the need for sovereign control over it.

This feudal/military competition for control over productive estates and operations turned out to be a transitional phase of history. It arose in the last stages of feudalism, around 1300, and disappeared in the great worldwide expansion of the sixteenth century that immediately preceded the emergence of capitalism. During this period certain new relationships emerged. Armies not only marched on their stomachs, as Napoleon later said; they ran on money, and more and more, they depended on technology. Gunpowder and artillery ended the ability of feudal lords to take refuge in impregnable castles; success came to depend on control of trade and technology. Hence merchants and markets took precedence over feudal relations; wealth became the key to power; and military competition took second place to economic within nations, though not between them. (The subordination of military to economic competition was only established on an international scale in the nineteenth century by the Pax Britannica – later reconstituted under American auspices.)

The shift from feudal military struggles to economic competition marked the point at which the economic sphere developed a separate existence, thereby creating the independent arena to which the Machiavellian code applied. Crafts, professions, and the household were regulated by the co-operative morality, with its ideal of disinterested fairness. But as commercial competition replaced feudal struggles, cunning, sharp bargaining and fast dealing, and the careful calculation of advantage took the place of violence, which retreated to the background, too destructive to play a regular role. The struggle for wealth and power shifted to the market.

The effect was to unleash the forces of industrial innovation and growth. Innovation cut costs, and expanded markets. Growth, in turn, led to the use of new power sources, expanding the scale of production. Water power, and in some cases, wind, provided the earliest substitute for human and animal energy, then came steam power, and later on petroleum and electricity.

But this growth soon began to need raw materials and primary products in quantities and of a nature the industrial nations themselves could not supply, partly because of geography and natural endowment, and partly because industrialization had shifted their populations from the countryside into the cities. Thus there emerged a new scramble between the major industrial powers to establish colonies that would make it possible to control important sources of raw materials and primary products. Of course, this was not the only reason behind the nineteenth-century push into Africa, the Near and Far East and South America; social and political forces were at work, as well as economic interests. But the need for stable and secure supplies of primary products – not to mention markets for industrial output – was important then and remains important now, even though the colonies have long since developed, often disappointingly, into supposedly independent nations. In actual fact, with few exceptions, they have remained highly dependent, governed more often as dictatorships than democracies.

THE MARKET-DRIVEN SYSTEM

Once the market had developed, it quickly became the driving force of the system. This came about in two steps; first, market forces came increasingly to dominate and organize production, removing it from the natural economy – the economy of the village square and of artisanal production – and rerouting it into production for distant and anonymous sale. Once outside the natural economy, production had to adjust not only its timing, but also its content, to the requirements of sales, so that the design and nature of products as well as the methods of production came to be shaped by the market.

Yet this dominance of the market and market forces is necessarily constrained by the fact that innovations, both new kinds of work, and new products, must be fitted in to the 'system of natural intent'. That is, the new forms of work must be shown to be acceptable, and they will be judged under the old work ethic. Only if the new products are accepted in patterns of normal consumption will markets for them develop. These judgements of acceptability are social judgments; they concern the questions of propriety and respectability, of the correct, convenient and proper forms of life, of the lifestyles of the society. This is the domain of the traditional code.

Initially, the expansion of the market ran up against the regulations of feudal and mercantilist states. These had to be swept away in order for the market to develop its own patterns of adjustment. The Mercantilist State was replaced by the Night Watchman. This was possible since markets in this era tended to adjust in a stable manner, and market outcomes appeared to embody a certain degree of robust common sense. But as innovation moved forward, and Craft methods were displaced by Mass Production, market adjustment became unstable. The working of the whole no longer reflected the aggregated intentions of the parts. The whole needed conscious guidance. The State had to adopt an active stance. Moreover, with the advance of transport and communications mobility increased; with faster technological change, families could no longer educate their offspring. The State found itself with new responsibilities and new functions. The Night Watchman became the Welfare State.

The rise of Mass Production had another effect. Industrial production has always produced effluents and pollution. In the eighteenth century William Blake wrote of the 'dark, Satanic mills' that blighted 'England's green and pleasant land'. But the industries of earlier centuries were small by comparison to those of Mass Production; their effects could be isolated. But the effects of twentieth-century industry cannot be confined. They have to be controlled and reduced. Unfortunately, these effects are sometimes hard to measure, and it is often hard to predict just where and whom it will impact. As a result it is difficult to devise regulations.[4] The state tends to find itself under heavy pressure from lobbyists representing all sides.

Markets now occupy the predominant position in the reproduction of the social order, revolutionizing the way production, distribution and exchange have been carried on. The benefits have been obvious, as has been the increase in our power over the forces of nature. But competition and Machiavellian strategy have become a central feature of daily life, with a heavy toll in stress.

Nowhere has this been more apparent than in the international competition for supplies of raw materials, energy sources, and, not least, markets, a competition that certainly contributed to two World Wars. Yet even here the Machiavellian problem eventually found a Hobbesian solution. Given two disastrous World Wars and faced with the Bomb, the post-War era saw the emergence of a partly implicit, partly explicit concordat governing the economic relations between the nations of the world, a compact that appears to embody pristine Hobbesian thinking. It placed the US in a position with many advantages and opportunities, but it also imposed responsibilities and over time exacted a high price.

THE WORLD SYSTEM

To talk about the world system as a whole, we have to weave a fabric mixing the threads of politics and economics. There are 'articles of peace' governing economic competition, and there has to be a sovereign, to enforce the articles. And the sovereign must be disinterested (enough of the time).

On those Re-union nights, after the banquet, international questions would arise. I was asked, more than once, would not all this unrepayable international debt lead us to war? My husband tells me all the time, she said, that weak-kneed liberals have so sapped our morale and military strength that we can no longer impose peace on the world. Now, with unpayable debts, there is a cause for war.

I liked the implication of 'imposing peace on the world'. 'They make a desert and call it peace', said Cato of the war party in the Senate, who had wrought the destruction of Carthage.

Later, I decided that perhaps I had missed the point; her husband had indeed called attention to an important change – that the US could no longer impose its will on its allies, nor could the US and its allies reliably control the Third World countries in the Western sphere of influence. The entire Soviet system has collapsed, and Russia cannot control its former allies, or even the former component nations of the USSR. A major shift in the way the world works is taking place. Since the collapse of the Axis international economic relations have followed a systematic pattern, which can perhaps be seen the more clearly as it draws to an end. 'The owl of Minerva takes wing at dusk.'

So what was the post-War world system? It was a compact allowing for competition, but shifting it from dangerous war to markets, diplomacy and limited war. It was simple and very Hobbesian. Until the collapse of Communism, the post-War world was partitioned into a divided 'centre' – US, Western Europe, and Japan, on one side, and the USSR, including its most advanced satellites, on the other – and a contested periphery. The two sides were driven both by ideology and by economic/military interests. Then, allowing for over-simplification, the world worked as follows:

War

• There are no wars in the centre, only 'cold' war.

- Wars are fought in the periphery, if possible by proxy, and by conventional means.
- Wars must always be fought, but must never be won.

(Think of Korea, Vietnam, Cuba, Afghanistan.)

Politics

- Democracy is the favoured political system in the Western centre and increasingly in the Eastern, too.
- Dictatorships are the favoured political system in the periphery.[5]
- Democracy must always be supported, but never permitted, in the periphery.
- Each side has a dominant country, running a strong alliance, which tolerates no friction.

Economy

- Both sides operate mixed economies, with the state predominant on one side, the market on the other.
- The state-dominant economy operates an excess-demand system, the market-dominant economy an excess-capacity system.[6]
- Each major power has exclusive access to its dependent markets and sources of supply.
- Each major power defines the rules of trade in its bloc – market-based trade and convertibility in the West, and planned trade in the East.

This provides a clearly Hobbesian solution to the problem of nuclear war, on the one hand, and to the problem of securing stable supplies and markets on the other. The dependent nations of the periphery must be kept in line; dictatorships are useful to that end. But the centre must innovate and develop; a pluralistic political system is essential to encouraging innovation. Innovations have to be tested against public opinion, and their impacts must be allowed to ramify. Social change is inherent in an innovative system; a dictatorship cannot easily manage it. But the problem of the nations of the periphery (as seen from the centre) is to provide a stable atmosphere for primary production – easy access to materials and supplies, stable prices, reliable purchase and marketing arrangements, and so on. Democracy might well give vent to sections of public opinion that resented the influence of the dominant nation or nations, leading to policies restricting access or controlling prices. Dependent dictators are more reliable. Franklin Roosevelt said of Somoza, 'He may be a sonofabitch, but he's *our* sonofabitch.' Wars in the periphery are acceptable, until the cost rises too high, as in Vietnam or Afghanistan. (The mistake in Vietnam was not the war but the escalation.)

One reason the post-War system worked was that each side was dominated by a single power, capable of enforcing the rules of the game. Things came unstuck, not because of glasnost and perestroika – they could be regarded as confirmation that the centre required democracy of some sort – but because the relative power of the centres was declining. The very success of the system in providing a framework for economic development undermined it on both sides. The Eastern system was designed to build an industrial base, to develop heavy industry. This they did; the question then became how to use it, and how to innovate. To deal with these questions they realized they had to reorganize and perhaps allow some form of competition. But the reforms were misguided and the system too brittle; the attempt to introduce market elements led to a breakdown. So the dynamism of the centre has faded, at least for the moment. China has long been a potential threat to the dominance of the USSR; now that the Soviet Union has broken apart and apparently turned inward, there could develop serious rivalry as China's economic power increases.

In the West there have been a number of changes. The 'newly industrializing countries', Brazil, South Korea, Mexico, Taiwan, are seeking a new role, and new alliances. The small, weakly aligned, non-militarist countries, Sweden, Austria, Switzerland, Norway, have done extremely well but are concerned over serious ecological problems. They are also suffering from the impact of the increased liberalization of trade. These problems affect others, too, and are forcing a change between the mix of market and state regulation. Thus success has led to demands for change among a number of the lesser nations. Nearer the centre, both Japan and West Germany have begun to challenge the economic pre-eminence of the US, and this threatens to alter the rules governing trade within the bloc. Within the US itself, technological progress and productivity growth have stagnated as transformational growth has slowed, partly reflecting market saturation, while at the same time environmental problems have worsened, and financial speculation has intensified – all leading to a falling off of productive investment, with a consequent weakening of US leadership. Moreover, following Maastricht, if the integration is successful, the EU will present more than just a challenge to the US. It will eventually represent an almost equal economic power. With China in the East and the EU in the West, the world system will no longer be divided between two superpowers locked in Cold War. There is only one military superpower, but there are a number of potential economic competitors.

Realistically, despite its military superiority, the US has neither the economic strength nor the diplomatic skill, nor the wisdom, to preside over the world by itself, as a single dominant power. As the Iraqi adventurism showed there is a very real danger of small-scale wars. Moreover, the Third World is growing restive; far from developing, most Third World nations have experienced increasing economic difficulties. There will have to be a re-alignment, and new institutions for preserving the peace, though what the shape of this new order will be cannot easily be foreseen. The prospects may be ominous – the last slip of a dominant nation from the pinnacle of power brought on World War I.

MADNESS AND THE EMPIRE OF RUIN

The decline of the super-powers leading to the collapse of the bipolar world system may have been the inevitable result of the system itself. For each major power was driven by a similar inner dynamic. This can be expressed in an admittedly over-simplified, 'stylized' form: domestic problems engendered a push for the extension of empire, both to divert the public, and to win access to cheap materials and supplies, and also for geo-political strategic reasons. However, the costs of this push, military and economic, in turn, further intensified the domestic problems, causing shortages to worsen in the Soviet system, and absorbing capital, technical and scientific resources in the US and UK, lowering growth rates below what they could otherwise have been, and allowing nations without military spending to grow faster, undermining US hegemony.

However, given MAD – Mutually Assured Destruction – the extension of empire on the part of each met a limit at the borders of the other's 'sphere of influence'. These borders had to be tested, hence 'border wars', such as Vietnam and Afghanistan, were endemic. A bipolar MAD system is self-limiting; the expansion of each side has to stop at the borders of the other, and border wars must remain limited. But the system undermines itself gradually. Each side slowly declines as its military adventures and the maintenance cost of its MAD potential erode its economic base. Moreover, on each side, the dominant country is required to behave as a leader, and seek the general good of the system. So the other nations are then able to act as 'free riders', and can take advantage of the leader. Consider each in turn.

On the Soviet side military spending absorbs vital resources in a supply-constrained economy. As a result, shortages are intensified, cost over-runs become more frequent, more and more projects fail to reach completion according to Plan, and over time technological inventiveness recedes, as it becomes too risky, in view of the shortages and pressures. As such problems become worse, the pressure for reform mounts, leading to calls for the introduction of market mechanisms. This move, on top of the Cold War pressure for military spending, proved fatal. Price deregulation, in these uncertain circumstances, simply leads to hoarding and speculation, which worsens the shortages and disrupts the system. Repressed inflation begins to move into the open, and reformers, believing in the magic of the market, try to carry their project further. But the more prices are deregulated, and the more output is removed from the sphere of the Plan, the greater the uncertainty, and therefore the stronger the incentive to hoard, with the result that output and productivity shrink, while prices rise. Savings are wiped out, production is widely disrupted, and enterprises are thrown into chaos. The end came, as we know, with a system-wide breakdown.

At first glance the US and the West seemed better placed to run the Cold War's military race; the capitalist economy was demand-constrained, so in the short run military spending tended to create prosperity, supporting employment, spinning off technological achievements and sustaining a number of giant companies that might not have remained viable otherwise. But the Cold War arms race was a marathon; the short run economic boost turned into long run exhaustion. Vietnam plus the Cold War undermined the international exchange system, creating a source of instability that has still not been brought under control. Technological innovation was distorted; military technology did not have to be cost-conscious; spin-offs became fewer. The arms build-up created jobs, but it did not create productive capacity, and it proved a long run drag on productivity. Plus it enabled companies to survive because they were good lobbyists and established contractors, though no longer able to compete with the Japanese or Europeans. For most of the Cold War era military projects absorbed the greater part of US scientific and engineering talent. Given that, together with the political limits on taxation, and on the deficit, military spending effectively crowded out spending to maintain or improve the infrastructure. Perhaps the US *could* have done both, and would have been better off, had it done so – but the political constraints could not be ignored. For many reasons, the choice was made to support the arms race, and neglect the infrastructure.

A capitalist international trading system faces a perennial danger of Protectionist implosion. Each country wants to protect its industries, and maintain control over its domestic policies. As each country enacts protectionist barriers, its trading partners will retaliate, with the result that trade will gradually dry up altogether. The leading nation – the UK in the nineteenth century and the US in the twentieth – is responsible for preventing this. Hence the leading nation must take an unequivocal position in favour of free trade. As a result its markets will be open to penetration, while other countries can equivocate and delay opening themselves to trade. The trading position of the leading nation will therefore gradually be eroded; once its balance of payments becomes weak, its currency, which will be the chief reserve currency, will be in danger. It will therefore have to adopt measures to defend the value of the currency, thereby losing freedom of action in regard to domestic policy, and, in particular, being forced to adopt austerity.

The US economy, however, now finds itself in a relatively weak position internationally. Instead of a current account surplus, it tends to run a deficit. It has also become a debtor on capital account. The dollar is still the world's chief reserve currency, but its position is weak. Worse, however, faster growth in hi-tech may not benefit the US in the long run. Even though the US has more computers per head than any other country, and has the lead in hi-tech, both in software and in hardware, faster growth in high-tech will expose its dependence on education, thereby exposing a major US weakness. Only the top levels of the US labour force are adequately educated; at lower levels even elementary literacy is questionable.[7]

Moreover, the US economy has other serious weaknesses. The 'infrastructure' has been allowed to fall into decay, meaning that maintenance has been inadequate on virtually everything like roads, highways, rail systems, subways, city water supplies and sewage systems, harbours, rivers and canals, bridges. Most of the major aquaducts in the New York City water system are over 75 years old, some a century. The electrical power grids are ageing as are many of the major power plants.[8] The percentage of the population in poverty has been rising, and all major cities have terrible problems with homelessness, crime, run-down housing, inadequate city services, especially in poor neighbourhoods, to say nothing of the dangerous and appalling conditions in the schools, at a time when the family is breaking down. The next generation is likely to be even less skilled, less well educated – and among the poor, malnourished – but is likely to have to face the breakdown of the inadequately maintained infrastructure.

An important political factor underlies this: a large and vocal segment of the American middle, and especially, the upper classes, are unwilling to pay taxes. Among the advanced industrial economies, the US has by far the lowest tax burden, meaning tax revenues (at all levels of government) as a percentage of Gross Domestic Product. The US tax burden in 1992 was 31.6 per cent, Germany's was 46.1 per cent, France's 49.6 per cent, Sweden's was 56.2 per cent.[9] At the same time, however, the US has the largest military budget as a percentage of GDP, nearly 6 per cent. The European countries have less poverty, far less crime, better elementary and high schools, more effective government services, and a working infrastructure.[10] In the US there simply isn't enough money being directed to infrastructure, education and government services. To bring the US into line with other advanced industrial countries, a *major* increase would be needed – on the order 5–10 per cent of GDP! This would have to come in the form of heavier taxes on the well-to-do, and on wealth and corporate profits. But political campaigns are extremely expensive and must be funded by gifts to PACs, Political Action Committees; that is, campaigns are funded by the very groups who would have to pay the higher taxes.

Still, for the moment, the US is in the position of being the only 'superpower'. It provides the military force; it dominates the United Nations. The centre, composed of the advanced nations, co-ordinates its policies through various consultative systems – summits, the G7, etc. It is apparently prepared to act in concert. All advanced nations are democracies. Dictatorship in the periphery remains the rule, although experiments may now be tolerated. But defiance in the periphery, as in Argentina, Grenada, Panama and Iraq, will be punished. Austerity strengthens the centre, relative to the periphery. It supports the dollar, strengthens finance capital, and slows the growth of secondary powers. It seems to be called for, given the weakness of the dominant power, the US. But it is unfair, and inflicts hardship, especially on the poor and the weak. In the long run it is likely to undermine, rather than strengthen, government.

Economic policy raises moral issues, and as we have seen, in certain respects the working of markets rests on a moral consensus. But it does not appear that any nation today, least of all the US, has a 'public philosophy' that could guide it, as a disinterested enforcer, a 'sovereign' capable of guiding and influencing, other nations, in a general preservation of peace and pursuit of prosperity. Indeed, far from there being any sign of a consensus, public discourse on economic goals and means in the US has become highly rancorous.

So there are grave, and justified doubts about the ability of the US to provide global leadership at this time. To appreciate the full magnitude of this we have to understand the nature of the long term economic issues facing the world.

Part IV

A NEW WORLD ORDER?

The market has generated technological change at a pace unprecedented in world history. The static societies of the past have been replaced by a social order built around continuous innovation. In the early stages of this process the incentives of the market tended to move the production system to a state in which it operated at its best – the market tended to move towards the 'general good', at least in the limited sense defined earlier. But with the advent of Mass Production, the market began to work paradoxically under certain conditions. Government regulation became necessary to correct this; planning was needed to realize the potential inherent in the technology. But now the market is undermining government itself, while at the same time generating a rise in *collective* goods, relative to private. Yet market incentives operate badly, and sometimes not at all, in regard to collective goods.

Market pressures built modern society; now they are undoing it. The family has been reduced from extended to nuclear, and now the nucleus is splitting. Traditional moral codes no longer provide guidance. The changes come so fast they leave people unhinged, particularly since state institutions are too weak or fragmented to provide much assistance. One result is widespread and deep social anger, much of which is vented on the State. In addition, the forces of the market are undermining the State's ability to cope with economic forces, and establish policies that will guarantee prosperity for ordinary people. Yet, at the same time, the need for such policies is increasing.

This dilemma – the weakening of the state at a time when the need for strong and forceful state action is increasing – is not widely appreciated. A major reason is that the discourse on the market and its relation to the state is largely based on individualism. Individualism underlies econobabble. It is a fundamentally flawed conception of the way society works, and it prevents us from seeing our problems as they really are.

8

TWILIGHT IN THE
MARKETPLACE

Over the years the women were definitely more in tune, I thought. Not surprisingly, for they are still, as they have always been, the chief custodians of the household economy. My classmates tended to be realists in the Machiavellian pursuit of wealth and power, on the one hand, or idealists – poets and dreamers – on the other. By contrast, their wives were often realistic in a different sense: practical and efficient in the pursuit of modest goals for the general good of family or community. Yet this was also changing – several classmates had left the corporate world, and were now working for environmental projects. And more than one wife was embarked on a new career in business. In a certain sense, my classmates were choosing between the two codes. But even so, the household economy was less evident than in earlier years, partly because the children of our class are mostly grown, but mostly because of the high divorce rate. Plus, as we shall see, there isn't much left to do in the household. Under the pressure of the market, business and the state have taken over its functions.

In general, our society has judged this to be progress. But there are now a number of serious warning signs, suggesting that economic development in response to market pressure may be creating problems for households. As we shall see, similar problems can be found in production. On the face of it, these problems seem to call for some kind of state regulation or guidance. Unfortunately the state itself is suffering from related problems, which give it difficulties managing its present responsibilities, and does not appear to be in a position to take on additional ones. Progress is looking more and more ambiguous.

THE HOUSEHOLD AND THE MARKET

From its earliest beginnings market-driven industry has been guided by a central principle: appropriate the activities or products of the household, make them better or cheaper, and sell them back. The household economy of several hundred years ago, or even of the last century on the American frontier, bought or grew or traded its own products for raw materials – raw

161

produce, dry goods, skins, grain – and produced its own finished goods, for its own use or for trading in a local exchange system.

By the last part of the twentieth century it was clear that there was very little left in the way of household activities for the industrial system to appropriate. Birth and death, hospitals and funeral homes, nursing homes for care of the aged, craft activities of all sorts, the manufacture of household items in ordinary use, have all long since disappeared into the market, to return polished, improved, and advertised in colour. The household itself, stripped of its traditional functions, appears to be changing in nature. Moreover, technological developments have been intensifying these changes, as consumption has taken on an increasingly social character. Households used to buy food and cook meals, buy cloth and make clothes; food and clothing next became increasingly prepared or ready-made. Now more and more of us eat out and wear whatever is in style, both leaving households less to do and making them less the focus of activity. And the newest developments are in communications, transportation, and data processing – all social processes impacting on households in ways that tend to reduce their importance as centres of activity and decision.

Traditional society grew up around settled cultivation, organized through ties of kinship, which bound the peasant – and his masters – to the soil. These bonds were fixed at birth, remained through life and were passed on from generation to generation. The seasons rolled, the weather varied, the cycle turned, but nothing changed. The world went on forever, under the gaze of Heaven. The emergence of the market shattered the fixed and rigid peace of the countryside. Market pressures created unparalleled opportunities for geographic and social mobility; they also forced the development of new skills, opened opportunities for new talents, and in general broke apart the frozen stupor of rural life, bringing openings for initiative, and chances for adventure. In the process, of course, a lot was lost; the safety of custom, the wisdom of tradition, the ease of settled ways, and the closeness and good fit, the caring relationship, between human society and the earth.

But the gains were enormous. Individuals had the opportunity to choose their own paths of development, to choose careers, to try to become whatever they wished. Of course, it wasn't really possible except for a relatively few, but even the purely formal establishment of equality of opportunity changed thinking. People were no longer what they were born; birth no longer defined the horizon of the possible. There were choices and there were chances.

The technological dynamism of capitalism has required changes in the way children are socialized. The system of fathers passing along their skills to their sons, mothers to their daughters, could not be continued, once innovation became intense and widespread. The skills of the parents would be outmoded, out of date. Children needed to be taught things their parents never knew, skills their parents never could have learned. In traditional society the work of the world was the same generation after generation. But in capitalism the jobs of tomorrow may be nothing like the jobs of yesterday, and the skills and knowledge required may be altogether different. Under these circumstances vocational education cannot take place in the home. The consequence has been an enormous growth in the state.

Yet market pressures have also had terrible consequences for the development of people. The socialization institutions of the state and private sector provide nothing comparable to the family in regard to nurturing. Love can't be bought, nor doled out by a bureaucracy. The destruction of traditions and the withering of the extended family have left people lonely, isolated, afraid, subject to anomie, and rootless, subject to outbursts of apparently unfocused anger. A general spiritual malaise can be seen throughout Western society, a loss of values, of rootedness, of purpose in life, which no amount of entrepreneurship or calculated self-interest can overcome. Yet none of the 'commune' movements of the last century or so, whether religious or political, seems to have succeeded, either.

Before the rise of the modern economy the world was the world we found; now it is the world we have made. In traditional society the household fitted into the rhythms of the earth. The land and the seasons, and the cycles of animal life, provided a setting that had to be cared for, and to which human life had to adapt. But with the growth of industry and technology, the world can be changed in whatever directions the market calls for.

The incentives and opportunities for innovation and improvement have perhaps never been greater, yet today, at least in the US, but perhaps in many advanced economies, there is a sickness of spirit, and a despairing sense that greater and greater efforts are required to achieve the most modest improvements. Sometimes even to stand still! Innovations are dramatic and far-reaching, but the overall impact of the economy on the quality of life is uncertain, bordering on the undesirable.

NET NATIONAL PRODUCT OR NET ECONOMIC WELFARE?

One interesting way of looking at this is to re-examine our national income statistics. By official standards the economy, during the 1970s and 1980s, has continued to grow at a respectable rate, if slower than in earlier years. In the twenty-odd years from the early 1970s to the 1990s, GNP has doubled in real terms. But journalists, commentators and people in general, certainly don't feel twice as rich; in fact many people actually feel worse off. People in the middle and lower income brackets undoubtedly feel this way at least partly because the distribution of income has moved against them. Yet even if their share has declined, has not the whole grown enough to offset this? It's hard to tell; what is clear though, is that even the well-to-do, who have become relatively better off in the last decade, feel that their prosperity is precarious and their quality of life imperilled. Why do measured growth and perceived well-being diverge so markedly?

The chief reason seems to be that our measures of GNP do not include a number of important and measurable economic items that significantly affect our well-being, sometimes in negative ways. For example, there are costs of various kinds due to pollution, environmental destruction, loss of leisure, and the wearing out of the social infrastructure; on the positive side we ought to add in the monetary values of the services of housewives, and for non-market acitivities, including leisure time. When these are all included we end up with a much larger figure – because of the money values imputed to various activities – but one which, some time in the early 1950s, begins to grow much more slowly than GNP. As a result, a large and widening gap has opened up between the two measures, which is another way of saying that it is increasingly costly in terms of GNP to improve economic well-being. Production generates 'illth' as well as wealth, and illth appears to be growing faster.

TEXTBOOK GROWTH OR TRANSFORMATIONAL GROWTH?

It has often been pointed out before that economic growth delivers less than it promises, but explaining just why has not proved so easy. Indeed, growth generally has proved difficult for economists. The textbook model portrays 'steady' growth, regulated by flexible prices. A casual look at American history reveals how complex it actually is. Starting around 1900, agriculture has declined in importance, but first manufacturing and then services have grown. Self-employment and small business have fallen, and the share of corporate business in GNP has risen. Corporate profits have fluctuated; whatever measure is chosen, whether figured on capital, or as a share of revenue, profits fluctuate. The basic consumer necessities, food, clothing and shelter have declined in importance in consumer budgets, but medical care and education have risen. All these declines have their counterpart in economic hardship – growth destroys wealth and undermines welfare as part of the process of creating new wealth and increased welfare. New products – which usually displace older ones – have been introduced in almost every category of consumer spending, and new techniques in most categories of production, too. Once an innovation has been introduced the change has usually turned out to be irreversible. Yet throughout all these changes the composite price indexes for broad categories of goods, like 'food products', 'footwear', 'textiles', etc., have remained surprisingly steady. It's not that they haven't changed; they just haven't changed all that much, and the changes that have taken place are almost entirely accounted for by changes in labour productivity. In short, there have been great and systematic changes in the composition of output, the distribution of income and the rate of growth, during which prices have remained quite stable.

And what says the textbook model? The most common model, the one that appears in most textbooks, shows steady growth, with a *given* composition of output (the model assumes 'one good', which is to say that its composition doesn't matter because it doesn't vary) and an 'equilibrium' distribution of income. Declining sectors and the destruction of wealth play no role in the smooth expansion portrayed. Prices, however, are considered to be flexible, meaning that a deviation from equilibrium will be met at once with price changes, that will lead to appropriate adjustments. On the face of it, the textbook's preferred model – for which the Nobel Prize was awarded! – paints a picture almost the exact opposite of the reality. As art this might be acceptable, but as science it leaves one breathless.

Understanding the processes of growth may give us some insight into why it has ceased to deliver well-being. Production and consumption have not expanded according to the swelling-up-in-proportion fashion of the textbooks, beloved because the mathematics is easy. Their growth has been a mixture of expansion, contraction and qualitative change. An intractable problem, the mathematics are formidable. But looking out the window I can see some tulips I planted last fall. A brownish bulb went into the ground; then a couple of weeks ago a green shoot appeared, then turned into long slender leaves; a stalk emerged in the centre with a tight green bud on top, which has now opened out into brilliant red and yellow flowers. Underground, the bulb has been destroyed by the growth of the stalk and the roots. Expansion accompanied by qualitative change – transformational growth! Not that gardening is all that easy, but if you pay attention to details, and take a realistic approach, you can bring about the kinds of growth you want. Not a bad way to approach the economy.

So we will start by looking at transformational growth in consumption and production; and this will take us into changes in forms of organization as well. In each of these we will find that there has been a progressive development in the nature of the characteristic activities, expanding from individual to social, simple to complex, and from a kinship base to a functional base. But these changes have brought with them progressively more intense dislocations and disamenities, a process that has gotten increasingly out of control.

THE TRANSFORMATION OF CONSUMPTION

To begin with consumption: a century ago, the management of consumption was a household project. The basic necessities of food, clothing and shelter, together with light and heat, made up the bulk of consumer demand. These and many other elements in consumption were bought or brought into the household in unfinished form and turned into final products by domestic labour. Foods would be bought in the market or grown; but meals were prepared, preserves put up, jams and jellies made, and food packed for winter storage in the household. Yarn and cloth would be bought at the dry-goods store; clothes would be sewn and spun at home. Candles, furniture, wood for heating, and many other necessities and conveniences were produced at home.

The history of modern capitalism is, to a large extent, the history of the transformation of these household activities into industries, in which products serving the same functions, but better, are turned out more cheaply by mass production. Canning replaces home preserves, modern textiles home sewing, prepared foods home cooking, radio and TV 'home entertainment'; the old craft skills survive only as hobbies, which, in turn, have become an industry as well, so that the old craft tools are now made by modern precision methods. The household is deskilled, stripped of its traditional functions. Women are thereby set free, but they may also be left at a loss as to what to do next.

In the process of moving the final stage of production – the finishing – of consumer goods out of the household and into industry the nature and relative importance of these goods changed. This went through several stages. At first, under Craft Economy conditions, a great deal of both production and consumption took place in the household, in ways that involved only household members. Much artisan production was organized by the household; the shop and the farm were household affairs, the home was also the workplace. And the most important goods, food and clothes and other household basics, could be considered 'individual' goods in the sense that the textbook Robinson Crusoe could in principle both produce and consume them in isolation. Growing food and making clothes involve traditional skills that one person could master – even if a larger number might do the job more efficiently. Consuming food and wearing clothes are likewise individual acts. No one else has to eat along with you. You can buy a shirt and wear it without anyone else having to wear the same thing. Many household goods, at least in their primitive forms, have this character. No one else has to use a washtub or an iron or a stove for you to use yours.

But with the development of the factory system, even in its early stages, production became separated from the household, so that its organization could adapt to functional needs, rather than reflecting kinship and family relationships. Consumption, however, remained as before. But all this changed with Mass Production and the emergence of standardized products.

Mass Production changed the supply side, redesigning and standardizing the goods, replacing Robinson with Henry Ford. Production requires an organized collective effort, independent of the family system, and Mass Production requires a Mass market. Yet though the goods must be manufactured socially, they are still intended or assumed to be consumed individually. I can open a can of beans whether you do or not; I can buy a suit off the rack whether you do or not – but there is a difference. The goods are finished in the factory; they do not have to be completed at home, and they will not be produced at all unless there is enough of a market to justify mass production. The act of consumption remains individual, but the social dimension is implicit.

Advertising and marketing, interacting with product design soon lead to further changes, adding a social character to personal consumption. Clothes, furniture, household appliances and food acquire symbolic status, and come to express the style and social position of the household or individual.

Transformational growth thus changes both production and consumption from activities performed in the household, under the aegis of the kinship system, making them into collective and socially defined projects, practised according to public criteria and governed by the rules of the marketplace. But besides this, there is another dimension to the change in consumption.

Some economic activities cannot be individual, in principle. That's why even the textbook Robinson needs Friday. Services, for example. But there are many others; you can't make a telephone call unless someone else answers; you can't play the game unless the other players – and the other team – show up. If you're going to see a Broadway show, you'd better get there just before the curtain rises, along with the rest of the audience. In other words, these acts of consumption are inherently social; they cannot in principle be undertaken by one person alone. At least one other person is involved, and because the act establishes a relationship, the timing has to be coordinated. Moreover, even though a customer pays the telephone company for the call, the most important benefits come from the *other people using the service*, not from the company. The club receives a fee for the use of the sports facility, but without other players they wouldn't be worth much. The same holds for schools, if not so strongly; a student learns from the teachers, but part of the benefits come from the company of the other students. And the Broadway show? Who would want to be the only one in the audience – the ambience would be all wrong. So it is not just that these goods and services are jointly consumed; it is that what each consumer wants is partly provided by *other consumers* – even though payment goes only to the 'provider'.[1]

In the earlier stages of capitalism, the basic items, whose consumption remains an individual act even when it comes to have a social dimension – e.g. food, clothing and shelter – made up the major part of the household budget. Later the proportions shift, as collectively consumed goods, and goods with a social aspect, make up a progressively larger fraction of household expenditure. Transportation, communications, entertainment, and education all increase with industrial development. Moreover, the last three all merge together in the new hi-tech sector of the past twenty years!

Goods and services in these five areas are produced by a mixture of private and public institutions, under the watchful eyes of government regulators. In each case market pressures have generated innovations; but they have also resulted in serious distortions. Private schools are sometimes excellent, but can also be committed to discrimination or absurd religious beliefs. Entertainment produced for profit often provides a diet of violence and glossy sex. Private transportation serves the profitable routes, as private medicine serves the well-to-do. The Internet was developed on the basis of government subsidies. Public parks, public beaches and public marinas are designed to give people a sense of freedom, of open spaces and contact with nature. To fence them off and charge admission is to undercut the basic idea. The point is very simple: market incentives direct producers to find ways to *inhibit access* to their product, so they can charge a fee for use. But this is exactly what should not be done in the case of goods with a collective dimension, particularly when the benefits to each user are partly due to the other users, or when widespread use will lead to learning, innovation or to the opening of new opportunities.

The developments in communications and hi-tech have led to corresponding changes in the nature of expenditure. In the past consumption goods were purchased by means of direct payments, cash or cheques. Today cash is now largely confined to incidentals and/or illegal goods. Major purchases and regular household expenses are increasingly managed through the servicing of credit – charge accounts, cheques and debit or credit cards, often handled through electronic funds transfer. At the end of the month, as income is received, accounts are balanced. Again there is a collective dimension – credit cards and payments networks are more valuable the larger the number of affiliated businesses and users.

The different kinds of consumption together make up a lifestyle, and have to be increased or decreased in proportion. Once consumption has taken on social dimensions, the lifestyle becomes fixed in the expectations of others. Hence there is little room for substitution – we cannot make up for a deficient education with more entertainment or better transportation. (We can substitute potatoes for rice, but we can't get a balanced diet by substituting more potatoes for meat.) Given the categories that make up a lifestyle, we can't increase one without at the same time increasing others – we can't have more appliances without a larger house, or better appliances without more power. We don't need a better washer-drier unless we have better clothes; we don't need better cooking utensils unless we plan a more gourmet menu – but we may need all of these if we plan to live in a certain style, a style, which in turn, goes with a certain level of education.

This tendency on the part of different categories in consumption to stick together implies that even large changes in price may not lead to very noticeable changes in demand. In these circumstances, the price mechanism isn't going to work very well; on the other hand changes in the level of income will rather easily lead to proportional changes in all forms of consumption. So the multiplier will work. Which means an economy in which the paradoxes hold. The market will not reliably tend to realize the aims, the natural intent, of the system of production.

The tendency to shift from largely personal to largely social consumption not only undermines the ability of the market to adjust, but also prevents it from reaching socially efficient outcomes. For with these developments consumer preferences tend to become interdependent, not only with each

other, but also with those of producers. What consumers of entertainm_
want to see and hear is inextricably interlocked with what entertainers w_
to produce. The same holds for educators, and somewhat differently, for t_
planners of transportation systems, which will strongly influence future
growth. Nor can preferences be taken as 'given'; they are the result of complex
interactions, in which the power of money is not to be underestimated.
Consequently, many markets will not be competitive in the classic sense, and
if costs and benefits are not independent, the market will certainly not be
able to balance them.

Think back, now, to the earlier chapter in which we outlined the traditional
theory of value. According to this conception, the theory took as given
the endowments of basic resources, the preferences of individuals, and the
technology. On the basis of these givens, equilibrium prices and outputs were
determined, and, supposedly, shown to be socially optimal. The traditional
problems that have filled the pages of the professional journals are that
equilibria may not exist at all, or there may be multiple equilibria (so which
one is best? which one will be realized?), some or all of the equilibria may
be unstable, and so forth. But what we have just seen is that, for the system
as a whole, *none* of the traditional theory's 'givens' can be taken as given.
There are no 'endowments': the system creates the world as it goes along.
The development of technology is a response to the problems of the marketplace. And preferences evolve in response to the changes brought about by
market pressures and new technologies.

To put it another, simpler way: traditional markets were composed of
private producers and private consumers, where each agent was assumed to
be small and to act independently, taking the world as given. This is the
model that provides the basis for the claim that market relations are optimal
and consumers sovereign. In the era of the Craft Economy firms were small
and family run, consumers and producers were independent of each other,
production processes did run into 'diminishing returns', the world changed
slowly so 'endowments' could be taken as given, and so on. But in the modern
world none of these conditions are met. Economies of scale are widespread;
firms are corporate bureaucracies. Consumers are interdependent both with
each other and with producers; large groups of agents typically act together.
We are simply in a different world. In the simple 'private agent' models, the
external environment could be treated as given; but when the system as a
whole is considered, that is not possible. The traditional claims for the market
are just irrelevant.

THE TRANSFORMATION OF PRODUCTION

The changes in the technology of production have run along parallel
lines. Just as households have been de-skilled by the development of mass
production, so have the traditional crafts. Entire crafts have been embodied

in machinery, as mechanical energy has displaced human, and mechanical skills manual. The result has been an enormous increase in the productivity of labour, and a reduction in both work hours and in the intensity and effort required. But the very processes which at first helped the market to develop, and then transformed it into Mass Production, now, as we move to hi-tech, may be undermining its ability to function.

Artisan production was small scale, and depended on individual skills. Craft work reflects the skills of the craftsman, and the individual item often bears the mark of its maker. Mass Production, by contrast, is anonymous, produced by a large workforce, each member of which is a mere cog in the machine. As far as possible all items produced are identical. Long production runs of a single item or short list of items allow economies of scale to be realized. However, Mass Production depends on sophisticated engineering, which in turn requires the development of appropriate suppliers, especially for machine tools. The system cannot develop – or even maintain itself – without the high-level engineering sectors. Artisan production in a given line depended on the skills of the artisans in *that* sector. Mass Production in any line depends on the sophistication of basic engineering and machine tools.

More recently, processes initially producing a single product have increasingly developed into joint production, as uses have been found for by-products and wastes. (A mundane example: when my family first began to summer in Maine the local lumber mill gave away scraps and ends; later they began to split them to sell for home heating; now they process all scrap and market them as wood chips.) Formerly separate processes have been merged or run in tandem to take advantage of synergy or mutually advantageous externalities. (Think of the construction of modular homes.) The result is that various goods are produced together; in traditional Mass Production, the proportions in which they were produced were fixed, or at any rate could only vary within limits. Initially this meant that they would somehow have to be consumed in those proportions – or the excess of some would have to be disposed of. Or, if this couldn't be arranged, the consumers of some goods might have to go short. But the development of flexible Mass Production has changed this; joint production processes have become increasingly able to vary the mix of products to respond to customer wishes.

Just as consumers have become increasingly interdependent, so have producers; just as different consuming activities have become more closely complementary, so have different outputs.

The implications are the same. The price mechanism cannot work effectively if large blocks of goods have to be supplied together, whether in fixed or flexible proportions. But this is perfectly consistent with the working of the multiplier. The paradoxes will therefore be reinforced. Interdependence of outputs requires producer interaction and strongly suggests coordination with consumers; under these conditions neither the traditional model nor its conclusions are relevant.

HIERARCHY, OWNERSHIP AND THE FAMILY

Finally, of course, Mass Production has traditionally implied economies of scale, and the growth of externalities and joint production has opened further possibilities of this kind. Such economies imply that costs fall as size increases, which in turn means that scarcity does not lie on the supply side. Greater demand means cheaper costs of production.[2] Firms will invest in marketing and sales operations in order to expand their markets; they will set prices so as to maximize growth. Markets will adjust in new ways.

The Mass Production firm is completely different from the family firm of the Craft era. As production and consumption have undergone both quantitative and qualitative changes, so have economic organizations. The family firm became the modern corporation, which then grew into the transnational conglomerate. This is hardly an isolated change: The Night Watchman State became the Welfare State; the standing army became the Military–Industrial Complex.

As technology has changed, so have the organizations that administer it. These have grown both larger and more complex, and have become less rooted in the kinship system. Growth in size follows from the general growth of the system in conjunction with economies of scale; growth in complexity from the synergy which leads to the combination and joint operation of processes, and from the development of joint production through finding uses for by-products and waste. The problem of coordinating different kinds of activities makes the hierarchy more complex.

At one time most businesses were controlled through the family and were handed down from father to son. Many family firms still exist, though most are small and, perhaps regrettably, short-lived. But the major form of contemporary business, the modern corporation, has become independent of the kinship system, and represents a different principle of social organization. The family firm determines control and fixes succession through a patriarchal hierarchy. The father who runs the family runs the business, and the oldest son inherits, subject to various qualifications and special circumstances. But a corporation is an independent entity – a legal 'person' – completely separate from its 'owners', who do not and cannot own it directly. Instead they own shares, entitling them to vote for directors and officers; a controlling interest is therefore 51 per cent of the shares. But a controlling interest does not own the corporation or its assets. An individual or a family may own a controlling interest, and the shares may be passed on from generation to generation. But here again the market intervenes: it will seldom if ever be in an individual's interest to keep his funds tied up in the assets of a single corporation. If a portfolio is to be managed to maximize its growth/earnings, it will have to be diversified. Hence the family's interests over time will very likely lead to the loss of its controlling position. But in any case, stock positions are determined by portfolio management, on the basis of professional criteria for performance.

A corporation is controlled by directors and officers who are elected to represent certain interests; the actual directors are often selected by the interests on the basis of their knowledge and expertise. Corporations are actually run by managers who are appointed and promoted on the basis of their qualifications and experience. In contrast to the family, where appointment and succession is determined by birth, in the corporation it is determined functionally, by performance.

Interestingly, exactly the same can be said about the managers of portfolios. They are chosen on the basis of qualifications and performance, i.e. professional competence. Thus both the management and the control of the modern corporation are determined on the basis of functional, as opposed to kinship criteria, even when the assets are still in the hands of a family. Further, when the assets are professionally managed, it will usually be advantageous to convert them into a trust, making the former owners into beneficiaries. In other words, the ownership itself becomes an independent corporate person, controlled by trustees, who are elected by the beneficiaries and some overseeing institutions according to some formula. This is a far cry from determining control by birth, or through family.

The picture can be taken a step further. Consider a corporation, all of whose stock is held by other corporations, banks, insurance companies, each of whose stock, in turn, is held only by other institutions. The set of these institutions, taken together, constitutes a unit of capital completely independent of ownership by any individuals or families. These institutions own each other and taken together, own themselves. They form a self-perpetuating, self-subsistent independent entity, operating in the market in pursuit of profit. (Self-perpetuating so long as raiders can be fended off! But raiders just represent other blocs of capital.)[3] In other words, capital has created a new vehicle for ownership, to replace the kinship system. Capital is now owned in the form of financial assets, which in turn are owned and managed by financial corporations. Ownership and control are more and more decided in the 'market for corporate control'.

The separation of business activities from the kinship system is momentous. Skills and trades are no longer passed on from father to son; nor is the family firm handed down. Ownership itself is becoming increasingly separated from the family. One consequence, to be explored in a moment, is a withering of the family, as it ceases to be the vehicle for basic functions. Another is the breaking apart and re-development of the class system. A third is the formation – in the corporate world – of a new kind of power, centring on financial markets, leading very likely to new political forces, no longer tied (so closely) to kinship or (in the same way) to class.

EFFECTS OF EXTERNALITIES

These changes have been going on for a long time. At first they simply reinforced the effect of Mass Production technology, in which the market began to adjust to variations in demand through adapting output and employment, rather than by adjusting prices. In other words they reinforced the multiplier. But before long other consequences began to emerge, and these became sufficiently important to slow the growth of Net Economic Welfare relative to GNP. The most important is the increase in 'external' effects in production and consumption, for example, the production of polluting waste products by industrial processes, and the generation of garbage, especially solid waste, as a by-product of consumption (part of this being discarded packaging, designed to increase sales and consolidate markets.) These external effects are both negative and positive, but both kinds undermine the ability of markets to adjust. The positive effects, as we have just seen, link preferences of different consumers and also interlock consumption activities with the prospective behaviour and preferences of producers, making it difficult for price adjustments to work. The negative effects either reduce productivity (smog increases sick days, lowers efficiency on the job) or undermine well-being by destroying beauty or ruining health. But the market attaches no price to either the positive or the negative effects; no one has to pay to get the benefits, nor do they have to pay for inflicting the costs. The community bears the burdens, but no one pays directly. From the point of view of economic incentives, this situation is a disaster. Positive externalities should be encouraged, but since no price is paid directly, there is no incentive to maximize them; negative externalities should be discouraged, but since the producer faces no costs, there is no reason to minimize them. The market is not designed to cope with these problems. But the state cannot deal with them either, unless it is sufficiently independent to approach the problem disinterestedly, and powerful enough to impose a solution.[4]

The growing interdependence between consumers, on the one hand, and between consumers and producers on the other, creates another set of coordination problems which the market cannot handle. These are problems of scheduling. Each economic agent chooses the best time for his or her activity; but because the activities are interdependent, the result is a rush hour or a traffic jam, or a crowded beach – often with underutilized facilities at other times.

To paraphrase the poet, again: the market's a fine and private place, though none, I think, do there embrace. Not the way the poet wanted, anyway; the market tends to corrupt anything immaterial or spiritual that comes into contact with it. The incentives in the market are Machiavellian; the object, the attainment of wealth and power through whatever means are efficient and arguably legal. Hence when the market comes to deal with public goods, collective activities or social consumption, it will attempt to privatize them, in order to make money. Ideas are patented, works of art copyrighted – for once the language is perfectly clear, so they can be exploited. Every time you sing 'Happy Birthday' you owe a royalty, at least if you do it in a commercial setting. To privatize a public good or collective activity means to establish boundaries, fence it off, charge admission or user fees – in short to limit access to it. Inevitably this sets up two classes, those who can afford it, and those who can't. Exclusion tends to breed envy and frustration, which in turn breed anger and resentment, feelings very much in evidence today.

The growth in size and complexity of organizations makes the notion of a 'labour market' obsolete. More and more people pursue careers, rather than take jobs. A career involves regular promotions, which follow good performance, creating the paradox known as the 'Peter Principle', namely that promotion will cease when the job-holder reaches a level he or she can just barely handle. People will rise to the level of their marginal incompetence – and stay there. But they will be promoted out of any job they do really well. This picture is exaggerated and oversimplified, but there may be a dangerous element of truth in it.[5]

It also calls attention to the ubiquitous hierarchy that pervades modern life. Almost everyone has a 'boss' and manoeuvres for a pay rise or a promotion, or perhaps to supplant their boss. Many are called, but few are chosen, thereby adding further to the pool of frustration.

IMPACT ON THE WORLD

And the results are increasingly disastrous. Power is generated by market forces; evidently, wisdom is not. There are holes in the ozone layer, the average global temperature appears to be rising, the forests are disappearing and the oxygen level of the atmosphere may be endangered. Cancer is epidemic in the advanced industrial world. Products are produced and marketed on the basis of immediate appeal, regardless of long-term dangers. Beef tastes good, but too much causes heart disease. Not only that, the world has too many cattle, far too many, so many that now 'bovine gas emissions' are endangering the planet. Cow farts! Methane is a major greenhouse gas, and cattle produce an estimated 20–25 per cent of the annual emission. What kind of a world have we created, in which we have allowed *cow farts* to become so serious a problem that they figure on the agenda of international meetings! Is satire possible anymore?

But it's not funny. Whole areas of the earth are becoming uninhabitable, and species we have hardly discovered are dying out. Pollution of the oceans, rivers and lakes is killing off species at an unimaginable rate. Extinction is forever. We will never know what they could do for us – or against us!

Think of it this way: earth, air, fire and water – the four elements of the world, according to antiquity, are each being endangered by the contaminants generated as the by-products of industrial civilization. The soil of the earth is being eroded, blown away or washed into the deltas of the great river systems, or is being contaminated by nuclear by-products and chemical wastes. Air is polluted by industrial smoke, by the burning of garbage, and by automobile exhausts. For fire, read energy. Nuclear power has generated wastes we cannot find ways of storing, and emissions that threaten many forms of life. Even electrical transmission poses dangers – electro-magnetic fields apparently cause cancer. Coal-fired generation releases pollutants; high dams destroy ecological systems. As for the sun, our basic source of fire, the holes in the ozone layer are making sunlight dangerous and cancer-causing. Finally, water: ground water is being polluted by chemical waste, by run-offs from solid waste disposal and rivers and lakes are being destroyed by acid rain, while the ocean is polluted by dumping and oil spills. Each of the four elements of the world is endangered.

This is bad, but it's not all. These effects interact. Environmental degradation can become a self-reinforcing process, as for example in the formation of deserts, where growing aridity reduces vegetation, leading to changes in climate that reduce rainfall. Another example: soil erosion reduces vegetation, and therefore the absorption of polluting gases; air pollution and acid rain then increase, further reducing vegetation, which in turn promotes soil erosion.

Even worse, however, environmental degradation appears to interact with population pressure in many parts of the world. As the environment deteriorates, farming becomes more difficult, and the social services of poor governments are strained as people unable to support themselves on the land move to city slums. Here economic life is harder and more precarious, and the ties of the extended family are weakened. Children are the only asset poor families have. They can work, beg and/or steal. Being cared for by their children is the only hope for old age; to ensure this enough children must survive. Paradoxically, as conditions worsen, families will continue to have more children. But a growing population increases the pressure on the environment and on government resources.

Another set of problems that may become serious and world-wide, centres on the development of diseases. World travel has shifted bacteria and viruses from their normal habitats to new areas, where they have interbred with local strains, producing new and sometimes deadly variants. Regulation and restriction of travel for public health reasons conflicts with the desire to earn foreign exchange. The problem is compounded by a side effect of widespread antibiotic use. The market-driven use of antibiotics and 'wonder drugs' has led to a kind of natural selection: the strains of bacteria that survive are those resistant to antibiotics. The result is that new and deadly forms of old diseases are emerging. Restricting the use of antibiotics, however, runs against the interests of powerful drug and medical lobbies – to say nothing of what the public's reaction might be, if denied access to effective medication. These problems are likely to transcend national boundaries.

These vicious cycles must be confronted by policy, and it is unlikely that many Third World governments will be able to mount effective programmes unaided. Leadership will have to come from the advanced world – but the institutions of the advanced world are facing serious difficulties of their own. Advanced nations will have to reconsider many basic policies. Consider the market, to take a fundamental example.

GROWING DYSFUNCTIONALITY

In the past the pressures of the market generated innovations, growing productivity, greater control over nature and the environment, all of which contributed to growing affluence, for many, perhaps at times for all, households. Much of this remains true today, but the negative side effects and externalities may now be growing faster than the positive benefits. As an experiment, we can apply the market's own rules of calculation to this problem, in a rough and ready way, to see if and to what extent the pressures of the market will continue to benefit something like the 'average household'.

Consider on the one hand, the amenities and benefits that flow from the forces and pressures of the market, and let us suppose that we can aggregate them in monetary terms. These amenities will increase as the per capita wealth of the society expands, but certainly after a point, they will begin to increase less rapidly. That is, in the language of economics, diminishing returns will set in, since material incentives can be expected to weaken as people become richer (marginal utility declines) and in any case such incentives will work less effectively as consumption becomes increasingly collective, and therefore increasingly subject to social pressures other than monetary ones. As social goods, and goods with a collective aspect, increase as a proportion to all goods, market incentives will become less effective.

On the other hand, now consider the disamenities and negative effects of market pressures and forces, disamenities such as those we've just discussed. These can also be aggregated in monetary terms, and they can be expected not only to increase, but very likely to increase at an increasing rate, as per capita wealth rises. This will be particularly obvious in the case of pollution, the costs of which may well rise exponentially, if pollutants combine multiplicatively, but it may also apply to the growth of additional social costs in market situations – for example misinformation and/or corruption associated with marketing and selling, the costs of dangerous or unsafe but profitable goods (cigarettes, alcohol, cars 'unsafe at any speed') and so on.

Thus as wealth per person increases, the benefits of market pressures rise, but at a diminishing rate while the costs of such pressures also rise, but at an increasing rate. It should be inituitively clear that at some point these must balance – and at this point the market system will no longer be socially advantageous from the point of view of households, although it may continue to be profitable according to market calculations. Even earlier, however, that is, at an even lower level of wealth, there will be a point at which the *additional* (rising) costs of the system are no longer offset by the additional (falling) gains from it. So at that level of wealth per capita it would be desirable to cease to rely on market incentives as guidelines for further investment.[6]

What next? To say the least, the market is a hard act to follow.

9

INDIVIDUALISM AND THE DILEMMA OF THE STATE

And what lies ahead? How much further can we go down this road? The economy has pursued essentially the same path for six centuries now – can we go on forever? Or can we see the outlines of a new course emerging, even if only dimly? I would have to think carefully about this, to wrap the book up properly.

I let the water run through my hair, leaning back into the barber's bowl. Some light colour in my hair? I'm blond, I keep telling myself, and every summer while I worked as a lifeguard the sun turned my hair almost white. Only now it doesn't darken again in the winters. No colouring though; Vitamin E – and exercise. That will put the colour back; the natural way.

There's also the question of Monoxidil.

I don't want to think about it. Vitamin E – and L-cysteine . . .

'Man, have you seen the new patches, like the buttons, man, but better colour. Look, outta sight.' A patch to be sewn on a jacket, with a life-preserver, white on a dark background, around the earth, bright blue seas and green continents. 'Save the Earth' written on the life-preserver. The button had been produced last year, and was very popular, but he was right, the colours on the patch were even better.

'We're movin', my friend, rolling, rock and rolling. Musicians coming outta the woodwork. Maybe it won't be Woodstock II, but we're gonna have something, something big. Gonna be for the earth, man, and we're starting in New York, on Earth Day. It's all set, the whole day.' There had been a huge legal tangle over which of various groups, if any, would be allowed to use the Woodstock name for a concert this coming summer, the Twenty-fifth Anniversary. A reunion, I thought, just like Princeton. I like reunions. Maybe some of the same people? Perhaps not many.

'The brothers are going to Vermont,' I was in the chair now; some of my hair looks quite bushy, seen from the right angle. Haircuts are beginning to be quite trying; is he taking too much off, will it grow back? 'Going to the top of the mountain, for the gathering, night of the full moon. A lot of strong medicine, power-full. The north means white and wisdom, the east, yellow and illumination; the northeast is real power, magic.'

The 'gatherings' are spiritual events, as well as social ones, communions as much as communal. In Woodstock they are held the night of the full moon. A bonfire is built in Magic Meadow, and people gather at dusk, with musical instruments, drums and horns, pipes and guitars, but especially drums, and as the sun sets they begin to play and dance, gradually building up a shared spirit that expands and deepens as the moon comes up over the shoulder of the mountain. People come from all over the world, California, Texas, Mexico, Japan, Germany – everywhere. Woodstock is not only an artists, and writers, community; it is seen as a spiritual centre as well.

Environment and spirit, outer and inner well-being. These are the concerns of the new age. The earth is our home and we've been fouling our nest. 'Don't shit where you eat', says a local badge. And why do people continue to pollute the planet when it doesn't take much sense to know better? One answer, and an important one: because they have no spirit, because their sense of humanity is weak or non-existent. They're trying to possess the world and have lost the ability to feel it. In the pursuit of material wealth, they have failed to develop their spiritual sense. The two concerns go well together; the drop-outs of the 1960s and early 1970s certainly sought both.

In the parking lot in the centre of town, to one side, against a tall wooden fence, stood a rusted van, with a hand-painted sign in once-brilliant colours, decorated with flowers, showing a pig dressed in a dinner jacket and a tall hat, making a speech. On the panels of the van were scenes of the riot at the Democratic Convention of 1968. The sign read, 'NOBODY FOR PRESIDENT', and below, half-legible, could be seen a list of qualifications:

• Nobody can manage the deficit.
• Nobody understands the economy.
• Nobody can stop war.

There were more, many more, but the wood was warped and the paint had peeled. Still, I reflected, the ravages of time had not impaired the truth of these claims.

A different sort of local concern, worldly rather than spiritual, was on display in the parking lot. A table carried leaflets – there would be political workshops this summer in town, to celebrate the coming Anniversary. Subject: 'political empowerment', apparently the middle-aged version of 'power to the people'. Like the bewhiskered, white-haired flower children on the green in the middle of town. They're dancing as fast as they can, but the 1960s were a long time ago. Never mind, the 1990s are well under way. I looked over the list of topics, would I take part? In spite of the backlash represented in Congress, it revealed how far we had come: democracy, CIA and drugs, eco-feminism, US economic interest in the Third World, Media Disinformation – and also how far we still had to go. Certainly, I'd be delighted. The parking lot had the same problems as the barber shop

– environment, pollution, poverty, oppression – but the approach was to revive political activism rather than to re-awaken spiritual energy.

But, wait a minute. To go back to those famous re-union dinners, if the speakers were right, we can't afford this sort of thing. Cleaning up the environment and raising our spiritual awareness, let alone a new politics that would eliminate poverty, are luxuries. Look at the twin deficits – we can't pay for our own government, and we can't pay our way in the world. We need to cut back on everything in order to make resources available for growth.

We have seen that there are lots of things wrong with this line. Cutting back, for instance, is not the way to stimulate growth, and resources are not scarce. Far from it; many are unemployed. The problem is to generate enough demand, without upsetting the applecart on prices and starting inflation. Cutting back is exactly the wrong thing to do. Yet there's a problem which the pundits haven't considered at all, but which is very well understood in Woodstock. Growth has gone hand in hand with a deterioration in the quality of life. The goods delivered are no good, the services don't serve, things fray at the edges, the colours fade and the plastic curls and warps in the sunlight. Nothing has solidity, weight, soundness; the economy no longer gives us value for money. Even worse, we can't breathe the air, drink the water, or fish in the rivers. When I was growing up we always ate snow – it was so clean. Now it tastes terrible, and I warn my kids to be careful of it. We grow and grow, but how much better off are we?

CHANGES IN THE WORKING OF THE ECONOMY

A capitalist economy has to grow – there has to be investment – simply for it to function. But, as we have seen, growth is not simply a swelling-up of the system. In the present era as in the past, it leads to profound trans-formations in production and consumption, which, in turn, have further consequences for both households and businesses. Moreover, the eventual impact of these changes will be to change the way the economy works – for the very simple reason that once the present transformations have gone a bit further, the market system will face great difficulties trying to function unaided. Even with support from governments, it may prove unable to perform its traditional tasks. This at a time when markets are celebrated as never before! Yet it is apparent that, even today, significant intervention is needed to keep the system afloat.

Consider some of the problems lying in wait. Taking an obvious danger, inflation is likely to prove ingrained, for several reasons. For example, the increasing size and complexity of organizations means that jobs will continue to be arranged in differentiated hierarchies, in which rank is indicated by salary. But the incentive system requires that increases in productivity be rewarded with increases in pay. So if production workers raise their output and are rewarded, the wage–salary differentials will be eroded, leading to a loss of morale among lower-level managers. To maintain these differentials, salaries will have to be increased. Thus a particular rise in productivity can lead to a general increase in pay, to underwrite which, without reducing profits, there will have to be price increases.

On the other hand, it might seem that if primary production were to come more and more to resemble manufacturing, primary goods would tend to be less sensitive to changes in demand. This would tend to reduce an important cause of inflation. But if technical progress takes place only in manufacturing, it could make things worse. Increasingly sophisticated production will allow output and employment to adapt more quickly to variations in demand. This is all to the good, but what if technological development in manufacturing were not matched by corresponding progress in primary production? A rise in the speed of adjustment in the centre means that its level of demand for raw materials and primary products will change more rapidly. If primary production has not developed, it will have trouble adjusting. If the changes are also large, they will be likely to exhaust inventories and set off price increases, which will then enter into the manufacturing sector as cost increases, thus starting a round of inflation.

Unemployment is likely to become a more serious and widespread issue, for old and new reasons. First, as in the past, governments will try to control inflation by reducing demand. Second, improvements in technology will make it possible to increase output by improving or reorganizing present plant; whenever this happens investment will be less necessary. New technologies, on the other hand, may require scrapping and new construction. So, as always, investment is likely to fluctuate as these pressures alternate.

But at this juncture a new consideration may enter: the new technologies are not all simply improvements – some, the information systems, represent a change in kind. If they are to be adopted the scrapping and overhaul will be nearly total, and the firm's Table of Organization will very likely have to be changed. This is a big decision, and a risky one. Very reasonably, firms may be reluctant to make such changes – but, on the other hand, since the new technologies are on the horizon, it may not be worth while investing much in older systems, either. In short, investment may be drying up: it's too risky and entails too much reorganization to go all out for Information Systems, but the older technologies are no longer competitive, so not worth further investment. This may help to explain the slowing down of growth and the deepening stagnation evident even during the so-called 'boom' of the 1980s, but actually dating back to the early 1970s.

Investment is also becoming more international, as a consequence both of the increasing interdependence of consumption and production, and of the ease with which production can be controlled at a distance through information technologies. This is bound to stimulate world trade; but as world trade increases as a percentage of world GNP, the balance of payments blems of chronically deficit nations will worsen. To deal with these deficits, they will be pushed to adopt austerity policies requiring cutbacks, which in turn will have depressing multiplier effects on world capacity utilization. Thus a rise in world trade as a percentage of world GNP is likely to mean a rise in stagnationist pressures.

UNEMPLOYMENT AND HI-TECH

But there is a completely different set of reasons for unemployment to increase. The new information technologies will lead to labour-displacing innovations, and there is no guarantee that investment and aggregate demand will rise enough to offset the displacement. Not only is there no guarantee; it is highly unlikely in the long run that demand will rise sufficiently to create as many new jobs as innovation eliminates.

The conventional view is that this cannot happen. If a substantial number of workers are displaced in some area of the economy, the resulting unemployment will drive down real wages, leading firms in other areas to hire more workers, that is, to adopt labour-using methods of production, thus absorbing the displaced labour. Voila, no problem! But this is just the same old 'supply and demand' story again. This time the price mechanism supposedly works through the real wage. The first problem, of course, is that even where the labour market works through supply and demand (that is, where there are no contracts, tenure systems, collective bargaining procedures, etc.), what is established is the *money* wage, not the *real* wage. And why does this matter? Because the traditional argument about substituting labour for capital, or vice versa, is couched in terms of changes in real costs, money costs deflated by a price index. Employers are smart enough to know that what counts is not the current dollar cost, but cost in terms of real purchasing power. So nothing can be proved one way or another by an argument that shows how supply and demand will lead to a fall in the money level of wages. (In fact, traditional theory will tell us that if money wages come down, other things being equal, competition will force prices down, too!)

Labour costs are only one among many pressures that lead to technical innovation. Other costs are also significant; so is product improvement. But all the various pressures focus on the competition for markets, in which cutting labour costs ranks as one of the chief strategies. As a consequence there are always innovations to cut labour costs; and labour is always being displaced. Over the long run capitalism has dealt with this by reducing both the working week and the working day. There are pressures to reduce both – although the working week for many managers and professionals has been increasing! But in the short and medium term, hi-tech innovations are likely to lead to 're-engineering' and 'downsizing', bringing substantial unemployment.

PRIVATE POWER AND PUBLIC POLICY

Power and wealth can hardly remain unaffected by these changes. The growth of complexity in organizations and the shift away from kinship changes the nature of power. Ascent to the pinnacles depends more and more on effective performance, evaluated by the market; power itself comes to reside in the organization, and tends to be exercised through a system of committees. Control over the organization, in turn, is established in financial markets. Wealth, in its turn, tends to take on a larger and larger multiplicity of forms, increasingly market-managed and collective, that is, likewise residing in organizations. In short, as power and wealth become more institutionalized, they tend to be directed by committees, and to function more and more through markets. And for the most part, the controllers of power and wealth will wish to minimize the degree of government oversight.

But the changes taking place in the economy are generating problems that call for a greater, not a smaller, role for state intervention. The unaided market will be less likely to realize the potential in the 'system of natural intent', and indeed, will tend to lead the development of that system increasingly in problematical directions. This is perhaps becoming evident in the development of what has been called the emerging 'Information Economy', in which both manual and white-collar labour have been extensively replaced by computerized processes. As a result, companies become top-heavy with fixed costs; having displaced labour with automated, computer-run processes, they have comparatively few variable costs, so when demand falls, they cannot reduce their costs to match the drop in sales. Such companies are therefore more vulnerable to recessions.

So pressure for state intervention and policy control will develop, to try to realize the potential of the system of production. But this pressure will have to work through the system's political arrangements, which can be expected to reflect the underlying philosophy of individualism; in which the whole is simply the sum of the parts, implying therefore that the whole will work in the same way that the parts do. This is just what the paradoxes show to be wrong. If the political system is grounded on this belief, basic to the working of the market, then it is unlikely to be able to correct the impulses of the market.

TRENDS AND POLICY PROBLEMS

We can sum this up by pointing to five trends that have become increasingly evident in the last few years:

- the emergence of a new 'Hi-tech' sector;
- the decline of Manufacturing relative both to Services, and to Hi-tech;
- the decline both of middle management and of high-paying manufacturing jobs;

- the growth in size and importance of finance, and especially international finance;
- the increased mobility of capital both within the US and internationally.

These are all well-documented.[1] Each presents new policy problems, or makes it more difficult to carry out traditional policies.

- Hi-tech creates new pollution and workplace safety issues, e.g. chemical run-offs in the manufacture of chips and computer boards, and 'carpal tunnel syndrome' and eyestrain among keyboard operators. It has also increased the ability of capital to monitor and even control production from a distance, contributing to capital mobility. Electronic funds transfer makes it possible to shift huge sums of money rapidly. These shifts are hard to track – and impossible if security software is used. It is therefore easier to evade taxes and regulations.
- Capital mobility makes it harder to impose taxes on business: if taxes are raised, businesses may leave. It makes it harder to stimulate investment – the benefits of a tax credit may be a new factory across the border. Worse, capital mobility has meant that communities have had to face sudden losses of large numbers of jobs.
- The changes in the labour market brought by hi-tech have involved the phasing out of many high-paying mass production jobs. These have been replaced by lower-paying service jobs. This has contributed to the rise in poverty, and to the worsening of the income distribution, both of which contribute to stagnation.
- The growing importance of finance capital, and its increasingly international nature, have made it more difficult to use monetary policies to stimulate the economy. High interest rates, which contribute to stagnation, are often necessary to prevent short term capital flight. Lowering interest rates to stimulate the economy could lead to a run on the dollar.

In short, all these developments have weakened the traditional policy tools available to governments. Indeed, it could be argued that Keynesian policies could only be effective at the world level now – but there is no world authority that could impose such policies. This leaves world markets mired in austerity.

ANGER

Yet there is more to it. Not only does the market system seem to work less well than even two decades ago, not only don't we feel better off, a great many of us feel frustrated and angry, and some of us are murderously angry. GNP per capita may be the highest in history, and by some measures – though not others – may lie above that of any other country, but the level of social violence, always high in the US, has never been higher, and likewise exceeds that of any other advanced nation! Why is this?

The breakdown of the family, together with the rise of large organizations, and the attendant frustrations, intensified by largely uncompensated economic malaise, may be a root cause of the extensive social anger among large sections of the population. In Europe the breakdown of the family has been offset, at least in part, by the rise of extensive and comparatively well-funded professional social services. But in the US, anger is compounded by the lack of such services, as well as by perceived unfairness, which is by no means confined to the underclasses. The middle classes are just as frustrated and just as angry. Workers are angry with employers, as they lose their jobs, get laid off, or fail to get a pay rise or promotion. Students are angry with their teachers, teachers with school boards. Everyone hates the government and 'the bureaucracy', whatever it may be. Men are angry with women, as they leave the home, take jobs, compete, and assert their independent sexuality. Blacks and Whites and Orientals; Protestants, Catholics and Jews; WASPS and everyone else; rich and poor – whatever the divisions, civility has broken down under the rising tide of frustration. Teenage 'wolf packs' roam the parks and streets of cities; comics and TV stress violence and sadism, and so do the movies – but both are just based on the news. Statistics of violent crime are at an all-time high, and stand at an almost incredible level compared to any other advanced country – although a similar tide of anger, frustration and violence can be seen beginning to rise in Tory England.

JOTTINGS FROM WRITER'S NOTEBOOK – OVERHEARD IN THE BAR OF THE P.......N CLUB:

'Which d'you think is better, a 357 Colt Magnum or a 10mm [unintelligible]?'
'Depends on the price, I suppose.'
'$359 against $487; but I've already got a 357, stainless steel. Question is a new one.'
'Whaddaya want two guns for?'
'Shoot my wife.'
'Don't need two guns for that!'
'Maybe, maybe not. Other's for work, get people at work.'

Much of this anger finds its outlet in drug and alcohol abuse or in violent crime; some of the rest of it finds an outlet in society's reaction to drug abuse and crime, namely violent repression.

EITHER/OR

But neither the substance abuse nor the repression are simply reactive. Both also have a basis in the philosophy of individualism. For, as we shall see, that decrees two and only two possible responses to social issues: laissez faire, or prohibition. Either/Or. The individual can do whatever he or she wants to do, so long as they do not intrude on the similar rights of others. Buying and selling, using your property, saying whatever you like – it's up to you. Nobody can tell you to put on a seatbelt or a helmet. The State cannot regulate the choices of the individual. It can only enforce the basic rules of property and contract. From this perspective, then, drugs, sex, alcohol, abortion, whatever, are similarly up to the individual. Anything goes; the cowboys ride the range, land is free and so is life.

But on the other hand, the State must defend the basis of the social compact. Anything which will undermine this must be prohibited. Hence some things are beyond the pale; and in that case there is complete Prohibition. The Moral Law – derived from the social compact – places certain acts out of bounds; there is no argument and they are forbidden absolutely. Therefore they must be outlawed. War must be declared on these acts and on those who engage in them – as in the 'War on Drugs'.

Of course, there is no agreement about where to draw the line – a woman has rights over her body, a foetus has a right to life. Anyone has a right to consume anything, drugs, liquor, candy, whatever; on the other side, drugs, alcohol are immoral, absolutely. If it is permissible, then it is your *right*. You can choose, it's your business and no one else's. So no one, least of all the State, should interfere. But if it runs counter to the fundamental law, then it must be prohibited absolutely, since it is a violation of *everyone's* rights.

The idea that the problem is to regulate a market for something much-desired, which, however, has a number of seriously undesirable side-effects or ramifications – 'externalities' – simply does not enter the discussion. If it is your right to choose to do or buy something the State has no business interfering, at all. There is no ground for disapproval or discouragement. If it isn't wrong, that is, such as to undermine the foundation of everyone's rights, then it is permitted, and the State has no business taking a stand on the matter. The gospel: markets should not be regulated, and immoral goods should not be marketed. As for why drugs are desired, why life is so unsatisfying, why there is so much anger – those questions are not only not raised, they are positively buried. How can life be generally unsatisfying when everyone is doing what they have freely chosen in the marketplace? How can people be angry and frustrated when they are doing exactly what they want to do?

There is an important corollary, however. When individual freedom and prohibition are the twin policy attitudes of the state, a substantial market in forbidden fruit can be expected. And compared to the previous century, trans-formational growth has had an impact on communications and transport, reducing the costs and increasing the mobility of traffickers in illicit goods. Large cities provide anonymity. Everything is faster and less costly. Concealment is easier. The technological improvements seem to have helped the growers and sellers of forbidden fruit more than they have assisted the police. The impact of police efforts is chiefly to drive up the price.

CRIME AND CORRUPTION

During my Junior year in High School Joey G.....'s family moved from Cicero into a large new house in Riverside. Joey joined our class; swarthy, fat, soft, and unprepossessing, he was hardly a candidate for the popular circles – except that, courtesy of his father, he drove a brand-new, white Cadillac convertible with plush red leather seats. And he was all too willing to drive us anywhere, anytime, just to be included. That was what his father, a larger, tougher version of Joey, wanted; 'just take him along; any expenses, you come to me', a thick wad of notes in one hand, 'no problem'.

Indeed, money seemed to be no problem. Joey always had plenty, and was willing to share it, as long as he was included, as quickly happened. Our parents were less accepting, and more sceptical. It seemed that Joey's father was a 'labour leader'. A *labour* leader?! Riverside had stockbrokers, not union members. Why would a labour leader move to Riverside, and where would he get that kind of money?

Then Senator Kefauver came to town, holding hearings on the mob and racketeering, and the headlines told us what kind of a 'labour leader' Joey's dad was, and where he got his money. After the indictments they sold their house, and we never saw Joey again.

A *labour* leader. We usually think of organized crime as a business supplying forbidden fruit, providing what we as a Puritan society regard as illicit pleasures – sex, drugs, liquor, gambling and the like. And that is indeed the foundation of crime as a business. Individualism permits everything that is not explicitly forbidden – but to guarantee freedom it establishes checks and balances on the power of the state, ensuring that the various Prohibitions cannot be effective. Indeed, the checks and balances tend to turn into paychecks and bank balances for well-placed officials. Prohibition drives up the price and creates huge profits, with which the successful entrepreneurs can corrupt public officials in order to maintain and expand their domain of operations.

But this is only the tip of the iceberg. Once established, organized crime becomes a part of capital – a very special part, however, providing important services to other parts of capital and to the state. Labour racketeering is one such service. For example, during World War II the OSS (forerunner of the CIA) cut a deal with Lucky Luciano to obtain the help of the Mafia first in keeping discipline in the New York docks, then in gathering intelligence for the invasion of Sicily; later the deal was expanded to include services fighting the influence of the Communists in Italian and French unions. In return, it has been suggested, the CIA – or some officers acting 'deniably' – agreed to help clear the way for the restoration of the New York heroin trade, which had pretty much dried up during the war. As for labour racketeering, the Mob's services in breaking strikes and preventing the rise of radical or political unions has been well documented.

The Mob. Like the outlaw of the wild west, the image carries a resonance of glamour and romance, it exudes resolution and enterprise, hot blood and cold cash – the very stuff of Hollywood Americana. The outlaws have gone the way of the buffalo; not so the Mob. It is omnipresent, everywhere, in fact, that there is something prohibited – drugs, gambling, sex, you name it, and from such bases it spreads, offering corruption and special services to those in need of either. The effect is to weaken the state; it no longer has a monopoly on violence and force. The police are not masters in their own house, regional governments are not in full control. It also undermines civic spirit – who can take pride in a corrupt city? It weakens labour, and prevents the development of effective unionism, capable of exercising constraints on the prerogatives of capital, thereby contributing to abuses of corporate power. And it contributes to the growth of a pervasive cynicism.

The pervasiveness of organized crime will make it more difficult for the state to control and direct the evolution of technology and the market. Individualism poses a dichotomy between liberty and prohibition, which gets embodied in the combination of a constitutionally fragmented government and a set of absolutely prohibited activities. But the fragmented government is incapable of enforcing the prohibition, and the consequence is widespread, endemic and highly profitable corruption.

DEMOCRACY IN DECAY

Endemic corruption, coupled with economic stagnation and an inability to project a convincing vision of the future – the 'vision thing' in President Bush's typically eloquent phrase – breeds a contempt for politics and politicians. With the end of the Cold War there is no external threat to pull people together; the system has no excuse for not delivering the goods. But to maintain the prerogatives of capital – control – it must pursue austerity; yet if austerity is the policy, it can't deliver full employment and a rising standard of living.

From another perspective: the new technologies offer wonders. There are fabulous opportunities, in bio-tech, computer control of production, new products in information and communications, and all the rest. Genetic engineering will transform our ability to control diseases; it may enable us to choose (some of) the characteristics of our children. We will certainly be able to alter the characteristics of domesticated animals. Genetics and computers may interact – biological computers are possible, and computer programs have been shown to evolve! And advances are being made in the application of lasers, in the formation of new materials, and on many other fronts.

To take advantage of these amazing new technological possibilities, to experiment and open up markets, business seeks the maximum freedom from restraint and regulation. But the public requires protection from defective and dangerous products, and from potential environmental disasters. And people have to come to terms with the moral implications of the new possibilities. Should we choose the characteristics of our children? Should we create new animals? Who should make these decisions? Who will be responsible if, or better, when, things go wrong? (As an example, one hypothesis about the origin of AIDS, reported in the *Economist*, suggests that it may have spread from monkeys to humans via a vaccination serum developed from monkeys using new bio-tech methods, then widely used on an experimental basis in Africa. Even if this is wrong, it suggests the magnitude of the dangers inherent in the new technologies.[2]) Capital wants full steam ahead (thoroughly outdated metaphor!); the public needs time and protection. The interests of Capital and the Public are in direct conflict; an exceptionally skilful diplomat might weave a policy that could satisfy both, but a stalemate, leaving both unsatisfied, seems more in tune with the times.

A lot of industries do not want effective regulation in the public interest, since it would mean down-sizing or eliminating them. Tobacco, for example. Cigarettes kill over 400,000 Americans a year; cocaine, crack and heroin combined, at most a few thousand, and marijuana none. But the media trumpet the dangers of drugs – and hardly mention tobacco. Of course, the tobacco companies and their subsidiaries have large advertising budgets. Then there is beef; it is not good for us, and the world's huge cattle population is an ecological nightmare. Another example: the US government has been successfully trying to revive the American auto industry – yet the *annual* deaths and injuries due to traffic accidents are on the scale of the *total* deaths and injuries in the Vietnam War! Moreover, cars are the worst polluters; ribbon development, shopping malls and highways figure among the worst destroyers of scenic environments. A rational approach would try to gradually reduce our dependence on and use of, products like tobacco, beef and automobiles – among many others – replacing them with alternatives less deadly and destructive. But this is not happening, and is not going to happen as long as politics is dependent on private donations for campaign funds, and people know it.

A crisis of legitimacy appears to be in the making, and not only in the US, though it may be further advanced here. All through the advanced industrial world voters are registering protests and polls indicate dissatisfaction with the options the system presents. Voting participation is down, indicating that potential voters are not happy with the choices facing them. As this is written, neo-Fascists are on the march in Europe, winning elections in France, Austria and Italy, and street battles in the cities of the former East Germany; military coups have been threatened in Venezuela, long the most stable democracy of Latin America, and civil war has ravaged Peru, while democracy is weak and unstable elsewhere. In the US a right-wing revivalist movement has captured Congress. The Welfare State no longer seems satisfactory, even in Scandinavia. Something is rotten, and not only in the state of Denmark!

THE DILEMMA OF THE STATE

We can now pose what may be the central issue of our times, the dilemma facing the state in the advanced industrial world. On the one hand the problems of ecology and potential environmental catastrophe, together with the increased need for regulation, in the interests of safety and for direction in the development of technology, call for a more active and interventionist state. Such needs are underlined by the weakening of family and community ties, which make it clear that the burden of caring for and socializing children is likely more and more to fall on the state, or on other collective agencies. But on the other hand, the opportunities for market development, for capital investment and restructuring and for innovation call for cutting back red tape and regulation, especially in outdated or corrupt and out-of-touch bureaucracies. The world is changing, new markets are emerging, and governments, responsive to the status quo, tend to stand in the way. Yet given the rise in collective goods relative to GNP, the market will increasingly give wrong signals.

To cope with the terrible problems facing us governments have to expand, modernize, develop new powers and new programmes. They will have to take the lead in defining and solving the problems facing the *system as a whole*. These simply cannot be handled by private markets or by non-profit institutions. And at stake is no less than the project of saving the earth! But at the same time the powerful incentives of the market system will lead business and the profit-driven, development-oriented classes to try to cut back on regulations and interference. Business must modernize, capital must become international, must develop new institutional forms, as new technologies, and even whole new industries, like bio-tech, are forming.

A danger point is approaching. The system faces a crucial stage where markets, families, the moral code, and even the state itself, are subject to pressures that will force major changes in their nature and functioning. Yet these are the foundations of society; moreover they are interlocked. The state rests on the market and the family – taxes are collected from market activities, and citizenship is defined by birth; the market depends on the moral code; family expenditure is one side of the market. The market is regulated by the state, the family is supported and the moral code enforced by it. The family inculcates morals and loyalty to the state. And so on. But all are simultaneously under pressure from forces that are largely generated at the level of the system as a whole. But the effect of these pressures has been to weaken both the state and the institutions that support the state.

The dangers go well beyond breakdown of the economy, bad as that would be. To restore the moral code, there may be a turn towards religious fundamentalism; to re-establish the authority of the state, a turn to neo-Fascism. To restore the strength of the market, regulation might be stripped away. These all fit together, and can be supported by nationalism and familiar doctrines of ethnic or racial superiority. A failure to handle today's economy – a widespread crisis that hits hard – could well bring political disaster tomorrow!

(To add to the complexities: repressive political regimes may prove self-defeating in the era of information technologies. Competitive success will very likely depend more and more both on a large market and on innovation, of a kind resulting from interaction with the market. Such an interactive market, in turn, depends on education and communication, which will have to be uninhibited and widespread, if not universal, conditions that would tend to undermine a repressive regime.)

These are the problems and conflicts that will shape the politics of the future, that will create the drama of our age, yet we hardly heard a whisper of any of this those nights at the Princeton Club. And why not? Because the terms in which we discuss economic and political issues don't recognize the problems of the whole. The larger forces shaping the movement of history cannot be seen, because history itself is defined in terms of individual rational choices, grounded in given preferences. Markets are aggregates of individuals, driven by self-interest. Markets sum up dollar choices, politics voter choices. Markets must be free of interference, politics must be free of corruption. Then the outcomes will truly reflect the preferences of individuals. Consider the favourite phrases of the speakers: Supporting 'private enterprise', encouraging 'consumer confidence', being 'free to choose', having 'self-reliance', relying on 'private initiative', responding to 'incentives' – these catchwords all reflect the centrality of the individual. There is an underlying philosophy here. 'Econobabble' is individualism!

Individualism

The philosophy of individualism may have provided both a useful way of thinking and practical guidance in life at an early stage in the development of capital. The seamless world of traditional society was breaking apart, and the pieces were being recombined. To think of social wholes as composed of individuals associating through free choice fitted well with events, and provided both a critique of the old order and a justification for the new. But with the flowering of both production and consumption into social or collective forms it is no longer appropriate.

Individualism plays such an important part in the way we understand the world and our place in it, that it is worth a moment to examine it in a systematic manner, starting with the foundations of being and knowledge, and carrying through to the world of social life.

Ontology

- To be, as object, is to be perceived by an individual.
- To be, as subject, is to be an individual; to exist, is to be able to perceive, to think, to make decisions.

The ultimate constituents of the world are objects and subjects, where objects are known only because perceived by individual subjects, a sort of Berkeleyan dualism. The individual subject is the ultimate knower, whose existence is attested by the *cogito*.[3]

Epistemology

- Knowledge arises from the perceptions and thinking of individuals.
- Knowledge is carried by, resides in the minds, of individuals.

Knowledge is a construction, by individuals, out of sense-data and perceptions, a position which gives rise to the problems of solipsism and the puzzle of induction. Theories are perceptions of regularities among facts; other minds are known because the outward manifestations in behaviour are similar to our own. We posit the feelings and thoughts of others because such posits explain what we perceive.

Social Theory

- Society is the sum of the individuals who compose it, and does not exist apart from them, their preferences and their (implicit) contracts.
- Society's values and mores are the sum (or product) of individuals' preferences and choices.
- Value arises from individual preferences and choices and is best expressed through the market or through democratic voting.
- Motivation is governed by self-interest.

This is the position of methodological individualism, and is reflected in the way mainstream economics thinks about markets. It is the basis of mainstream thinking on democracy.

Moral theory

- Individuals ought to be free to do as they choose, subject only to the right of all others to do likewise.
- Acts which undermine the ability of individuals to freely express themselves and freely associate are immoral and must be prohibited.

This is the point at which the dichotomy of liberty versus prohibition arises. The latter is simply the mirror image of the former; if liberty is absolute, anything which undermines liberty must be absolutely prohibited. Individual freedom plus motivation by self-interest, of course, leads to behaviour in accordance with the Machiavellian code, modified by Hobbes.

History

- Innovation springs from the ideas of individual geniuses.
- History is shaped decisively by the decisions and actions of great men.

Certain connections almost jump out. If everything that exists is an 'individual', or an object of an individual's perception, then knowledge has to be knowledge of individuals by individuals, and, most importantly for our purposes, society *must* be (nothing but) the sum of the individuals that compose it. It follows that the correct method of social inquiry must be to examine the preferences and choices of individuals – or so-called 'methodological individualism'. Institutional acts and rules will have to be explained as shorthand for a full description of the acts and relationships holding between the individuals involved. In particular, the market must be a construct derived from individual choices and acts, and value must be a projection of individual preferences. We can only learn the laws of the market by studying the behaviour of individuals and aggregating. (There cannot be any such thing as 'the natural intent of the system of production'.) Similarly the state must be based on contracts between individuals, and its actions and laws, will be a construct out of their choices. And if individuals are what exist, then history has to be the history of individuals.

As both production and consumption shift from individual to social, and as organizations shift from a kinship to a functional basis, the philosophy of individualism becomes harder and harder to sustain. The family itself, both extended and nuclear, loses its central place, as its functions are progressively stripped from it. This is symbolized by the shift in the meaning of the word 'private', formerly denoting the sphere of the family, the household, self as opposed to other, now signifying the sphere of business as opposed to government. The private world of today is not a world of individuals; it is the world of corporate business, indeed, of what are properly called public companies, ironically enough. The social position and power of a person today is defined largely by his or her job, i.e. place in an organization. There is very little scope for autonomy, even for the rich, whose money has to be managed professionally if it is to be kept intact.

The philosophy of individualism is defective at its roots. It suffers from the logical flaw that individuals – persons – are *produced* – they don't spring into life full-blown and live forever. They, or rather, we, are conceived, born, grow up, learn, work and live and die, to be replaced by others. We 'individuals' are social creatures, and what we are, what we can do, what we know and what we value, all are the results of social interactions, with our parents, teachers, friends and employers. And books and movies and radio and television. Far from society being a logical construct out of individuals, individuals are the products of society. This is not to *deny* the autonomy of the individual – but it certainly limits it. Genuine autonomy is rare, but all the more important for being so. In short, individualism has it the wrong way around.

As a result, it meets problems at every level in understanding social issues. To take some examples: philosophically, the apparent existence of other kinds of entities – 'universals' like colours, ideas, forms – has to be explained away, showing that these are dependent on individuals and not vice versa. In treating knowledge as arising from and residing in the individual's mind, the problem of solipsism – 'other minds' – is created. In social theory, there is the matter of 'reducing' institutions – rules, laws, official decisions or acts, roles, obligations and powers of offices, etc. – to purely individual behaviour without covertly presupposing other institutions. Individualistic economics requires the reduction of the social relationship 'capital' to a marketable commodity with a price (the rate of interest). In general, production and consumption both have to be explained in terms of choices, rather than in terms of the duties, obligations and privileges that go with socially defined (class and organizational) positions in a structure that reproduces itself and, in the process, develops. The movement of history must be the simultaneous outcome of the free choices of independent individuals. And so on.

When a theory serves an important social function (something hard to explain exclusively in terms of individual preferences!) it comes to no harm as a result of having serious logical problems. Far from it; such problems simply define the research programme for the theory's well-padded adherents.

The social function of individualism has been to explain and justify the central role of the market, and to mediate its relation to the state. Individualism as a philosophy explains the derivative nature of both state and market, as constructs out of individual behaviour and preferences, which are fundamental. The better and more freely individual choice is expressed, the more the result deserves to be respected; thus the market should take priority over the bureaucrat. The state should interfere only when it is clear that the market mechanism has broken down or is functioning improperly.

But the advent of Mass Production created widespread need for state regulation and intervention; moreover, it changed the working of the market dramatically, creating the paradoxes of individualism. The on-going processes of transformational growth are now carrying these changes further, to the point where the market may not be able to function effectively in respect to the system of natural intent. But none of this can be understood in terms of individualism. For the individual the world is given, for the whole it is in the process of being created. Nothing is given at the level of the whole – the world which we, as individuals, must take as given, is created as we develop collectively. That is the paradox of transformational growth!

The Philosophy of Individualism which once helped people involved in the market to see clearly and make constructive decisions, now stands as a barrier to our ability to understand what is happening and how the system is developing.

THE ANSWER ... AND A NEW QUESTION

So we can now turn to the Question from which we began on that fateful evening at the Princeton Club, the Question I had so rashly posed, and then found myself unable to answer. Why can't our leaders understand the larger significance of what they are doing? Why can't they see the dilemma facing the state today? Because they examine their own roles and behaviour through the lens of the Philosophy of Individualism, they assume that the whole functions in the same way, according to the same laws, that regulate the parts. They assume that the development of the institutions of society can be explained by understanding the psychology of individuals, and that economic development in particular results from the interaction of individual choices made under the constraint of natural scarcity. Nor do they make these assumptions lightly; indeed, they could make no other. This is the philosophy, the world-view, on which they – and we – have been brought up, which we imbibed along with, perhaps not our mother's, but certainly our school milk, which we spelled out in our term papers and senior theses at that great and idyllic University that haunts our collective past, the philosophy that underlies every reference to the market on the evening news, that props up the pomposity of every pundit.

So, that is the Answer. But what do we do about it? Ah, now that is a new Question. One at a time, please. Of course, if you must ask, there is a simple answer to this new question: we develop a new philosophy, something like Social Humanism, and then we persuade everyone that it is both the best and the most useful way to understand the world, and we begin to reorganize our affairs accordingly.

And what would this philosophy be? It would start from the existence of universals, as well as individuals; it would find knowledge based on transcendental laws of thought; it would establish that social wholes can function according to different laws than social parts, including 'individuals'. It would examine the evolution of these social wholes, and seek to grasp the underlying forces driving this evolution. It would develop a new morality, based on the 'constructions of reason', to adopt the phrase of perhaps the leading thinker in the field. And it would draw on this morality to guide the forces driving the evolution of the system. There are many forms such a philosophy could take, many different emphases. But however it develops, it would have to establish the independent existence of the social structure, and the determining relationship it has to the concrete individual, who is necessarily its product. It would have to relate people to the earth that is their home, and to each other in their common humanity. It must give us the rational foundation we need for a new ethics to replace the outmoded traditional code.

Simple phrases cover complex realities. 'We' can't begin to reorganize our affairs unless and until 'we' can take political control of them. And that means establishing a new relationship between those with power and privilege and those who are affected by the decisions of the powerful and privileged. Forty percent of American children today are growing up in poverty. The Princeton Club needs to be opened up a little – or perhaps a lot. Whatever the merits of our democracy it is too easily manipulated by money. Nearly three-quarters of American adults today cannot read or do arithmetic at the sixth-grade level! The well-to-do in America pay lower taxes than the wealthy in any other advanced country. Yet the speakers at the Princeton Club that evening were unanimous that there was no conflict between the demands of profit and the needs of people.

Back in the parking lot they were working on the political consciousness of the next millennium. 'We' can't persuade people that there is a better way to think about the world unless and until 'we' can touch their hearts, make them feel the world in a new awareness, make them love it as the home of humanity. Back in the barber shop they were playing music and working on the spiritual re-birth that would happen with the turning of the century.

Is this going to happen? Will the Woodstock Nation ever join the Princeton Club? Or vice versa? Could they ever be happy together? We'll have to wait and see.

EPILOGUE
The world as seen from Woodstock

The world system is changing; the US is no longer supreme and unchallengeable. The Cold War is ending, but paradoxically, the danger of hot war may be greater than ever. Unless the next half century sees significant development in the Third World the turmoil there may engulf us all. But if Third World industrialization follows the same course as that of the First and Second Worlds, we will be lucky to survive the environmental disasters that will follow. This is the dilemma of our times, and it has to be managed at the level of the whole.

Yes, yes; this is all true. But that is not it; it's not the right note to end on. How can I finish? What is the *message* that I want to leave with the reader? The one thing they will really remember? Walking up the hill, following the winding road, the brook to one side, I tried to put my thoughts in order. The mountain stream sparkled in the dappled sunlight. You couldn't see the dying fish. The mossy rocks glistened; the moss had grown so much from the run-off of chemicals that walking in the stream was dangerous. A tourist up from the city, wading on a recent Fourth of July, slipped and broke his ankle, he said – and then sued my neighbour for possessing an 'attractive hazard'. Up to that time my neighbour, a genial socialist and famous sculptor, had permitted bathing in the rock pools dotting his portion of the stream. No longer. His insurance company settled out of court, cancelled his policy, and advised him to put up a chain-link fence! He drew the line at that, but there are plenty of 'No Trespassing' signs everywhere. Not even my children can swim there now.

Not that they're here all that much. I just got a post-card from Bali – forked-tongue lizards with double-jointed penises. Symbolic of what? Just what an 18-year old on his trip around the world would send. His older brother, now at Oxford, sent post-cards from Khajurao. I liked those better. The girls – children of my second marriage – spend most of the year at boarding schools. They want to come home all the time, but I travel a lot. As the cliche says, family life is not what it used to be.

The top of the hill was graced with a birch grove and a view, as a steep cliff fell down to a forested valley. The highest mountains of the Catskills

197

rose a lush and leafy green in the middle distance. I remembered a peak in the Bavarian Alps looking West to the Black Forest, great patches of brown blotching the evergreen slopes. 'As far as you can see,' said the Professor of Political Economy from Frankfurt, 'one-third of all the trees are dead or dying.' Acid rain is killing the Catskill fish, but has not reached the trees.

But the message is not to be found in forests and streams. Ecological devastation is nothing new – the Sahara is said to be man-made. Our relation to the earth is part of the equation, but not the whole. Nor does our issue lie with the tourist, or his simulated anguish, making money at the expense of the general interest – though he, too, shame of Machiavelli, plays a part. As do my children, scattered across the globe, longing to come home to a family that never existed.

The progressive destruction of our environment, erosion of traditional values, and disintegration of the family are usually treated in separate compartments. But they should be considered together, for they reinforce one another. As traditional values weaken, people are more inclined to trash the environment if they can get away with it; people care less about making their marriage work for the sake of the children. Disintegration of the family in turn means that traditional values will not be developed and passed along to the next generation. The erosion of the environment, in turn, destroys the traditional setting for the family, and intensifies the pressure to scramble for whatever can be had in the twilight of the age. The result is a progressive society-wide deterioration in the quality of life, materially, socially and spiritually.

Even more important is the fact that all three stem from the same pressures that have so stimulated the development of technology and the growth of industry – the pressures that arise from the Machiavellian working of the market, the institution that has so largely forged the world we live in, but now bids fair to destroy it.

The family is disintegrating. What can replace the family? Traditional ethics no longer provides guidance. What can replace the traditional code? Markets give the wrong signals, and generate excessive social costs. In the development and reproduction of society, what can take the place of the market? A new family, new values, and a new economic order – without these we shall risk ending up impaled on the horns of our dilemma. But where are they to be found?

Well, Woodstock was a good place to start looking. Communes have existed here since the end of the nineteenth century. Radical groups including the American Socialist Party used to meet in the 1920s at Overlook Mountain House. The 'Woodstock Nation' was an attempt to establish a countercultural political movement, to put new values and a new consciousness into practice. To develop a new philosophy, beyond individualism, and build a new society. Woodstock, of course, is only a symbol. The search for new forms of family living and new institutions to educate and socialize children has a long history, from Plato's *Republic* through Israeli kibbutzim to the many and varied American communes. New thinking on values ranges all the way from progressive thought in the Churches across bioethics and ethics courses in medical and business schools to the teachings of New Age gurus. Some of this may be nonsense, just as some of the attempts at new forms of collective living may be disastrous. But it is imperative that we look critically at them all, for the old ways are in a state of irreversible decline. (As for reviving the traditional ways, the fundamentalist preachers seem to have adopted a strikingly simple criterion of success – making money.)

But not even Woodstock has given thought to how to set up a new economic order. Replace the market? A few of the early socialists wrote about it, but they were dismissed even by Marx as 'Utopians'. Some of the 1960s radicals talked about it, but never got past rhetoric. The Cambodian Khmer Rouge abolished money when they seized power; they drowned in the blood they spilled. The centrally planned economies did not provide an attractive model; and in any case they have collapsed. Besides, they operated according to Machiavellian rules, and often implicitly relied on markets.

But we earlier remarked on the success of the small, homogeneous and egalitarian 'intermediate' economies – Austria, Sweden, Norway – where detailed planning and regulation are mixed with market incentives. Their homogeneity means that planning can be governed by a consensus on values, while the existence of the market allows space for innovation and competition. This may be just what is needed – employment, fair incomes, safe working conditions, education and social services are guaranteed to all citizens, but there is also room for competition and the play of money and power, under the aegis of an overall framework that circumscribes the game and regulates the play, preventing it from endangering the public. Planning and regulation have to *contain*, not displace, the market; but planning and regulation must be carried out rationally and fairly, in accordance with a general consensus on values. In these circumstances the state can guide the development of the market – Alec Nove's 'feasible socialism'. In principle, the problem is easy; in practice, to say the least, it is quite another story.

Even so, this only handles today's problems; it replaces austerity with expansion. Yet even today this is difficult to sustain for individual nations. As the paradoxes show, the market gives the wrong signals at the level of the system as a whole, requiring correction. The 'whole' today is the world market – but there is no world authority to organize and impose a transnational policy of expansion. And by tomorrow the fundamental mismatch between the requirements of the 'system of natural intent', the structure of normal economic activity, and the day-to-day working of the market can only have worsened. In addition, the market is not equipped to handle joint production and collective consumption, yet that is where innovation is taking us. Circumscribing the market doesn't correct its misdirected movements. Yet even circumscribing the market is going to be difficult, given the growing pressure to cut back state intervention and power. The market generates incentives and innovations for private profit – but public goods are becoming more important. The market will no longer deliver what is needed; it will therefore have to be redefined. But how?

It is clear that the market is not going to be abolished, Cambodian style. Yet it could be changed. When it gives the wrong signals or generates the wrong results, corrective pressures are bound to arise. If these pressures remain *ad hoc* they will be ineffective, and the cumulative impact of market mis-direction will erode the economic base. Once these correctives become *institutionalized*, however, the market itself will begin to change, since anticipations of future developments will have to take the corrective forces into account. Costs are the reflection of rights and contracts in the mirror of economics, so that changes in rights or contracts will change the structure of costs, influencing market strategies, and the working of markets.

For example, if long term workers are given vested rights in their jobs and incomes, a large portion of labour costs become fixed. This both supports consumption spending, and reduces the ability of business to adjust costs when sales fluctuate. And by reducing the proportion of variable costs in total costs it reduces the multiplier. A correlative, however, might be changes in financial contracts, allowing for greater variability in interest and dividend payments. These two changes together would tend to shift the burden of adjustment to changes in aggregate demand from labour to capital, a major change in the working of the market – and a major gain in well-being for people.

Using pension funds to control capital in the interests of workers, consumers and citizens can help to establish 'industrial democracy', to me an old-fashioned phrase. But control is not much use without a sense of direction, and that can no longer be provided by the market. But it is not clear that the political system can fill the void. Taxes and subsidies are necessary to influence business to take account of externalities. A massive effort to develop non-polluting, renewable sources of energy is required. The world has to shift out of fossil fuels. But this would require a political system powerful enough to impose costs on – and grant benefits to – business, there-fore wise enough to choose winners and losers. It is not likely that the political system of the US will prove able to do this. Indeed, what is needed is a re-alignment of the 'public' and 'private' spheres. The bundle of rights we know as 'private property' will have to be increasingly broken up into compo-nents and devolved on various agents. The bureaucracies of the state will have to be broken down, and redefined to allow for 'customer' pressures and competition. As pressures build, groups will demand rights – the right to a job, for example, or to an education, to have clean air and safe water. Or even to an adequate or safe and reasonably priced supply of certain goods – petrol, cars, food, electricity. These rights, once institutionalized – as will surely happen in some or many advanced countries – will affect costs and market strategies, and the struggle over them may come to be more important than competition in the market. The game of wealth and power is bound therefore to shift increasingly into the realm of politics, for once capital development and employment are determined outside the market this is where the shape of the future will be decided. But the system cannot simply respond to the pressures of existing interests; it will have to look ahead and anticipate both problems and opportunities. Government will have to be 're-invented'. This will be hard for a nation whose political order is corrupt, weak and fragmented.

For the power to re-direct the market and re-invent government resides in the state, and the foundations of the state itself are eroding, under pressures arising largely from the market. Nations no longer have control over their domestic economies. New institutions, including and especially supranational ones will have to be built – as is happening in Europe now. Sooner or later – most likely later, after a depression – it will become clear that the world market will have to be controlled, requiring a supranational state. But how can that be constructed when nation-states are splitting up, and the US no longer exercises determined leadership?

The family, unaided, can no longer handle socialization effectively. Even in many advanced countries, especially in the US, children are short-changed. We have never confronted this explicitly; it calls for a complete policy on the reproduction of the population – a policy which would compel the society to make explicit its assumptions about morals, education and equality or inequality of opportunity. But such a policy would have to build new collective institutions, and where will they come from?.

Nevertheless, even if the political system cannot do the job effectively, decisions will still shift to politics, because the issues transcend the boundaries of the older system of markets and families. There will still be a market, or rather, markets, but their working will be a new mix of the economics we have known and the politics we are beginning to see, a fragmented politics of groups formed around single issues or bundles of related issues. There will still be families, but they will be increasingly unstable, and their functions will be reduced even further. How such a system will evolve, and whether it can be made to work in a large non-homogeneous society, lacking a consensus on values, remains to be seen. The future may well belong to those countries with more homogeneous populations, still able to maintain a consensus on the basic values of a traditional code, and flexible enough to adapt it to the modern world. They will therefore find themselves in a position to develop more effective collective institutions. But they will have to build these institutions at the world level – or develop effective protection from the world market.

There was another sign to be seen in the parking lot. It read, 'THE END OF THE WORLD IS NIGH', and only appeared occasionally, carried by an ageing, bearded figure, who spent a lot of his time digging a large hole, in which he sat for long stretches of time, meditating. I liked 'nigh'; it was satisfyingly arcane, and provided a touch of class, stirring remote memories: 'The great Proclaimer ... cried ... Heaven's Kingdom nigh at hand.' The shabby figure in a headband was a far cry from Milton's 'great Proclaimer', and it wasn't Heaven's kingdom he proclaimed. More blunt and less hopeful, a better message for the times, I thought, and surprisingly true, though not perhaps in the way intended by the messenger. For what else should we say, when the family has dissolved as the centre of personal life, when the market can no longer effectively organize production and consumption, when the nation-state has lost its position as the source of authority? These are the pillars of our world, and they are crumbling.

The message, then, is simple. In the past the market was the force driving progress. But today, the state, the family, traditional values and the environment are being undermined by the new development of the market. At the world level, the market is now spinning out of control; at the domestic level it is becoming unable to deliver its traditional services. We have no institutions at present capable of effectively restraining and re-directing it. But if we do not establish dominion over it, it may destroy us!

Golden light spread across the green mountaintops; the sun was setting in the Catskills, as on the world. The night would be dark, though not long. Then there would be dawn. Would we live to see it? On what world – and whose – would the new sun rise?

NOTES

1 MAINSTREAM OR BILLABONG?

1 This is *not* a textbook – readers are supposed to have one near at hand – so it is not appropriate to clutter it up with diagrams. Nevertheless, this is so important, and so simple, that we can make an exception here.

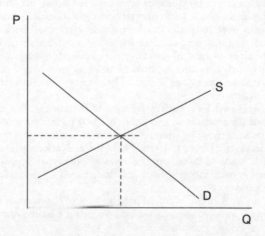

The axes represent different possible prices, on the vertical, and quantities to be bought and sold, on the horizontal. The demand curve, D, slopes down, showing that at a lower price more will be demanded, while the supply curve S, slopes up, indicating that at higher prices firms will be willing – eager – to supply more. The reasoning behind each curve will be explained more fully later in the text. The point at which the two intersect identifies the price at which the quantity demanded is just equal to what firms are willing to supply. At a lower price, demand would exceed what firms would be willing to supply, at a higher price it would be less. Prices will adjust until the quantity supplied equals that demanded.

2 In the early period the benefits of productivity increases were 'transmitted' to the economy in the form of lower prices; in the later, through higher money wages.

Keynes noted this difference, *General Theory*, p. 271, but failed to appreciate that, among other things, the second method of spreading productivity gains imparts an inflationary bias to the economy.

3 A classic case is the delay experienced during the Ford Administration in 1974. All signs pointed to the need for budgetary stimulus to offset the impact of the oil shock, especially since monetary policy had to be kept fairly tight to defend the dollar. When the stimulus finally came it was too late, and the economy had gone into a tailspin (Sorkin, 1988).

4 A great deal of modern neo-Classical work can be understood as attempting to escape from the 'local setting' that is so central to Marshall. Demand theory, in particular, first develops 'indifference curves', which make it possible to discard 'cardinal (measurable) utility', and then 'revealed preference', which, combined with simple axioms, allowed consideration of all possible combinations of goods. However, Hicks (1956), develops a hybrid theory that remains close to Marshall, in that he avoids assuming that consumers have complete scales of preferences (they can rank every conceivable combination of goods, e.g. they know whether or not they prefer 23 living room sofas and 786 light bulbs to 13 sofas and 4562 light bulbs) and that there are no alternatives they cannot rank, i.e. between which they are indifferent, cf. pp. 189–90.

5 Since the Marshallian approach takes current plant and equipment as given, it has been considered 'short-run'. This is not correct; it *starts* from current plant and equipment, but investment will change the capital stock. What it does not do is attempt to survey all possibilities at once, and choose the 'optimal' position. Instead it begins from one set of concrete circumstances and moves to another.

6 What if Robinson were to 'prefer' to keep some extra food back for himself, or if Friday 'preferred' a different kind of tool? We assume that all these problems are ironed out in the process of defining the *required amounts of input per unit output*. These requirements are supposed to hold, as an average, in normal conditions. Special circumstances don't count. Then, given the required inputs we can calculate the exchange.

7 Prices provide for growth by covering the costs of investment. But such investment will lie unutilized unless demand grows at an equal pace. The growth of demand, however, may be influenced by price. A sophisticated theory of the mark-up must take this into account, (Eichner, 1976; Nell, 1992) Notice the crucial point that in this approach prices depend on the *rates of growth* of supply and demand, whereas in conventional theory prices are determined by balancing the *levels* of supply and demand.

8 In particular, we will argue that Marshallian S&D describes the pattern of adjustment – in response to various 'shocks' – around a basic position determined by the Robinson–Friday exchange.

9 Defoe's book is better understood as a parable of how imperial domination is established. Robinson makes Friday his servant, and then with Friday's help extends his sway. Robinson is always extremely careful to calculate exactly how to maintain his position of dominance (Defoe, 1948; Hymer, in Nell, 1980).

10 An economic interpretation of The Theorem of the Alternative runs as follows: If a commodity is produced in the optimal solution of the primal problem, then the value of the resources needed to produce a unit amount cannot exceed its unit price; and if a positive valuation is assigned to a resource in the dual optimal solution, then that resource must be used fully (Baumol, 1986).

11 Schumpeter distinguished between the normal behavior of business and the activities of 'entrepreneurs', whom he argued were responsible for the innovations that have changed the face of the world. Ordinary businessmen, in his view, tended to be conservative and timid, blindly following traditional routines. He held them

in contempt. By contrast, entrepreneurs, the innovators, were the aristocracy of business, knights in shining armour, the daring creators of new worlds.

12 It is worth emphasizing that optimizing models *can* be used, quite profitably, in descriptive analysis. They simply have to be plausible; that is, the agents have to see the world that way – which means that applicable models are never general. But the postulate of self-interested behaviour which underlies such models is quite powerful and illuminating – it cuts through hypocrisy and posturing. The point in the text is not that such models cannot be used descriptively; it is that whenever they are, they *also* tell us which of the givens it would be most useful to change.

13 Sraffa's famous (1926) critique of Marshall is relevant in this context. Two fundamental points were made. First, if many sectors all employ the same 'fixed factor', fixed for the economy as a whole, then varying supply in a given industry will change the marginal returns to the use of that factor, and therefore its price. Hence costs and earnings in other industries will be affected, with the result that the demand curve to the given industry may be affected. Hence the 'fixed factor' must be specific to the given industry. Second, if there are increasing returns, they must be external to the firm though internal to the industry. Otherwise the size of the firm will be indeterminate. So Marshallian analysis requires industry-specific fixed factors and increasing returns external to the firm, but internal to the industry. These conditions are certainly not widespread and perhaps not found at all in modern industry. But, in fact, they *are* found in Craft Economies. Land is the chief fixed factor in agriculture, and is specific to it. Traditional skills and 'secrets of the trade', passed down from father to son, make up the 'fixed factor' in most crafts. Increasing returns external to the firm are common in agriculture – when output rises new forms of storage and transport will be introduced. When the output of crafts rise enough, bulk buying and storage will be introduced (Cf. Nell, in Bharadwaj and Schefold, 1992).

14 The ratio of aggregate net output to the aggregate means of production is known as the Standard Ratio, or sometimes as the Von Neumann Ray (Sraffa, 1960; Pasinetti, 1977; Bharadwaj and Schefold, 1992).

2 INVISIBLE HANDS

1 Markets interact and affect one another, giving rise to three analytical problems: the existence, uniqueness and stability of equilibrium. When a price rises in one market, and people buy less, this can affect many other markets. The good is more expensive, so there will be more demand for substitutes and less for complements. All these changes are likely to affect factor incomes, with further ramifications for demand. The first question, then, is: can we find a position in which all markets are simultaneously in equilibrium – all markets clear. Second: will there be only one such general equilibrium, or might there be many? Third, will will market incentives tend to move the system towards the equilibrium – or equilibria – or will it move away? Or oscillate endlessly around it? This third problem is the question of stability. If equilibria are not stable, the market is not going to bring about desirable results. In standard neo-Classical theory the system will be stable so long as *substitution* effects outweigh *income* effects. (The interested reader will have to look up these terms in a textbook – there isn't space to explain them here.) Unfortunately, there are no economic grounds why this should be so. If the owners of a factor, say labour, demand proportionally more of labour-intensive commodities, then an increase in the supply of labour could lead to a *rise* in labour's remuneration, instead of a fall. It can be shown that such an upward-sloping demand curve will create reactions,

spreading from market to market, tending to move the economy away from equilibrium. However, there are no grounds to rule this out – it is not implausible in some circumstances that labour should demand labour-intensive goods, or owners of capital, capital-intensive ones. Further investigation distinguished 'static' and 'dynamic' stability – the latter includes a specification of *reaction times* to changes in market – and 'local' and 'global' stability. (An equilibrium is locally stable, if a small deviation will set up corrective forces, and globally stable, if the system will converge to it starting from absolutely anywhere.) As the dimensions of the problem emerged, it also became clear that there were no solid economic grounds on which to base a claim for the stability of general equilibrium.

2 Somewhere in the *Structure of Scientific Revolutions*, Thomas Kuhn (1970) remarks that textbooks imprint a stamp of official approval on their contents, as if they represent all that is right in the profession, while dismissing all previous – or alternative – thinking.

3 Frank Hahn, a leading analyst of general equilibrium theory, and one of the first to show that the usual competitive assumptions do not and cannot guarantee stability, has argued that this implies that, in practice, even apparently competitive markets require regulation (Hahn, in Bell and Kristol, 1981). Alternatively one could argue that the theory, neglecting institutions and technology, and inappropriately basing itself on RC, does not accurately portray market realities.

4 The price mechanism may have provided stable adjustment processes for markets for goods and services in the nineteenth century, but the monetary system was decidedly unstable (Kindleberger, 1978; Deleplace and Nell, 1995). By contrast, until the 1980s, the post-War monetary system has tended to be fairly stable.

5 The book is by B. Traven, the movie, directed by John Huston, stars Humphrey Bogart. A classic.

6 For a more detailed account of the mechanism, see (Nell, 1992, ch. 16). Explorations of the Craft Economy in Japan, the US, Canada and Germany confirm the inverse relationship between real wages and employment in the years before World War I; there is good evidence for Japan, and suggestive evidence for the rest, that investment and consumption varied inversely in this period (Nell and Phillips, 1995; Nell et al., 1996).

7 Marshall's production function should be understood as a kind of utilization function. When demand drove up prices, money wages remained relatively unaffected, since employment was difficult to change. Real wages therefore fell, making it worthwhile to undertake the disruptive process of adding to the work teams – disruptive because new working patterns had to be developed.

8 The difference is that in the case of the Keynesian or macroeconomic multiplier, the funds withdrawn from circulation each round are known as a precise fraction of the level of expenditure. Such funds are saved by businesses or households, and the saving propensity is assumed known and fixed. In the case of bankruptcy, however, the 'withdrawal' is involuntary, and neither the amount withdrawn nor the moment of its occurrence can be known reliably in advance.

9 In actual fact in the second half of the nineteenth century governments played a considerably larger role than the expression suggests. Think of 'eminent domain' and the building of the railroads, or the canals, to say nothing of managing, or mismanaging, the currency. But even so, the size of government in relation to GNP, for most advanced nations, tended to lie between 5 per cent and 10 per cent right up to the years before World War I, and below 5 per cent for the US.

10 Suppose for simplicity that shop assistants and factory workers both have the same wages, and that the productivity of their labour is the same. Assume further that workers spend all and only their wages, and that their consumption falls to zero when they are laid off and are no longer paid. Let the wage be w, and

the labour per unit of output (or sales) – the inverse of productivity – be n. The initial decline in sales will be ΔC_0. The next round of declines will be ΔC_1 = $wn\Delta C_0$, followed by $\Delta C_2 = wn\Delta C_1 = (wn)^2\Delta C_0$, and so on. Elementary algebra shows that

$$\Delta C_0 + \Delta C_1 + \Delta C_2 + \ldots = \Delta C = \{1/[1 - wn]\}\Delta C_0.$$

The multiplier is $1/(1 - wn)$; it depends on the real wage and the productivity of labour. It thus differs from the Keynesian multiplier of the textbooks, which depends on household's 'psychological propensity to consume'. In fact household savings are quite small; business savings, which the textbooks ignore, are much larger. The approach here focuses attention on business withdrawals. (Nell, 1988; 1992, ch. 20)

11 Structuralist macroeconomics sometimes suggests that investment should be seen as depending *both* on profit potential – costs and prices – and on expected demand. So a fall in costs/rise in productivity would, or might, *increase* investment. This seems to imply that higher potential profit would call forth more investment, even if expectations of sales were weak or declining. *Replacement* investment, maybe – it makes sense to replace old equipment with new and better stuff. But businesses that tend to build new factories in the absence of new markets, just because construction costs are low, are not likely to be around very long. Nevertheless, the structuralist approach has much to recommend it; it's a well-worked-out breath of fresh air blowing through the musty, stale classrooms of conventional macroeconomics (Taylor, 1991).

3 INSTITUTIONS

1 And the role of genetics? If we are discussing the production of the next generation, surely genetics has something to offer? Perhaps, but there are two reasons to think that it may not. First, the gene pool from which will spring the next generation of a particular class or sector is itself defined by the rules for selecting marriage partners. The genetic possibilities are *socially* determined. Second, in all eras prior to the modern, limitations of diet, education, medicine, and public health so constrained the realization of human potential that neither (small) expansion nor contraction of genetic possibilities would have mattered much. In the coming post-modern era we may reach our genetic limitations, but we are also learning how to alter DNA!

2 Think of the University again: suppose we raise either pay or perks to make everyone better off – students, faculty, administrators, alumni, clerical staff, library staff, and janitors. Maintaining standards – grades, course evaluations, teaching evaluations, evaluation of research – can take a great deal of time in committees and staff meeting. Cutting these back will save the money to provide the raises. But one of the university's *intangible* missions, to maintain high standards, will have been sacrificed. Its component parts are all better off but the university has suffered.

3 The 'general good', as defined here is the (very likely non-unique) proper working of a total system of social re-production. To increase the general good is to make the system work better. This is an *entirely separate* question from whether the social system is a good, or proper, or just system in the first place. Note that *judging* such a system cannot be carried out on the basis of the interests inherent in an agent's current position or role, since such interests are themselves created by or dependent on the system. Nor can an agent's preferences, tastes, likes and dislikes be involved in judging the system, since those tastes, etc., will or may

have been formed or influenced by the agent's training and upbringing, which will have been in the system's socialization processes. (This appears to be analogous to Kant's famous 'refutation of heteronomy'.)

4 The market's ability to single out the efficient, sift wheat from chaff, of course, rested on the fact that participants could accurately judge the worth of products and the quality of services. As technology and products have grown more complicated, so has judging them. Adam Smith inveighed against licensing; he saw it as a form of monopoly. Today it is protection for a public which lacks the time and the expertise to judge competence and quality in many technologically sophisticated fields.

5 A note on methodology: Here we have defined production and socializing institutions (firms and families, for instance) in terms of their objectives, the activities they undertake to pursue those objectives, the skills they require of those who accept appointment to roles, and so on. Markets, in turn, are another kind of institution, in which monetary gains are pursued, according to various strategies, governed by competitive rules. Firms, families and markets are defined independently of one another. The contrast with, for example, Ronald Coase could not be sharper. The question Coase raised, was, why do firms exist to determine the division of labour and allocate equipment to various tasks, if markets are the most efficient method of allocation? His answer was that transactions costs were larger in the market than in the firm, by an amount that exceeded the difference between the efficiency of the market and the lesser efficiency of 'command' by firms. The approach rests on a particular theory of the market – generalized abstract RC – which we have suggested is highly questionable. When markets are considered realistically, they are seldom efficient at all, especially in regard to allocation. Their power lies in generating incentives – raising productivity, calling forth innovations, etc. Moreover, the market is a selection mechanism – it rewards profitable and productive innovations, and squashes others, and punishes the inefficient. Bureaucratic hierarchies are quite efficient at allocation and planning, but generate a lot of negative incentives, and tend to quash innovations. Bureaucracies do not favourably select innovations; quite the reverse, they tend to punish anything that threatens to upset established routines. 'Transactions costs' are important, but are often over-stated. The evolutionary contrast is far more significant.

6 It is a hallmark claim of free market conservatism that Big Brother cannot have Invisible Hands, that is, that the market can never encourage tyranny or aid in the abrogation of freedom. Hayek and Friedman have strongly argued for the close connections between markets and freedom. But it is possible to see another aspect of markets. Their tendency to destroy community and the family, and to concentrate political power in the hands of unscrupulous wealth, may lead to a social order fully as unpleasant and as constricting to individual choice as the worst communist regime. The Pinochet regime in Chile comes to mind. The working of a fully corrupt market system is developed imaginatively in the novels of Richard Condon, e.g. *Money is Love*. Neither left nor right have a monopoly on either freedom or tyranny. Big Brother can very well have Invisible Hands, and just might use them to pick our pockets!

4 THE PARADOXES OF INDIVIDUALISM

1 It should, of course, be abundantly clear that we reject the textbook story of supply and demand in the labour market. That story relies on a demand curve for labour which slopes down from left to right; such a curve is derived from

diminishing returns in production. So it makes sense in the Craft Economies of the nineteenth century, and, indeed, empirical studies of leading countries prior to World War I confirm that the real wage tended to move inversely with respect to output and employment. But in Mass Production economies returns tend to be constant or increasing. So there is no demand curve of the kind implied. Moreover, hiring, lay-offs and labour practices generally are quite different. As for supply, there is good evidence that in some circumstances, when real wages fall, household offers of labour rise, just the opposite of the textbook model.

2 Taxes on savings, e.g. on corporate earnings, fall on a *withdrawal*. To get the stimulative impact of the budget such taxes should be subtracted. Some kinds of payments, e.g. interest on the debt, do not enter into the circulation, i.e. are not outlays on goods and services.

3 Notice that taxes on funds *already withdrawn*, like savings or retained profits, do not reduce activity. Thus a budget balanced by taxes on savings and profits would provide the same stimulus as an equal amount of deficit spending, while not giving rise to interest payments. Since interest on the national debt is a significant and regressive item in the Federal budget, there is a case to be made in favour of taxes on savings, profits and capital gains. But this has nothing to do with the usual case against the deficit.

5 ALTERNATIVES

1 The early drafts of the Act committed the Federal government to the goal of Full Employment. But under heavy lobbying pressure from business, the language was watered down considerably. Nevertheless, the Act represents a consensus in favour of expansionary policies, something that would be unthinkable today.

2 Fiscal policy refers to manipulating taxes and spending in order to provide a net stimulus to, or a net drag on, the economy. A stimulus is provided when the government injects more spending into the economy than it withdraws in taxes, creating a deficit in flow terms, and vice versa for a drag. Monetary policy concerns manipulating interest rates and credit requirements – and/or the money supply – in order to encourage or discourage borrowing and lending. High interest rates, tight credit and a squeeze on the money supply will discourage borrowers and thus reduce activity; low interest rates, easy credit and expansion of the money supply will encourage borrowers – but there will only be expansion if potential borrowers think they can make money from business projects. Even if credit is cheap, there is no point to borrowing to start a business or set up a new project, if there are no prospects for sales once the new business is under way. This is the point of the old adage, 'you can't push on a string'. A credit crunch will kill an expansion; easing credit may not cure a recession.

3 Another source of cost-inflation can be found in the *machine tool* sector. Machine tools are fundamental in the development of Mass Production, and the machine tool sector has to make the tools to make the equipment that is operated on the assembly lines. But the machine tool industry itself cannot be a Mass Production operation – tools have to be devised for each project. The machine tool industry itself has kept many of the characteristics of a *Craft* Industry. Hence when demand rises, the machine tool sector may find it difficult to handle the increase – and prices may start to rise. This could be prevented by providing subsidies to the machine tools sector to maintain extra capacity, and by careful planning of expansions.

4 Having had an unemployment rate lying between 2 per cent and 3 per cent for most of the last fifty years, Sweden for the first time faces serious unemployment

– reaching almost 13 per cent in 1994. Much of this is the consequence of having joined the European Union; Swedish firms are investing in other countries. Sweden has also been forced to raise its interest rates. A small, open economy is very limited in its policy options.

5 Suppose the government is the captive of private interests: spending decisions will be made so as not to compete with private firms. Military and construction contracts will be awarded to the largest political donors, not to the most efficient producers. Interest rates will be set so as to maximize the earnings of those financial institutions that have contributed most to the electoral success of the government. Government will be leery of running deficits, because large Treasury issues depress bond prices, and make it harder for major Wall St firms to get good prices for their customers. (No, deficits do *not* drive up interest rates *over a period of time.* When we take into account the effects of the spending which raises activity and so increases savings, the activity stimulated by the government spending generates the funds to offset the borrowing. But at any given moment from the point of view of each individual player on Wall Street, a large Treasury offering will appear to depress bond prices. Without that offering, each trader will say, the market would have been much better. But the trader will not take into account that the counterpart of that offering is government spending that generates employment, output and profits, creating an additional flow of savings into the market.)

6 One way to deal with unemployment is to shorten the working week. This will create more jobs and, while it may be inconvenient for business, if managed carefully it could substantially reduce the misery of the present situation. This is an important proposal, deserving careful consideration. But it is not, or not necessarily, part of an expansionist programme. It is a way of reducing the social costs of austerity.

7 A familiar lament runs: but surely it is wrong to burden our children with such enormous debts? This overlooks the fact that government bonds are also assets, so while we burden our children as taxpayers with debts, as bondholders we bequeath them the corresponding assets. Of course, the children that get the bonds are generally much richer than the children who will pay the taxes. This inequity is easily corrected by a simple taxation scheme: levy a tax on wealth (productive assets) *of all kinds* at a rate just sufficient to pay the interest on the national debt. Let D stand for the total national debt, and W for total national wealth, of all kinds – real assets like buildings and factories, and financial assets like stocks and bonds. Clearly W will be much larger than D. (At present in the US, W is probably near 30 trillion dollars, and D about 5 trillion.) Then if i is the interest rate, iD stands for the annual burden of the debt that we must bear and will, all too soon, pass on to our children. So let us set a tax on Wealth, t, such that iD = tW. This tax, on the order of about 1 per cent, will then completely remove that burden! The rate of such a tax will be very low, and since it falls equally on all wealth it will have no distorting effects. As with all taxes many details would have to be worked out, e.g. a defining taxable wealth so as to exempt the assets of the poor, the unemployed, etc. Assessment procedures and collection systems would have to be developed. But because such a tax would be very general and quite low, it would have few, if any, distorting effects. Nor would it be likely to drive capital abroad – and if it did, an exit tax could be levied on capital flight. Such a tax is not likely to prove popular with the large campaign contributors on whom it would chiefly fall. But it is important to understand that the burden of the debt is not a problem that requires cutting one cent of useful government spending. The burden of the debt exists only

because wealth-holders resist paying taxes. In the long run there are no free lunches, not even school lunches. Perhaps we don't always get what we pay for, but *ex nihilo nihil fit* – if we don't pay anything we won't get anything. We are perhaps too concerned with our *rights* as citizens; maybe we should pay more attention to our *duties*, the first and foremost of which is to pay our way.

8 In round numbers: for 1991 Social Security Trust funds come to $268 billion, 401K Pension Plan assets are $448 billion, other Private Pension Plans, $110 billion, Federal Employees Pensions, $367 billion, while State and Local Government Employee Pensions add up to $783 billion, the whole totalling $1936 billion.

9 The more sophisticated econobabblers – the *Wall Street Journal*, the *Economist* – are inclined to claim at this point that the fall in A' s currency, coupled with the rise of B' s, will correct the problem. For A' s currency decline will curb its imports, and stimulate its exports, while B' s rise will do just the reverse. Hence A' s balance of payments will strengthen, and B' s will weaken, bringing them back to equilibrium. Like so much in economics – it all depends on the arithmetic. For if imports don't decline, or exports increase, when the currency falls, the country is *worse off*, not better off, and vice versa for a rise. More precisely, the proportional decline in imports added to the proportional rise in exports must be greater than or equal to the proportional fall in the currency's value, for the country to break even or gain by a devaluation. (This is known as the Marshall–Lerner condition.) Imports may be essential goods, or may be necessary inputs into exports; so they could be price-inelastic. Exports may depend more on quality than price. In practice, all too often, the Marshall–Lerner condition fails to be satisfied – and devaluation makes things worse.

6 MARKETS, BUREAUCRACY AND MACHIAVELLI

1 However, as we have repeatedly noted, the textbook model is a reasonable approximation of the world of business prior to World War I. The Craft Economy of family firms and family farms did look rather like that.

2 A takeover raider buys a large set of shares in a company, and then, lining up backing from a bank or financial institution, makes a hostile takeover bid at a high price. (The raider may have neither the intention nor the resources to carry out the takeover, but management cannot be sure.) To fend off the bid, management must make a counter-offer, raising the price of shares even further. The raider then sells out his initial holding, making a bundle.

3 In short, Machiavelli's advice must be supplemented by that of Mephistopheles, with whose help Faust founds industries and builds cities. Mephistopheles even appears to be an early Keynesian – faced with a depression in the Empire he advises Faust to have the Emperor issue paper money, secured by as yet undiscovered supplies of gold and minerals, still in the earth. At first this greatly stimulates commerce and industry, but ultimately leads to inflation (Goethe, *Faust*, II).

4 Fred Hirsch, 1976, emphasized the *conflict* between a traditional code, derived from cooperation in the household and in collective activities, and grounded in status, and the individualistic, maximizing ethic of the market. He saw that the market tended to undermine the traditional ethic, but he also saw that the market *depended* in many ways on that ethic (Cf. esp. Part III, 'The Depeleting Moral Legacy'). But he did not see that in other ways the two codes *reinforce* each other, or that the interaction beween them is an important part of capitalism's dynamic.

7 MORAL CODES AND MARKET FORCES

1 From his fundamental considerations, developed in ch. 13, Hobbes derives nineteen 'natural laws' which make up the articles of peace, and are presented in chs 14 and 15. The first of these, and most basic, is 'Every man ought to endeavour peace, as far as he has hope of obtaining it, and when he cannot . . . he may seek and use . . . war'. From this he concludes, the second law, 'That a man be willing, when others are . . . too . . . to lay down this right to all things; and be contented with so much liberty against other men, as he would allow other men against himself.' This leads Hobbes directly into a discussion of contracts (current transfer of rights) and covenants (one or more parties will perform in the future), since for a man to lay down his natural right to all things on condition others do likewise is to enter a contract or covenant. Hobbes notes that what gives a covenant force is fear of retribution if it is violated. The third law, then, is justice, 'That men perform their covenants made', the fourth is gratitude, the fifth, mutual accommodation, 'Every man strive to accommodate himself to the rest', the sixth is pardon, 'A man ought to pardon the offences past of them that repenting, desire it', because to pardon is nothing but granting of peace. The seventh states that in contemplating revenge, men should consider not the evil past, but only the future good; the eighth states 'that no man by deed, word, countenance, or gesture declare hatred or contumely of another'. In today's terms this could not be more 'politically correct'. The ninth demands recognition of general equality, that every man acknowledge others to be his equal, while the tenth declares that 'No man . . . reserve to himself any right, which he is not content should be reserved to every one of the rest'. The eleventh is equity, or distributive justice, 'If [one judges] between man and man, . . . he [must] deal equally between them', which implies the twelfth, requiring the equal use of things held in common, and the thirteenth, when such things cannot be divided, or used jointly, that they be used alternately, with first use decided by lot. This, for some reason, is then thought to justify primogeniture, a 'first use' determined by 'natural lot'. The fifteenth then allows mediators safe conduct, the sixteenth, submits controversies to arbitration, the seventeenth forbids men to judge their own cases, the eighteenth disallows judges who are partial or have an interest, and the nineteenth allows no partiality in assigning credibility to witnesses. Hobbes makes no effort to show that this is a complete list; only that it is enough. Obviously many are of general significance; others seem almost trivial by comparison.

2 Hobbes, chs. 17, 18. The Sovereign must be understood as an artificial person, bearing one will, uniting all, and using the strength and means of all for the pursuit of peace and common defence. The Sovereign therefore *cannot* be a self-interested party; the conduct of the Sovereign, *as* Sovereign, must be governed by the general good – just as the 'auctioneer' in Walrasian economics cannot be a profit-seeker.

3 Both Ricardo and Friedman propose their policy rules in part *because* they fear that allowing more discretion might tempt the Monetary Authorities in various ways. The simple rules will help to keep them from self-interested or partisan actions. By contrast, I have argued that the monetary system has an inherent and inescapable tendency to instability, which has to be controlled by State policy. There must therefore exist an Authority with the responsibility for managing the monetary system, which it must do disinterestedly.

4 Economists have sometimes argued that pollution should be stopped only if the damage to those affected is greater than the cost of stopping it. But if this is so, then, if markets were 'perfect' – or a reasonable approximation to those of theory

– brokers should emerge to collect fees from those affected by pollution, which would then be used to bribe the polluters to stop. Then if the fees were less than the damage, but greater than the cost of stopping, everybody would be better off, including the brokers, who, of course, would earn a commission. This doesn't happen, it is usually argued, because 'transactions costs' – contacting everyone, coordinating fee schedules, etc. – are too high. Very likely they are. But in addition, much of the impact of pollution becomes apparent only over long periods of time, and will initially only be evident to scientists. Moreover, the impact is likely to be statistical; a certain percentage of people or places will be damaged, but there is no way of telling exactly which ones. By the time cancers appear it is too late.

5 *Obviously* many individual citizens – to judge from the opinion polls, a large majority – would prefer to see democratic regimes in the periphery. That is not the point. Nor is it relevant that politicians and the foreign policy establishment reverently pay lip service to the desirability of democracy everywhere. What counts is what they do, not what they say. Allende was elected democratically – but the US helped to organize the coup against him, and then strongly backed Pinochet, its leader and a vicious dictator. Currently the US is backing the PRI in Mexico; a memo from Chase Manhattan bank making the rounds in Washington urges us to support rigged elections. The same story can be repeated for virtually every country in Latin America – the US overthrew Arbenz in Guatemala, and supported the military in El Salvador, backed dictators in Bolivia and the generals in Brazil, supported Somoza and Papa Doc, opposed the Sandinistas and Aristide. The same holds elsewhere in the Third World, e.g. Mossadegh in Iran. Foccart's book has detailed the behind-the-scenes way the French ran many countries in Africa. The reason is simple: authoritarian regimes are easier to deal with and more likely to be friendly to American business interests and security concerns. Of course, there are exceptions.

6 'Socialism on Earth', the Soviet system, tended to generate a permanent state of excess demand – not unlike the war-time economy of the US 1941–5. Given price controls this tended to produce repressed inflation and shortages. It also led to imbalances, with the paradoxical result that along with excess demand, and shortages, there could be found idle capacity – idle because of lack of spare parts or lack of materials to work with. But the Soviet system never developed policies to control aggregate demand pressure. Indeed, they never seemed to recognize that they faced a *Keynesian* problem (Nell, 1992).

7 It is estimated that over two-thirds of the US labour force cannot read and perform basic mathematical skills at the sixth-grade level. This is the level needed to read an ordinary newspaper and fill out income tax forms.

8 Breakdowns of these systems could interact – conceivably, a major water breakdown could bring on a power grid failure, which would, of course, shut down the subways and much of the rail system. The potential for really major, expensive and prolonged disasters is there.

9 In the late 1980s and early 1990s, Denmark, Norway and Sweden all had tax burdens of over 55 per cent. Finland, Belgium, the Netherlands and France were all near 50 per cent. Austria, Italy and Germany were above 45 per cent, while Spain and Great Britain were in the high 35–40 per cent range.

10 It should be noted, however, that the US has the world's leading system of *higher* education – junior colleges, colleges and universities. Among the advanced countries, the US and Canada have the highest percentage of student-age population attending college, 18.5 per cent, and about 16 per cent, respectively, in the late 1980s. To some extent the US makes up for its poor high schools in its colleges, although many US colleges have much lower admissions standards

and lower level courses than comparable institutions elsewhere in the advanced world. Of course, none of this helps those who don't attend college – still a large majority.

8 TWILIGHT IN THE MARKETPLACE

1 Fred Hirsch 1976 developed the idea of 'positional' goods (and services), as a complement to the economist's long-standing category of public or collective goods. In the case of a positional good it is not just that others must be involved in the act of consumption also, as with the telephone, but the value of the good to each consumer depends on their *position* relative to each other. A hamburger is a pure private good, clean air in the city a pure public good (no matter how many people breathe it, it is still of the same value to each). Positional goods are those whose value to each consumer depends on what others are doing; the value of a road to a traveller depends on how many others are using it at the same time. The value of a seat in a theatre is diminished by the tall lady with the bouffant hairdo in front. The public park, noisy and crowded, is one experience; quiet and empty, another. Increasing access reduces the value of such collective goods. But above all, Hirsch stresses the fact that a large part of competition, e.g. in education, is competition for *place*, that is, for *relative* position. Everyone wants a front row seat in the theatre of life. Everyone wants to win the race. These goods cannot be increased, and in positional competition one person's gain is another's loss.

2 Among some schools of economists, this has stimulated a fruitless search for a 'fixed' or scarce factor of production, one subject to diminishing returns. The chief candidate has been something like 'entrepreneurial talent' or 'organizational skill'. As development economists have noted, in some societies such talent *is* scarce, but not because it is a given factor. Such talent is *produced* by the society's system of socialization. Postulating scarce entrepreneurship is not a useful way to think about the development of economic organization.

3 Do such blocs of capital owned or controlled only by other blocs of capital exist? Evidently. Institutional holdings and bank trusts together make up a solid and growing majority of all stock holdings; private and government pension funds alone are worth more than 50 per cent of the value of all stocks listed on the New York Stock Exchange in 1991. Families and individuals have been a minority of total stock holdings since the 1960s.

4 Economics textbooks will suggest imposing taxes to discourage negative externalities and to provide the means to compensate those adversely affected, and by the same token, subsidies for positive externalities. This is surely a step in the right direction; but in addition incentives are needed to develop the technologies away from negative in the direction of positive externalities.

5 This is one of the reasons for the new interest in 'networks' and 'cells'. A hierarchy where information flows up and decisions down may be inefficient in an age in which market conditions are changing rapidly. By the time the information is processed into a decision, the situation may have altered. Local variations may be important, and may be difficult for distant decision-makers to judge. Hence the power to make decisions may be devolved on 'cells' – groups of workers, who manage themselves, and are responsible for an outcome, which they can achieve in any way they like, taking into account whatever information they deem relevant, and adjusting to local conditions. The cells, in turn, are co-ordinated into networks. Great successes have been reported – and significant failures. (The *Economist*, 17 December 1994) Different cells establish different routines, making

coordination difficult. Cells can break down because of internal bickering. Economies of scale are lost. Nevertheless it is clear that the old pattern of large-scale hierarchy is no longer the corporate norm.

6 This can be illustrated with a simple diagram:

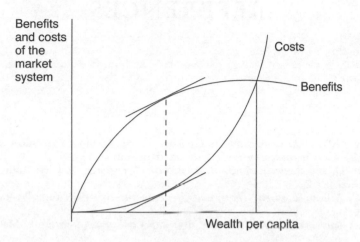

9 INDIVIDUALISM AND THE DILEMMA
OF THE STATE

1 Since 1980 investment in hi-tech has grown more rapidly than any other form of investment, but the size of manufacturing, measured either by percentage of labour employed, or by percentage of value added in GNP has declined (Nell, in Eatwell, 1995). For the loss of high-paying jobs, cf. Gordon, in Eatwell, 1995. The growth of finance capital is analyzed by Minsky, and further in Dymski and Pollin, more popularly by Greider, 1987. The statistical picture is clear in the rising burden of debt in the US economy, cf. Nell, 1988. Capital mobility is evident from the rising ratio of international investment to domestic, and in the movement of short term capital.

2 A more ominous theory suggests that the AIDS virus may have been genetically engineered. In the 1980s the Soviets claimed that the AIDS virus had escaped from US 'germ warfare' labs. No convincing evidence was proferred. It was believed that all these claims could be put to rest, when the preserved organs of a Manchester, England, man who mysteriously died in 1959, of a disease unknown to doctors, were supposedly shown to be infected with the HIV virus. But it has now been demonstrated that the organs come from two different individuals, and that HIV is not present at all in one, while the strain of HIV present in the other is a very recent development, suggesting contamination (*NYT*, Tuesday, March, 1995).

3 Descartes argued that '*cogito ergo sum*' – 'I think, therefore I am'. This was the fundamental starting point for philosophy – a proposition no sceptic could deny, since to deny it would require thought. Hence the existence of the individual thinker was affirmed and placed at the centre of the philosphical universe.

REFERENCES

Andrews, P.W.S. *On Competition in Economic Theory*, London: Macmillan, 1964.

Aristotle. *The Nichomachean Ethics* (any standard edition).

Bartlett, D. and Steele, J. *America: What Went Wrong?* Kansas City: Andrews and McMeel, 1992.

Baumol, William. *Economic Theory and Operations Research*, New York: Prentice Hall, 1986.

Beard, Charles and Mary. *The Rise of American Civilization*, New York: Macmillan, 1927.

Bharadwaj, K. and Schefold, B. *Essays on Piero Sraffa*, London: Routledge, 1992.

Braudel, Fernand. *Capitalism and Material Life: 1400–1800*, New York: Harper & Row, 1967.

Brockway, George. *The End of Economic Man: Principles of Any Future Economics*, Harper Collins: Cornelia and Michael Bessie Books, 1991.

Chandler, Alfred. *Scale and Scope*, Cambridge, MA: Harvard University Press, 1990.

Chomsky, Noam.

Coulton, G.C. *The Medieval World*, Oxford: Oxford University Press, 1945.

Defoe, Daniel. *Robinson Crusoe*, New York: Modern Library, 1948.

Deleplace, G. and Nell, Edward J., eds., *Money in Motion: the Circulation and Post-Keynesian Approaches*, London: Macmillan, 1995.

Dymski, G and Pollin, R. *New Perspectives on Monetary Theory*, Ann Arbor: University of Michigan Press, 1994.

Eatwell, J. ed. *Unemployment and Markets*, London: Edward Elgar, 1995.

Eichner, A. *The Megacorp and Oligopoly*, Cambridge: Cambridge University Press, 1976.

Eisner, Robert. *How Real Is the Federal Deficit?* New York: The Free Press, 1986.

Gandolfo, G. *Economic Dynamics: Methods and Models*, New York: North Holland, 1983.

Gemmell, Norman. *The Growth of the Public Sector: Theories and International Evidence*, London: Edward Elgar, 1993.

Goldethorpe, J. E. *Family Life in Western Societies*, Cambridge: Cambridge University Press, 1987.

Greider, W. *Secrets of the Temple*, New York: Simon & Schuster, 1987.

Hahn, Frank. 'Equilibrium', in Bell, Daniel and Kristol, Irving, eds. *The Crisis in Economic Theory*, New York: Basic Books, 1981.

Hahn, Frank. *Equilibrium And Macroeconomics*, Cambridge: MIT Press, 1984.

Heilbroner, Robert. *An Inquiry into the Human Prospect*, New York: Norton, 198?.

Heilbroner, R. and Bernstein, P. *The Debt and the Deficit*, New York: Norton, 1992.

Hibbert, C. *The Rise and Fall of the House of Medici*, Harmondsworth: Penguin, 1967.

216

REFERENCES

Hicks, J.R. *A Revision of Demand Theory*, Oxford: Clarendon Press, 1956.

Hirsch, Fred. *Social Limits to Growth*, Cambridge: Harvard University Press, a Twentieth Century Fund Study, 1976.

Hobbes, Thomas. *Leviathan, or the Matter, Forme and Power of a Commonwealth, Ecclesiasticall and Civil*, ed. M. Oakeshott, Oxford: Basil Blackwell, 1957.

Hollis, Martin. *Models of Man: Philosophical Thoughts on Social Action*, Cambridge: Cambridge University Press, 1977.

Hollis, Martin. *The Cunning Of Reason*, Cambridge: Cambridge University Press, 1987.

Hollis, M. and Nell, E.J. *Rational Economic Man*, Cambridge: Cambridge University Press, 1975.

Hunter, Louis C. *A History of Industrial Power in the United States*, 3 vols, Charlottesville: University Press of Virginia, 1985.

Hymer, Steve. 'Robinson Crusoe and the Secret of Primitive Accumulation', in E.J. Nell, ed. *Growth, Profits and Property*, Cambridge: Cambridge University Press, 1980.

Kant, Immanuel. *The Critique of Pure Reason*, tr. N. Kemp Smith, London: Macmillan, 1958.

Kant, Immanuel. *The Critique of Pure Reason*, tr. Abbot, London: Longman, 1959.

Keynes, John Maynard. *The General Theory of Employment, Interest and Money*, London: Macmillan, 1935.

Kindleberger, Charles. *Manias, Panics and Crashes: a History of Financial Crises*, New York: Basic Books, 1978.

Koopmans, T. *Three Essays on the State of Economic Science*, New York: Yale, 1953.

Kuhn, Thomas. *The Structure of Scientific Revolutions*, 2nd edn, Chicago: University of Chicago Press, 1970.

Kuttner, Robert. *The End of Laissez-Faire*, New York: Knopf, 1991.

Laslett, Peter. *The World We Have Lost: England Before the Industrial Age*, 3rd edn, New York: Charles Scribner's Sons, 1984.

Machiavelli, Niccolo. *The Prince*, intr. C. Gauss, tr. L. Ricci, New York: New American Library, 1952.

Machiavelli, Niccolo. *The Discourses*, ed. B. Crick, tr. L.J. Walker, rev. by B. Richardson, Harmondsworth: Penguin, 1970.

Mankiw, N.G and Romer, D. *New Keynesian Economics*, 2 vols, Cambridge: MIT Press, 1993.

Marshall, A. *Principles of Economics*, (ed. C.W. Guillebaud), 9th Variorum Edition, 2 vols, London: Macmillan, 1961.

Minsky, Hyman. *Stabilizing an Unstable Economy*, New Haven: Yale Univserity Press, 1987.

Morone, James A. *The Democratic Wish: Popular Participation and the Limits of American Government*, New York: Basic Books, 1990.

Nell, Edward. *Growth, Profits and Property*, Cambridge: Cambridge University Press, 1980.

Nell, Edward. *Prosperity and Public Spending*, London and New York: Routledge, 1988.

Nell, Edward J. *Transformational Growth and Effective Demand*, London: Macmillan and New York: New York University Press, 1992.

Nell, Edward J. 'Transformational Growth and Learning: Developing Craft Technology into Scientific Mass Production,' in R. Thomson, ed., *Learning and Technological Change*, London: Macmillan, 1993.

Nell, Edward J. 'On Transformational Growth: An Interview', *Review of Political Economy*, vol. 6, no. 1, 1994.

Nell, Edward J. 'Stages in the Development of the Business Cycle', in H. Hagemann and H. Kurz, *Essays in Honour of Adolph Lowe*, London: Edward Elgar, 1995a.

Nell, Edward J. 'Unemployment, Aggregate Demand, and Government Policy', in J. Eatwell, ed. *Unemployment and Markets*, London: Edward Elgar, 1995b.

The New Palgrave: a Dictionary of Economics, eds John Eatwell, Murray Milgate and Peter Newman, London: Macmillan, 1987.

Nell, Edward J. *et al. Transformational Growth and the Business Cycle*, London and New York: Routledge, 1996.

Nell, Edward J. and Phillips, T. 'Transformational Growth and the Business Cycle', *Eastern Economic Journal*, vol. 21, no. 2, Spring, 1995.

Ollman, Bertell. *Class Struggle is the Name of the Game*, New York: Morrow, 1982.

O'Neill, O. .

Osborne, D. and Gaebler, T. *Re-Inventing Government: How the Entrepreneurial Spirit is Transforming the Public Sector*, New York: Plume (Penguin), 1993.

Oxford Analytica. *America in Perspective*, Boston: Houghton Mifflin, 1986.

Paehlke, Robert. *Environmentalism and the Future of Progressive Politics*, New Haven: Yale University Press, 1989.

Pasinetti, Luigi. *Lectures on the Theory of Production*, New York: Columbia University Press, 1977.

Peterson, Wallace. *Silent Depression: The Fate of the American Dream*, New York: Norton, 1994.

Phillips, Kevin. *The Politics of Rich and Poor: Wealth and the American Electorate in the Reagan Aftermath*, New York: Harper Perennial, 1990.

Plato. *Republic*.

Ponting, Clive. *A Green History of the World: The Environment and the Collapse of Great Civilizations*, New York: St. Martin's Press, 1991.

Reich, Robert B. *The Work of Nations*, New York: Vintage Books, 1992.

Robinson, E.A.G. *The Structure of Competitive Industry*, Cambridge: Cambridge University Press, 1931.

Roeder, Ralph. *The Man of the Renaissance: Four Lawgivers; Savonarola, Machiavelli, Castiglione, Aretino*, New York: Viking Press, 1933.

Rorty, R. *Objectivity, Relativism and Truth*, Cambridge: Cambridge University Press, 1991.

Rousseau, J.-J. *The Social Contract and Discourses*, New York: Dutton, 1950.

Smith, Adam. *The Wealth of Nations*, New York: Modern Library, 19xx.

Sorkin, A. L. *Monetary and Fiscal Policy and Business Cycles in the Modern Era*, Lexington Books: D.C. Heath & Co., 1988.

Sraffa, Piero. 'The Laws of Returns Under Competitive Conditions', *Economic Journal*, vol. 36, December, pp. 535–50, 1926.

Sraffa, Piero. *Production of Commodities by Means of Commodities*, Cambridge; Cambridge University Press, 1960.

Strawson, Peter. *Individuals*, London: Methuen, 1959.

Taylor, L. *Income Distribution, Inflation and Growth: Lectures on Structuralist Macroeconomic Theory*, Cambridge, MA: MIT Press.

Varian, Hal R. *Microeconomic Analysis*, 2nd edn. New York: Norton, 1988.

Walras, Leon. *Elements of Pure Economics*, ed. W. Jaffe, London: Allen & Ulwin, 1954.

Walsh, Vivian. *Introduction to Contemporary Microeconomics*, New York: Mcgraw-Hill, 1970.

Weintraub, E. Roy. *Microfoundations: The Compatibility of Microeconomics and Macroeconomics*, Cambridge: Cambridge University Press, 1979.

INDEX